Literary Histories in Portuguese

Tagus Press
Center for Portuguese Studies and Culture
University of Massachusetts Dartmouth
Portuguese Literary & Cultural Studies (PLCS) 26

PREVIOUS ISSUES

Fronteiras/Borders (PLCS 1)
Edited by Victor K. Mendes, Paulo de Medeiros, and José N. Ornelas

Lídia Jorge in Other Words / por outras palavras (PLCS 2)
Edited by Cláudia Pazos Alonso

Pessoa's Alberto Caeiro (PLCS 3)
Edited by Victor K. Mendes

2001 Brazil: A Revisionary History of Brazilian Literature and Culture (PLCS 4/5)
Edited by João Cezar de Castro Rocha

On Saramago (PLCS 6)
Edited by Anna Klobucka

A Repertoire of Contemporary Portuguese Poetry (PLCS 7)
Edited by Victor K. Mendes

Cape Verde: Language, Literature & Music (PLCS 8)
Edited by Ana Mafalda Leite

Post-Imperial Camões (PLCS 9)
Edited by João R. Figueiredo

Reevaluating Mozambique (PLCS 10)
Edited by Phillip Rothwell

Vitorino Nemésio and the Azores (PLCS 11)
Edited by Francisco Cota Fagundes

The Other Nineteenth Century (PLCS 12)
Edited by Kathryn M. Sanchez

The Author as Plagiarist—The Case of Machado de Assis (PLCS 13/14)
Edited by João Cezar de Castro Rocha

Remembering Angola (PLCS 15/16)
Edited by Phillip Rothwell

Parts of Asia (PLCS 17/18)
Edited by Cristiana Bastos

Facts and Fictions of António Lobo Antunes (PLCS 19/20)
Edited by Victor K. Mendes

Garrett's Travels Revisited (PLCS 21/22)
Edited by Victor K. Mendes and Valéria M. Souza

Economies of Relation: Money and Personalism in the Lusophone World (PLCS 23/24)
Edited by Roger Sansi

Lusofonia and Its Futures (PLCS 25)
Edited by João Cezar de Castro Rocha

Portuguese Literary & Cultural Studies is a multilingual interdisciplinary peer-reviewed journal published semi-annually by the Tagus Press in the Center for Portuguese Studies and Culture at the University of Massachusetts Dartmouth. The journal addresses the literatures and cultures of the diverse communities of the Portuguese-speaking world in terms of critical and theoretical approaches.

Manuscript Policy

Portuguese Literary & Cultural Studies welcomes submission of original and unpublished manuscripts in English, Portuguese, or Spanish appropriate to the goals of the journal. Manuscripts should be in accordance with the *MLA Style Manual and Guide to Scholarly Publishing* (latest version) with parenthetical documentation and a list of works cited. The author is responsible for the accuracy of all quotations, titles, names, and dates. Font and sizes as close as possible to the style of the previous issue of PLCS should be used throughout the text. All of the information must be in the same language (e.g., abstract, body of the article, bio-blurb). Updated guidelines are available at http://www.portstudies.umassd.edu/plcs/editor.htm. PLCS encourages submission of manuscripts in the form of a single attached MS Word document. Please send submissions to João Cezar de Castro Rocha, Editor in Chief, at jccr123@yahoo.com.br.

PORTUGUESE LITERARY & CULTURAL STUDIES 26

Literary Histories in Portuguese

Edited by JOÃO CEZAR DE CASTRO ROCHA

Tagus Press UMASS DARTMOUTH / DARTMOUTH, MASSACHUSETTS

PORTUGUESE LITERARY & CULTURAL STUDIES 26
Tagus Press at UMass Dartmouth
www.portstudies.umassd.edu

Manufactured in the United States of America
Managing Editor: Mario Pereira
Copyedited by Jason Warshof
Designed by Richard Hendel
Typeset in Quadraat and The Sans by Integrated Publishing Solutions

Tagus Press books are produced and distributed for Tagus Press
by University Press of New England, which is a member of the Green Press Initiative.
The paper used in this book meets their minimum requirement for recycled paper.

For all inquiries, please contact:
Tagus Press at UMass Dartmouth
Center for Portuguese Studies and Culture
285 Old Westport Road
North Dartmouth, MA 02747-2300
Tel. 508-999-8255
Fax 508-999-9272
www.portstudies.umassd.edu

ISSN: 1521-804X
ISBN: 978-1-933227-60-3 (pbk.: alk. paper)
Library of Congress Control Number: 2014930504

5 4 3 2 1

Contents

Reviews

Fiction

JOÃO CEZAR DE CASTRO ROCHA

Introduction
Possibilities of Literary History

(Im)Possibilities?

A reader looking at the cover of this issue of *Portuguese Literary & Cultural Studies* may wonder: how to propose nowadays a collection of essays devoted to *literary histories in Portuguese?*[1] Is it not true that a reasonable consensus exists regarding the impasses of the genre of literary history?[2] Indeed, David Perkins's rhetorical question—"Is literary history possible?"—seems to have synthesized the present state of the discussion. Perkins goes on to explore "the aporias of the form or, in simpler terms, the insurmountable contradictions in organizing, structuring, and presenting the subject; and the always unsuccessful attempt of every literary history to explain the development of literature that it describes."[3]

Nonetheless, recently some experiments have been attempted in the once tranquil realm of literary history. The goal of this issue, therefore, is to contribute to this contemporary discussion. *Literary Histories in Portuguese* also aims to engage in dialogue with the series of literary histories published by Harvard University Press since the release of *A New History of French Literature* in 1989.[4] Volumes to follow included those edited by David Wellbery[5] and then by Greil Marcus and Werner Sollors.[6] Thus, to produce a literary history implies establishing an intertextual dialogue with the literary history genre itself. Accordingly, *Literary Histories in Portuguese* intends to problematize both the normative concept of literature as well as the act of writing literary history. In its monographic section, the contributors have developed an array of new possibilities and focused on relevant case studies concerning this relevant topic.

Indeed, a set of theoretical assumptions governs the organization of this issue of *Portuguese Literary & Cultural Studies*, which tries to offer alternatives to the composition of and reflection on literary histories. Therefore, we should start by rendering clear the theoretical framework we are proposing. In particular, the essays in the monographic section are committed to shedding light on a theoretical dimension in order to broaden the usually narrow understanding of the task of writing literary histories.

First and foremost, the very concept of "literature" should be an object of reflection, instead of being understood as a given whose history could then be narrated in linear terms. In other words, rather than assuming a normative understanding of literature, which could be "applied" to different historical circumstances, the diversity of historical meanings taken by the concept of literature should be brought to the fore and properly discussed. This principle should allow for an active rereading and thus rewriting of key controversies of cultural history, as they should be associated with conceptual disputes over the definition of literature.

At the same time, the idea of literatures in Portuguese as an "autonomous" entity should be called into question, in order to denaturalize the automatic association between one given language and its literary manifestations. We propose that literature has to be studied from and within an axis of cultural, political, and economic relationships, characterizing a comparative as well as an interdisciplinary approach. Literary history, in fact, should always be of a comparative nature—especially when it deals with only one national literary history.

We should emphasize, within that horizon, relationships that are formative of literatures in Portuguese, stressing their relative location in the world of Portuguese language. Instead of privileging the writing of the national literary history of Portugal, or of Brazil, or of Mozambique, or of Angola, and so forth and so on, we should privilege the study of the interrelations and crossings that constitute the lusophone predicament. Therefore, we should attend closely to the Portuguese presence in Brazilian and Portuguese-speaking African literatures; the Brazilian presence in Portuguese and Portuguese-speaking African literatures; the growing and welcome influx of Portuguese-speaking African literatures in Portugal and Brazil. Last but not least, we cannot forget an increasing wealth of literature produced by Portuguese-speaking immigrants, usually in a foreign language, especially English.[7]

In other words, our task is to produce an ever more complex portrait of literary exchanges, including the need to acknowledge the plurality of conceptions of literature itself.[8]

Another question relates to modes of appropriating diverse literary traditions developed within the universe of lusophone culture, stressing the associations of these forms with similar techniques of appropriation engendered in other cultural universes. We could, among many possible examples, put Oswald de Andrade's *antropofagia* and Fernando Ortiz's *transculturación* side by side, casting light on the uniqueness of a given cultural strategy precisely by the contrast with another cultural circumstance.

Finally yet importantly, we should privilege the study of the emergence and consolidation of the literary system in Portuguese, a phenomenon that necessarily transcends national borders and engages several languages and national literatures. Once more, this broadened perspective would allow for a much-needed reconsideration of key moments in the lusophone cultural history. Machado de Assis's strong and polemical reception of Eça de Queirós's *O Primo Basílio* deserves a detailed analysis,[9] which should unveil a moment of tension in the emergence of a lusophone literary system,[10] especially within the hegemonic centers of the so-called Republic of Letters.[11]

The concern with the establishment of a literary history with an emphasis on a comparative approach does not mean neglect of the uniqueness of particular experiences. Rather, such an approach should allow, even through contrasting lenses, for the renewed clarification of that specificity.

Criticisms and Alternatives

In a relevant essay for this issue, Paulo Franchetti reflects on the "apogee and decline of literary history." After analyzing the crisis of the genre, he raises some criticisms concerning an effort focused on literary and cultural history previously sponsored by *Portuguese Literary & Cultural Studies: Brazil 2001*.[12]

In Franchetti's words: "It does not seem to me that the outcome can eliminate the aporia in the title, which brings twice the national factor. In the assembled essays, the question of national identity emerges repeatedly, and Brazilian Literature is portrayed as the main character."[13] The criticism is sound, and this current issue of *Portuguese Literary & Cultural Studies* tries to advance an alternative to the seemingly unavoidable obsession with the national factor.

Precisely regarding this dilemma, Helena C. Buescu and Miguel Tamen edited *A Revisionary History of Portuguese Literature* with an innovative approach. This effort—especially the introduction by Tamen, "Ghosts Revised: An Essay on Literary History,"[14] and the afterword by Buescu, "Literary History: Are We Still Talking"[15]—remains an important instance in the necessary effort toward developing a theoretical foundation for the project of writing literary histories in Portuguese. Tamen's warning regarding the aporias of traditional literary history must be taken into account: "It can therefore be said that literary history, from its inception, and by definition, has been *national*, *communitarian* and *cul-*

tural, as its main result was the formation of a specific, teachable knowledge of national cultural communities."[16]

Paulo Franchetti's reservations, it is worth repeating, are correct, once the omnipresence of the national determination has indeed limited the scope of the genre of literary history. Helena C. Buescu's suggestion seems to open up new paths of thought: " . . . if we consider literary history to be also a process of questioning itself, that is, if we mainly understand it as an epistemological activity."[17] The epistemology of literary history should question both a normative concept of literature and the naturalization of the national determination in the definition of the task of writing literary histories.

As a matter of fact, the essays gathered in the present issue of *Portuguese Literary & Cultural Studies* try to cope with the challenge of reflecting on two key points. On the one hand, there is the narrative character of every literary history.[18] On the other, there is the association with a unique national space—or with a wider locus, engendered by a common language or by the constant and constitutive access to the same cultural and literary repertoire. Indeed, *Literary Histories in Portuguese* aims to provide a theoretical framework within which the narrative of the historical process of a given literature may be conceived under a new perspective.

As the subject is complex, we must move forward gradually, analyzing previous examples of alternative literary histories.

Experiences and Impasses

In his reading of Denis Hollier's *A New History of French Literature*, David Perkins coins the term *postmodern encyclopedia*.[19] The term synthesizes the fragmentary organization of this new literary history. In tune with the criticism raised by Franchetti, such an organization purports to refuse national determination, while maintaining the geographic space of the nation as a nonassumed axis of the myriad entries that make up the volume.

Hollier defines the problem eloquently: "One of the most selfless of today's humanitarian institutions is called Médecins sans Frontières, Doctors without Borders. Literature, however, selfless or not, never comes without borders. Not only, as Rousseau said, does language distinguish humans from animals, but also, as he added, languages distinguish nations from one another."[20]

Thus, the three assumptions that supported traditional literary history would be questioned by the model of the postmodern encyclopedia as an effort to escape national determination. David Perkins didactically summarizes the issue: " . . . literary works are formed by their historical context; that change in literature takes place developmentally; and that this change is the unfolding of an idea, principle or suprapersonal entity."[21]

Therefore, to say it more directly, the postmodern encyclopedia would go against a normative conception of literature and, above all, it would reject the teleological notion associated with the predominance of the concept of nation. Therefore, against totality, a frequent discursive effect of normative conceptions, the postmodern encyclopedia invests in the fragmentary, and incompleteness becomes an important value. However, ultimately, at least according to Perkins, Hollier's experiment was not wholly successful.[22]

Likewise, the project of *A New History of German Literature* sought to move away from the ghost of totality. In the words of David Wellbery, this gesture implies "a forceful critique of traditional literary history: a critique that proceeds not from a formalist rejection of history but from a radicalization of the idea that literature is historical. The date each poem or work of literature bears is internal to the work itself, the temporal center around which it crystallizes."[23] This statement on the radical historicity of literary history is particularly important and should allow for an innovative understanding of the problem.

The patron of this literary history could be Paul Celan, with his sharp aphorism "Jedes Gedicht ist datierbar." The radical singularity of the experience of both the writing and the reception of a literary text is thus recovered, for *every poem is datable* both in the act of its creation and in the countless moments of its reception.

The patron of this literary history could also be Erich Auerbach, especially in his thoughtful rejection of abstract concepts and theoretical, grandiloquent transhistorical overviews, which subtly he links to the structure of the legend as opposed to the writing of history.[24] In Auerbach's perception: "To write history is so difficult that most historians are forced to make concessions to the technique of legend."[25] According to Wellbery's insight, this is the case for most literary historians.

However, a decisive question remains to be discussed: how could one qualify a text as being literary, once regulatory concepts are rejected? If we radicalize the principle of contextualization, then how to rely on a concept of literature that paradoxically would remain identical to itself throughout history? In seeking to provide an answer, David Wellbery adopts a dual strategy. First, he defines the traits of traditional literary history that are to be avoided: "continuous narrative time, the cultural space of the 'nation,' and imaginative writing."[26]

It is worth rendering explicit the naiveté of this threefold naturalized association. Actually, it is grounded upon a tautological movement that equates geographical boundaries with a given language in order to create a fixed image of national identity, always identical to itself; therefore, it is immune to historical changes, although paradoxically rooted in a particular historical development. Against this framework, Wellbery proposes an equally threefold and yet symmetrically inverted articulation: " . . . the changing conceptions of time and tradition that inform the self-understanding of writers and readers. Historical time is not a homogeneous medium that the historians can simply presuppose, but is itself in flux . . . the larger linguistic, cultural and political unities within which literary activities operate . . . the changing configurations of the media of storage and transmission."[27] This model of literary history encompasses the changing conceptions of the object while keeping an eye open to the transformations that occur in the materiality of communication,[28] stressing the interaction between new media and the social process of production of texts and their reception. Wellbery also establishes a productive dialogue with the groundbreaking approach inaugurated by Friedrich Kittler's *Discourse Networks*,[29] one of the most thought-provoking books produced in the complex crossing among several disciplines: literary history, media theory, cultural and intellectual history.

In 2004, the same year as Wellbery's publication, another important development emerged for the project of producing alternatives to the writing of literary history: *Literary Cultures of Latin America: A Comparative History*, edited by Mario J. Valdés and Kadir Djelal. In the general introduction, symptomatically entitled "Beyond Literary History," Valdés proposes, "The people of Latin America have diverse and extremely rich literary cultures that bring together three traditions into one heterogeneous flux."[30] In other words, instead of a normative concept of literature, the reconstruction of this complex flux demands the simultaneous incorporation of different traditions.[31]

Therefore, the complex junction of Amerindian, European, and African legacies would have produced a radical heterogeneity with which traditional literary history would be unable to cope. The concept of literary history is then replaced by that of literary cultures—and, here, plurality is a key concern. In this context, it is possible to associate, among many other possibilities, the concepts of cultural cannibalism (Oswald de Andrade); transculturation (Fernando Ortiz); literary transculturation (Ángel Rama); heterogeneity (Antonio Cornejo Polar); Macunaíma's literature (Mário de Andrade); cannibalistic literature (Roberto Fernández Retamar); cultural heritage (Pedro Henríquez Ureña); and multiple temporalities (Antonio Candido).

Indeed, the creation of potential dialogues among variegated critical traditions may be an alternative to the discipline of literary history. After all, such parallels would at least trigger a constant and healthy reevaluation of one's own theoretical presuppositions. Recently, Dobrenko and Tihanov have given theoretical and empirical concreteness to this possibility: "In order to grasp the difficulty of the subject, it is sufficient to compare the different dimensions of the concept of *literary criticism* in various Western cultures."[32] This comparison leads to a much more complex perspective on the history of the concept of literature itself.

Actually, the act of going beyond literary history, in its traditional discursive practice, had already been outlined in another attempt, aimed at writing the history of Spanish literature after the civil war. The book's title is revealing, *A New History of Spanish Writing: 1939 to the 1990s*. The outstanding change stands out: *Writing* instead of *Literature*. According to the editors: "This *New History* looks at 'Spanish literature' in the period 1939 to the 1990s, but also at frontier genres, such as the journalistic essay, and at texts so loosely—or recently—connected with the notion of literature that we have chosen to leave the word 'literature' out of our title and to avoid rehearsals in our narrative of caveats and redefinitions."[33]

The broadening of the scope deserves to be highlighted, for it is a main theoretical drive of the recent experiments in literary history, whose common ground, in spite of remarkable differences, is the detachment from any concern with the search for a supposed *literariness*. This concept, omnipresent since its coinage by Roman Jakobson within the context of so-called Russian Formalism, has lost favor from the 1980s onward, and remains valid today only as a synthesis of the sort of theoretical approach that ought to be avoided.

The logical consequence of this attitude is found in the latest volume published by Harvard University Press, *A New Literary History of America*. The difference in the title, only subtle in appearance, represents an authentic requiem to traditional literary history and, to some extent, it radicalizes the replacement of the term *literature* by *writing*, as we saw in the previous models. Its editors claim: "This book is a reexamination of the American experience as seen through a literary glass, where what is at issue is speech, in many forms."[34] The vantage point is literary, although the emphasis is on *speech, in many forms*—and, once more, plurality becomes a value in itself. The explanation may seem sophisticated, but the underlying reason is more traditional than the most traditional literary history! Comparing their project with the previous ones, edited by Denis Hollier and David Wellbery, the editors justify their choice of *a new literary history of America* instead of *a new history of American literature* as follows: "The earlier projects began in the eighth century and moved forward to trace the organic literatures of organic societies that long preceded the emergence of the modern French and German nations. *A New Literary History of America* begins early in the sixteenth century; the nineteenth and twentieth centuries dominate the story it tells, and this is the story of a made-up nation that in many ways preceded its society. Its literature was not inherited but invented. . . ."[35]

In this case, it is as if the act of abandoning traditional literary history did not correspond to a sophisticated theoretical apparatus but rather to a hopelessly historical lack of historicity—in this predictable constellation, the redundancy imposes itself. Yet every nation is made-up,[36] it cannot be otherwise, unless we would indulge in an embarrassingly naive understanding of European cultural history as naturally superior just by being European. Indeed, this tautological reasoning belongs to a nineteenth-century mentality. After all, as Ernst Renan lucidly recalled, the *organic* character of a nation—let us adopt Marcus's and Sollors's vocabulary—is not a matter of an unquestioned heritage, which seems to imply a careful preservation of a common cultural memory, usually transmitted through a specific repertoire. Thus, a radically different process takes place in the invention of national feelings of belonging: "Forgetting, I would even go so far as to say historical error,[37] is a crucial factor in the creation of a nation, which is why progress in historical studies often constitutes a danger for [the principle of] nationality."[38]

By the same token, all traditions are invented,[39] and therefore that cannot be the decisive factor in establishing such a key distinction between proposing "a new history of American *literature*" and engaging in the production of "a new *literary history* of America."

Of course, the contributors to this issue of *Portuguese Literary & Cultural Studies* move in a very different, almost opposite, direction.

About this Volume

Let us now clarify a fundamental theoretical inspiration for *Literary Histories in Portuguese*, namely, the vision proposed by Wlad Godzich and Nicholas Spadaccini in a book titled *Literature among Discourses*: "If the construct of literature . . . is to be the focus of our inquiry, this inquiry can proceed according to its own structure, a structure that has the value of a periodization: a) before literature; b) literature among discourses; c) the institution of literature; d) the hegemony of literature; e) literature under attack."[40]

This structure of thinking is even clearer than the model put forward by David Wellbery, and may indeed provide an innovative ground upon which to develop future projects of literary history. After all, if any transhistorical notion of *literariness* is rejected, at the same time is preserved a decisive concern with the reconstruction of discursive constellations in order to seize the particularity of the production and reception of "literature." Instead of relying on an a priori definition, Godzich and Spadaccini concoct what could be called a definition a posteriori of "literature"—therefore, literature *among* discourses.[41]

Finally, as we write this introduction, Noé Jitrik is serving as general editor of an ambitious project, which is producing *Historia Crítica de la Literatura Argentina* (Critical History of Argentinean Literature) in several volumes. The third volume, *El Brote de los Gêneros* (The Emergence of Literary Genres), shares this approach and reconstructs the process of differentiation of genres, the result of which is the clarification of what is conceptually meant by and, above all, socially received as literature in a given historical moment. In the words of Alejandra Laera: "This volume considers the history of Argentine literature, in a critical sense, from certain general assumptions. Firstly, it is understood as a process. . . . Finally, this perspective aims to reveal, in the emerging processes it studies, the constant elements, precisely in contrast to the diversity and the variations."[42] In other words, the aporias and dilemmas of literary history have to be fully acknowledged, and yet they may be faced creatively. It is our hope that *Literary Histories in Portuguese* will become a relevant reference in this contemporary debate.

In the monographic section of this issue, Remo Ceserani, a leading scholar on literary theory, discusses the recent changes in the theoretical and practical approaches to literary history, providing an indispensable overview of the problem. Carlos M. F. da Cunha develops an important reflection on two recent histories of literature, introducing the category of literary geography in conjunction with the consideration of asymmetrical cultural relationships. Frans Weiser studies Rubem Fonseca's short story "Intestino Grosso" (Large Intestine) in order to propose the thought-provoking notion of *internal literary history*. Isaac Lourido aims at contributing to the renovation of the discipline of literary history through the development of a historiographical model grounded in systemic theories. Jobst Welge focuses on the paradoxical relationship between particularity and synthesis in the practice of literary history, highlighting the central role of the modern novel for the contemporary epistemological situation faced by the genre of literary history. José Luís Jobim keenly calls into question the issue of national affiliation, mainly through a critical appraisal of some key categories, such as "imitation," "autonomy," "originality."

The reader, therefore, will be able to reevaluate the (im)possibilities of the genre of literary history through the rich and diverse collection of essays assembled in this issue.

The three subsequent permanent sections provide a wealth of perspectives and topics.

"Essays" and "Reviews" offer a broad spectrum of themes and approaches, reiterating the commitment of *Portuguese Literary & Cultural Studies* to voice the plurality and diversity of the lusophone universe.

The final section, "Fiction," features two young and already consecrated names. Carola Saavedra, one of the most acclaimed young authors of Brazilian contemporary literature, offers a powerful short story, "Brief Beginning of the World (Episode in Three Movements)." Michel Melamed, an award-winning Brazilian artist, considered one of the most outstanding talents of his generation, closes the issue with an authentic manifesto, regurgitophagy, a radical linguistic experiment, which also unfolds a much-needed reconsideration of techniques of cultural appropriation in a globalized world.

NOTES

We would like to thank José Luís Jobim and Hans Ulrich Gumbrecht for their comments and criticisms on an earlier version of this introduction. We also would like to thank Jason Warshof for suggestions concerning the style.

1. Hans Ulrich Gumbrecht has deepened the dilemma by questioning not only literary history as a genre but also, and more broadly, the discipline of history: "It's about time, at least for professional historians, to respond seriously to a situation in which the claim that 'one can learn from history' has lost its persuasive power. . . . In the closing

years of the twentieth century, people no longer consider history to be a solid ground for everyday decisions about financial investments or environmental crisis management, about sexual mores or preferences in fashion." "After Learning from History," *In 1926: Living at the Edge of Time* (Cambridge: Harvard University Press, 1997), 411.

2. The same scholar has written a voluminous history of Spanish literature, whose introduction is symptomatically entitled "*Noch* eine Geschichte der spanischen Literatur?" (*Yet* a History of Spanish Literature?). Hans Ulrich Gumbrecht, *Eine Geschichte der spanischen Literatur*, vol. 1 (Frankfurt: Suhrkamp Verlag, 1990), 9.

3. David Perkins, *Is Literary History Possible?* (Baltimore: Johns Hopkins University Press, 1992), ix.

4. Denis Hollier, ed., *A New History of French Literature* (Cambridge: Harvard University Press, 1989).

5. David Wellbery, ed., *A New History of German Literature* (Cambridge: Harvard University Press, 2005).

6. Greil Marcus and Werner Sollors, eds., *A New Literary History of America* (Cambridge: Harvard University Press, 2009).

7. See the Portuguese in the Americas Series, edited by Tagus Press, for a relevant overview of this literature. Representative of this voice are contemporary authors such as Katherine Vaz (*Our Lady of the Artichokes and Other Portuguese-American Stories*, 2008) and Luana Monteiro (*Little Star of Bela Lua: A Novella and Stories*, 2005).

8. See José Luís Jobim, *Literatura e Cultura: Do Nacional ao Transnacional* (Rio de Janeiro: EDUERJ, 2013).

9. See João Cezar de Castro Rocha, *Machado de Assis: Por uma poética da emulação* (Rio de Janeiro: Civilização Brasileira, 2013).

10. John Gledson proposes an insightful reading of the episode in "Machado de Assis e Eça de Queirós: A crítica de 1878 e a internacionalização do romance," in *Eça & Machado*, ed. Beatriz Berrini (São Paulo: Editora da PUC-SP, 2005), 115–32.

11. Of course, the reference is to Pascale Casanova's book *The World Republic of Letters* (Cambridge: Harvard University Press, 2004).

12. João Cezar de Castro Rocha, ed., *Portuguese Literary & Cultural Studies* 4, 5 (2001), *Brazil 2001: A Revisionary History of Brazilian Literature and Culture.*

13. Paulo Franchetti, "História literária: Um gênero em crise," *Semear*, 7 (2002): 262.

14. Miguel Tamen, "Ghosts Revised: An Essay on Literary History," *Hispanic Issues* 18: xi–xxi.

15. Helena C. Buescu, "Literary History: Are We Still Talking?" *Hispanic Issues* 18: 209–12.

16. Tamen, "Ghosts Revised," xix.

17. Buescu, "Literary History," 209.

18. Remo Ceserani thoroughly discusses this fundamental theme in "La storia letteraria come genere narrative," *Raccontare la letteratura* (Turin: Bollati Boringhieri, 1990), 17–32.

19. David Perkins, "The Postmodern Encyclopedia," *Is Literary History Possible?* (Baltimore: Johns Hopkins University Press, 1992), 53–60.

20. Denis Hollier, ed., "On Writing Literary History," *A New History of French Literature* (Cambridge: Harvard University Press, 1989), xxii.

21. Perkins, "The Postmodern Encyclopedia," 1–2.

22. See ibid., 60: "Encyclopedic form is intellectually deficient. Its explanations of past happenings are piecemeal, may be inconsistent with each other, and are admitted to be inadequate. It precludes a vision of its subject."

23. David Wellbery, "Introduction," *A New History of German Literature* (Cambridge: Harvard University Press, 2004), xvii.

24. After all, "legend arranges its material in a simple and straightforward way, it detaches it from its contemporary historical context, so that the latter will not confuse it. . . ." Erich Auerbach, *Mimesis: The Representation of Reality in Western Literature* (Princeton, NJ: Princeton University Press, 2003), 20. In the original: "Die Sage ordnet den Stoff in eindeutiger und entschiedener Weise, sie schneidet ihn aus dem sonstigen Weltzusammenhang heraus, so dass dieser nicht verwirrend eingreifen kann. . . ." Erich Auerbach, *Mimesis: Dargestellte Wirklichkeit in der abendländischen Literatur* (Tübingen: A. Francke Verlag, 2001), 22.

25. Ibid., 20. In the original: "Geschichte zu schreiben ist so schwierig, dass die meinsten Geschichtsschreiber genötigt sind, Konzessionen an die Sagentechnik zu machen." Auerbach, *Mimesis*, 23.

26. Wellbery, "Introduction," xxiv.

27. Ibid., xxiii–xxiv.

28. On this paradigm, see Hans Ulrich Gumbrecht and Karl Ludwig Pfeiffer, eds. *Materialities of Communication* (Stanford, CA: Stanford University Press, 1994). On page 7, Pfeiffer clarifies the breadth of the approach: "'Materialities' may also function as an overall metaphor for the joint impact of institutions (the church, educational systems) and the media they predominantly employ (rituals, books of special kinds, etc.)."

29. Friedrich Kittler, *Discourse Networks 1800/1900* (Stanford, CA: Stanford University Press, 1992). David Wellbery wrote the "foreword" to this translation of *Aufschreibesysteme 1800/1900*, originally published in 1985. The impact of Kittler's perspective on traditional notions of literary history may be better appreciated by Wellbery's appraisal: "What Kittler's reading shows, rather, is that the scene in which the origin is imagined is not an origin at all—the pristine moment of auto-constitution—itself derives from a non-origin, from a beginning that is intrinsically plural, empirical, and other The origin" (xxi).

30. Mario J. Valdés, "Introduction," *Literary Cultures of Latin America: A Comparative History*, Mario J. Valdés and Djelal Kadir, eds. (Oxford: Oxford University Press, 2004), xvii.

31. Ibid.: "Latin American literary culture partakes unequally, discontinuously, and without any uniformity of three different cultures: first, the Amerindian, especially in Mesoamerica and the Andean region; second, the European, predominantly Spanish and Portuguese (but also having some French and Italian characteristics); third, the African cultures, which are today still of major consequence in Brazil and the Caribbean region."

32. See "Introduction: Toward a History of Soviet and Post-Soviet Literary Theory and Criticism," in *A History of Russian Literary Theory and Criticism: The Soviet Age and Beyond*, Evgeny Dobrenko and Galin Tihanov, eds. (Pittsburgh: University of Pittsburgh Press, 2013), ix.

33. Chris Perriam, Michael Thompson, Susan Frenk, and Vanessa Knights, eds., "Preface," *A New History of Spanish Writing: 1939 to the 1990s* (Oxford: Oxford University Press, 2000), v.

34. Marcus and Sollors, *A New Literary History of America*, xxiv.

35. Ibid., xxiii.

36. See, among many titles, the always-quoted collection of essays *Nation and Narration* (London: Routledge, 1990), edited by Homi K. Bhabha. As the editor affirms, "Nations, like narratives, lose their origins in the myths of time and only fully realize their horizons in the mind's eye." Homi K. Bhabha, "Introduction: Narrating the Nation," 1.

37. Then, at once, literary history, "for approximately the first seventy-five years of the nineteenth century . . . enjoyed popularity and unquestioned prestige," although this implied the danger mentioned by Renan; after all, "because literary historians viewed texts in relation to their historical contexts, literary history could achieve . . . a juster interpretation and a more complete appreciation than was otherwise possible." David Perkins, "Introduction: The State of the Discussion," in *Theoretical Issues in Literary History*, David Perkins, ed. (Cambridge: Harvard University Press, 1991), 1.

38. Ernst Renan, "What Is a Nation?" in *Nation and Narration*, Homi K. Bhabha, ed. (London: Routledge, 1990), 11. The sequence of the text is even more revealing: "Indeed, historical inquiry brings to light deeds of violence, which took place at the origin of all political formations, even of those whose consequences have been altogether beneficial."

39. "Inventing traditions, it is assumed here, is essentially a process of formalization and ritualization, characterized by reference to the past, if only by imposing repetition." Eric Hobsbawm, "Introduction: Inventing Traditions," in *The Invention of Tradition*, Eric Hobsbawm and Terence Ranger, eds. (Cambridge: Cambridge University Press, 1992), 4.

40. Wlad Godzich and Nicholas Spadaccini, eds., "Introduction," in *Literature among Discourses: The Spanish Golden Age* (Minneapolis: University of Minnesota Press, 1986), xi.

41. The editors define precisely the aim of this new literary history: " . . . to replace

the very phenomenon of literature in a larger verbal luxuriance, one in which literature is never given but is constantly being forged through a dynamic of inclusions and exclusions as complex as the social dynamic itself" (xv).

42. Alejandra Laera, ed., "Introducción: El Brote de los Géneros," *Historia Crítica de la Literatura Argentina*, Noé Jitrik, ed., vol. III: *El Brote de los Géneros* (Buenos Aires: Emecé Editores, 2010), 9.

Literary Histories in Portuguese

REMO CESERANI
Translated by James Kierstead

Literary History

ABSTRACT: Recent changes in the theoretical and practical approaches to literary history: new interest in the relationship among literature, culture, and history, new attention to the narrative quality of this particular genre of history, new interpretations of the traditional problems: distinction between document and monument, distinction between the general and the individual. Some of the old approaches to writing literary history, such as the nineteenth-century examples of *Geistesgeschichte* or *Stilgeschichte,* have gone out of fashion. Newer suggestions have come from the French historians gathered around the journal *Annales,* the German school of *Rezeptionskritik,* and the American discussions on the canon. Among the types of literary history that are widely practiced today are those focused on the evolution of literary institutions, the development of a language, the history of ideas and ideologies, and the reconstruction of the biographical and sociological conditions underlying the production of a literary work. Two types of approaches seem to stand out: those that center on the development of literary forms and those that trace the changes in literary themes over time. The real achievement would be to provide, at the same time, a history of literary forms and a history of literary themes.

KEYWORDS: literature, culture, history.

The last three decades have seen a sharp change in the cultural and philosophical attitudes of many scholars, across many disciplines. For some time at the beginning of this period, structuralist linguistics held sway, penetrating many other disciplines with its influence and generating distinctive approaches in sociology, psychology, anthropology, and even in literary criticism, where texts tended to be treated as linguistic structures separate from their historical contexts. Now we have entered a new phase, in which structuralist linguistics has been replaced by psycholinguistics and sociolinguistics. In many disciplines, dialogical and hermeneutical approaches have dominated, while in literary studies, previously abandoned critical approaches and key words have returned in force: the study of themes, the analysis of narrative techniques in their historical development, the relationship between texts and contexts, the combination of specifically literary analysis and the broader study of cultures. The change has even reached the subdiscipline of literary history, whether in reopening the discussion about the relationship between literature and history or in giving encouragement to more analytic studies of the particular genre of narrative work constituted by literary histories, which had their greatest moment in the nineteenth century, an era of historiography and of novelistic narrative. Lending force to this change has been a widespread interest in narrativity, as attested by the interventions of a wide variety of thinkers and scholars, including the American biologist Stephen Jay Gould. According to Gould, "We are storytelling creatures, and should have been named *Homo narrator* (or perhaps *Homo mendax*) to acknowledge the misleading side of storytelling, rather than the often inappropriate *Homo sapiens*. The narrative mode comes naturally to us as a style for organizing thoughts and ideas."[1]

But what is the current state of the theoretical discussion about literary history? Here too the signs of change are easy to discern. One question raised on several occasions in the twentieth century made a renewed appearance in the title of a book published in 1992: *Is Literary History Possible?*[2] The question itself is evidence of a certain skepticism, a skepticism that has found many different forms of expression and a wide variety of theoretical and philosophical justifications on the many occasions throughout the twentieth century when the underlying principles of literary history have been subjected to critical scrutiny. It is nonetheless true that the very act of asking the question about the possibility of literary history invites and encourages us to search for a positive answer.

Critical debate on this topic has revolved around two distinctions of a conceptual nature. The first is the distinction between *documents* and *monuments*, an ancient distinction that has recently regained currency in an ongoing debate among historians. Imported into the field of aesthetics (especially the phenomenological schools), it has provided the basis for a division between those works that present themselves as *documents*, that is, as testimonies for a certain historical reality, individual or social, and those works that present themselves as valuable in themselves. These latter examples may of course, with the necessary caution, be employed as historical documents, but they have their real raison d'être in themselves, in the richness and density of their significations, in the brilliance of their formal achievement, and in their own aesthetic qualities.

Hippolyte Taine, at the high-water mark of the exaltation of the document, and inspired by a conception of literature that was drawn from the great romantic and Hegelian tradition, felt able to write that "if literary works provide documents, that's because they are monuments."[3] René Wellek, years later, and in a decidedly antipositivist climate, was far more drastic: "Works of art, I would argue, are monuments not documents (though they can of course be used and studied as documents)."[4] They are, according to Wellek, immediately present, whether Homer or Proust, the Parthenon or Picasso, Monteverdi or Janacek.[5] He also wrote that:

> A work of art is not simply a member of a series, a link in a chain. It may stand in relation to anything in the past. It is not only a structure that may be analyzed descriptively. It is a totality of values that do not adhere to the structure but constitute its very nature. The values can be grasped only in an act of contemplation. These values are created in a free act of the imagination irreducible to limiting conditions in sources, traditions, biographical and social circumstances.[6]

The other conceptual distinction is between *individual* and *general* (or *generic*, or *exemplary*). This is taken from classical logic and distinguishes between the interpretation and aesthetic judgment of individual works of literature, in which each text is often best treated in and of itself, and the formulation of generic and classificatory principles, an activity most familiarly associated with natural scientists but also required of historians, often guided by the principle that "a single swallow does not a summer make." This distinction, in reference to the problems of literary history, has been set out with great clarity by the German critic Peter Szondi precisely to establish a difference between science and literary history:

> Literary history, like the study of all art, is separated from history by the same gulf that divides it from the natural sciences. Literary history also tends to see the particular only as a specimen, not as an individual entity; uniqueness falls outside its purview too. Friedrich Schlegel had some harsh words to say on this score. He complained that one of the "basic principles of the so-called historical criticism [is] the postulate of commonness: Everything truly great, good, and beautiful is improbable, for it is extraordinary, and, at the very least, suspect." Such criticism of literary history by no means implies acceptance of the thesis that the individual, the particular work, is unhistorical.

> Quite to the contrary, historicity is in fact a part of its particularity, so that the *only* approach that does full justice to the work of art is the one that allows us to see history in the work of art, not the one that shows us the work of art in history. The latter point of view also has its justification: of that there should be no doubt. One of the tasks of literary study is to abstract from the individual work in order to arrive at an overview of a more or less unified period of historical development. Moreover, it cannot be denied that a deeper understanding of an individual passage or an individual work is sometimes facilitated by this general knowledge, however problematic it may be.
>
> Yet we must not overlook the fact that every work of art possesses a certain monarchical strain, that—as Valery put the matter—simply by its very existence it would like to destroy all other works of art.[7]

Around the key concepts that I have laid out here there raged, through the course of the twentieth century, a long and intense debate, which eventually resulted in the calling into question of the very legitimacy of literary history. In my book *Raccontare la letteratura*,[8] I reconstructed this debate and told how, after years in which formalist and structuralist styles of criticism were greatly in vogue and the legitimacy of any attempt to historicize or contextualize literary texts was put in doubt, there was a sudden return of interest in those approaches to literature, and hypotheses and theories were advanced on the historical richness of literary texts and on the various ways in which they could be contextualized historically. I recall here as one of the most significant episodes in this resurgence—along with the book by David Perkins and the reader he edited on the subject[9]—a special edition of *Annales*,[10] which added to an already healthy number of previous initiatives of a similar type (such as those mounted by two journals, the American *New Literary History* and the European *Poetics*, which published together in 1985, in a sort of organized dialogue, two issues on the theme of *Writing Histories of Literature*[11]). That the main organ of the prestigious French school of social history judged it necessary to dedicate an entire issue to this question was naturally of some importance. But it is also worth remembering that *Annales* itself printed an essay by Roland Barthes on the same subject as long ago as 1960, the somewhat conflicted quality of which is apparent even in its title, "History or Literature?"[12] And it is also worth remembering that literary history was for some time of considerable interest to the greatest of all the practitioners of the French school of social history, Lucien Fevbre, even to the point of motivating him to call for a "genuinely *historical* literary history."[13] Furthermore, in his review of Daniel Mornet's *Histoire de la littérature classique*, and in reaction to the failure of Gustave Lanson's attempt to bring history and literary history closer together, Febvre had written that a genuinely historical literary history would represent the history of the literature of a particular era in its relations with the social life of that era. It would reconstruct the atmosphere of the era, investigate who was writing, and for what audience, as well as who was reading, and for what reason. It would have to examine what education writers received (either in colleges or elsewhere) and at the same time what education their readers received.[14]

In the introduction of the special issue of *Annales*, Christian Jouhaud surveys current critical attitudes to the problem of literary history, both on the part of historians and on the part of literary scholars, and speaks of a "vast movement to rehistoricize the literary,"[15] endorsing a view that has become quite widespread. I myself have spoken of the "reversal of a trend" in recent theoretical attitudes,[16] and David Perkins has spoken of a "revival of literary history."[17]

The two trends in literary criticism and theory that attract most of the attention of the contributors to the *Annales* special issue are the German tradition of *Rezeptionskritik* or "reader-response criticism" led by Hans Robert Jauss, the principal representative of the School of Konstanz, and the American tradition of New Historicism spearheaded by Stephen Greenblatt. And the choice is unsurprising, since these are the two schools of thought that are for various reasons closest to the method and theoretical presuppositions of French social historiography.[18] As emerges, indeed, from the essays collected in this issue of *Annales*, all dedicated—and this was deliberate—to aspects of French literature of the seventeenth century, the main themes of research are: the publishing and circulation of literary works, with an obvious reference point in the French tradition of the history of the book (Lucien Febvre, Henri-Jean Martin, François Furet, Jacques Ozouf[19]); the reception of literary work and profiles of the audience these works were addressed to; the self-fashioning of writers and of their own social role as projected in their works.

Of course the full variety of critical and theoretical proposals that have been advanced inside this vast movement to rehistoricize literature is much broader than this. And one of the central approaches in the field, the School of Konstanz's attempt to do literary history as a history of literary reception, is now in crisis even in its German homeland (though it has undoubtedly stimulated discussions of some importance, such as that surrounding the "canon"). Undeniably, now that three or four decades have passed since the original formulation of the theory, and in view of the practical results that have been achieved and the various intellectual paths that some of the movement's leaders have taken (H. R. Jauss toward aesthetics, Wolfgang Iser toward problems of the imaginary[20]), a certain sentiment of discontent and frustration has grown among adherents of the school. After so many years of theorizing, not one actual literary history has been written along the lines set out by reception theory. As a consequence, the journal *Cahiers d'Histoire des Littératures Romanes—Romanistische Zeitschrift für Literaturgeschichte* has taken on a certain stature as an organ for alternative views. The journal was founded in the 1960s by Erich Köhler (shortly before his early death), a scholar of Romance literature and a colleague of Jauss who collaborated with him on the grand literary historical project *Grundriss der romanischen Literaturen des Mittelalters.*[21] Köhler's work on the troubadours, on Arthurian romances, and on many other aspects of medieval and modern literature[22] was often highly original, and his proposals to recontextualize the literary text seem to me to be still of great interest today, appealing as they do to a conception of a historical sociology of literature and of the imaginary more generally, an approach that is strikingly modern and sophisticated. Besides this, he had a fair number of students and followers, both in Germany among the contributors to the *Zeitschrift* he founded and in Italy among Romance studies scholars such as Mario Mancini and Nicolò Pasero, who edits a journal whose debt to Köhler's work is apparent in its name, *The Reflected Image.*

The problem of the literary canon, on the other hand, after having been of some interest to Jauss and his German colleagues, stimulating them to a series of discussions on the topic of the classics (both canonical works in general and, in particular, possible canonical works of the Middle Ages[23]), has gone through a remarkable development in the United States, where it has provoked unusually sharp debate and has come to touch on the very delicate question of the role of literature in schools and in the nation's common cultural foundations. The issue of the canon, in fact, has laid bare all of a sudden a very important aspect of any literary history—that is, the hierarchy of individual literary works (which determines how much space each individual work deserves in a literary history). At the same time, it has brought us face-to-face with the constant change, from one generation to the next, in our hierarchy of values and, with it, the possibility that each new generation will have to construct a literary history of its own. It is no accident that *New Literary History*, in celebrating its twenty-fifth year, opened the first of four projected special issues, all dedicated to the rehistoricization of literature, with an essay devoted to the question of the canon, and bearing the ironic title "Canonade."[24]

So much for the long series of theoretical proposals to which scholars have had recourse over the last few decades in their attempt to provide new and original answers to the question of whether it is possible to write literary history. I turn now to two different questions. First, *what* exactly is literary history about, or what exactly is it writing the history of? What choices are literary historians making, and what purposes do they have in mind, when they decide to tell us about a particular series of events in which, according to them, literary history consists? And second, how does one *do* literary history? What narrative techniques do literary historians have recourse to, or have at their disposal?

There are two types of literary history that stand no chance of being rehabilitated in our time. Though they both belonged to the genre's most glorious phase, writing in either mode no longer seems possible; no scholar today would feel comfortable in using them as a basis for his or her own work. The first type is literary history as the history of a national consciousness or of the identifying traits (whether cultural, linguistic, or even racial) of a particular national community. This is the model that inspired the great literary historians of the nineteenth century. Besides Francesco de Sanctis[25]—who probably wrote the single greatest work of this type in all of Europe—we should recall here the already mentioned Taine, along with Georg Gottfried Gervinus, Leslie Stephen, George Brandes, Émile Legouis, Louis Cazamian,[26] and many others. This type of literary history rests on particular philosophical foundations. Particularly fundamental is the idea that the nation should be conceived not only as an assemblage of political institutions but also as a set of common cultural norms; the idea that each nation has a particular Hegelian spirit or *Geist*, a particular national identity that can be isolated and reconstructed in telling the story of its past, and which found expression in all the various ways the nation had of representing itself, and especially through the representative modes of literature. Underneath this particular tendency in literary history was an even broader conception, widespread in the nineteenth century, of a history of the spirit, *Geistesgeschichte*, which should be involved in recovering the successive stages of the development of civilization in the various European nation-states. (And this is leaving aside the contemporaneous debate on the difference between civilization and culture.[27])

This nationalistic tendency depended upon the enabling condition of the birth, at the beginning of the modern age, of a very strong sense not only of the individuality of the bourgeois subject but also of the individuality of those collective subjects that constitute modern nation-states. It is therefore hardly surprising that, beside the development of a striking new narrative form, the *Bildungsroman*, involved in recounting the episodes that went toward the construction of an individual subject (his "self-education" or, to use Hans Blumenberg's[28] terms, his "self-affirmation" and "self-determination"), there arose the genre of literary history, whose task was to recount the episodes that went toward the construction of a collective subject, the nation-state, and to mirror its self-education and self-fashionings through time.[29]

Another type of literary history, also very popular in the past but now out of fashion and surrounded by doubts and criticisms whenever it makes an appearance, is literary history as the history of styles: not *Geistesgeschichte*, then, but *Stilgeschichte*. Examples include the periodic attempts to write histories of the neogothic, baroque, or neoclassical styles. In such cases the element in common that allows one to generalize, which provides a solid foundation for the reconstruction of a period of history, is some stylistic trait, some recognizable formal characteristic (such as openness and closure, horizontality and verticality, torsion, spirals, and so on), often chosen by analogy with the practice of art historians. This approach certainly has a notable past, and can be traced back to the example of Heinrich Wölfflin and other great art historians. It is motivated by the idea that a literary form has life and a development in time.[30] All the same, there are cogent reasons to doubt the theoretical coherence of this type of literary history, which hypothesizes a separate and autonomous life for literary forms,[31] and after projects like that of Arnold Hauser, who constructed his own model that combined the history of styles with the history of societies,[32] this type of literary history has rarely been attempted. When one comes across a book with a title like Jean Rousset's *La littérature de l'âge baroque en France*,[33] one should be on one's guard: Rousset's critique of the traditional idea that the Baroque was foreign to the spirit of the French people, and his attempt to show that there was such a thing as the French baroque, is based almost entirely on the demonstration of recurring *themes* (not stylistic tropes) in the literary texts of the *grand siècle*.

But there are other types of literary history that are more theoretically acceptable, more widespread, and more commonly practiced today, and today's literary histories tend to model themselves at times on one of them, and at times on another; sometimes they are even modeled on a combination of approaches. I will try to make a rapid survey of these types.

First and foremost, there is the history of literary institutions, which focuses on all the various sorts of institutions that have assisted in the production and distribution of literary texts in different historical periods. This type of literary history—not too far from that called for by Lucien Febvre—deals with the material supports for literary communication, from orality to literacy and from the manuscript to the book. It also deals with the contexts and circumstances of literary production, from the copyist's workshop to modern editing to electronic means for the conservation and distribution of texts. (It is, then, a field of inquiry closely related to the history of the book.) It further deals with places of encounter between writers and readers (the medieval university, the chancellery of a medieval city-state or *signoria*, courts, academies, literary cafés, editorial boards for encyclopedias, publishing houses, journals). Finally, it deals with the coming together of groups, schools, and movements, traditional and avant-garde, and with the formulation of programs and the writing of manifestos. This is a perfectly respectable way of constructing a literary history, and one that is readily connected to other aspects of social and cultural history. But its real subject matter is cultural institutions, which provided the backdrop and rendered possible the production, distribution, and consumption of literary works.

Related to the history of cultural institutions is another type of history, which is similarly concerned with the very conditions of literary production and which is particularly vital to it: the history of languages themselves. Carlo Dionisotti, for one, has argued (picking up some important insights of Antonio Gramsci[34]) that it is impossible to do Italian history—not only literary history but cultural and social history as well—without grappling with the question of the Italian language. The Italian language, in this view, is a fundamental aspect not only of the construction of the Italian national identity but also of the construction of Italy's civic, social, and political institutions.[35] The same can be said of many other nations.

Another type of literary history takes the circulation of literary works as its subject. This is a broad field and has generated a distinctive brand of literary sociology, which has occupied itself with publishing markets, the distribution of books, the reactions of readers, in sum with literature as practice and its various fortunes through history. To this field belong outstanding studies such as the history of the circulation of Boccaccio's *Decameron* by Vittore Branca, who was able to establish, by a careful study of the manuscripts, that it was Florentine merchants, more than the members of any other social class, who bought, read, and circulated the *Decameron* in the fourteenth century.[36] A quantitative sociology of reading has been elaborated by the German scholar Rolf Engelsing and the French scholar Robert Escarpit. The American Robert Darnton has complemented these elementary statistical studies with more intimate investigations, examining the internal effects on the mind and imagination of readers of the often exciting and emotional experience of reading a novel, from the eighteenth century to today.[37] And a good number of scholars have studied the market for books in the modern era, reconstructing the consequences that the internal differentiation of the reading public has had on the production of volumes of various sorts (e.g., highbrow and lowbrow literature) and on the formation of strongly defined and conventionalized genres built around the effects produced in readers (e.g., mystery, suspense, horror). (And from here a whole series of other histories can be written of the subgenres of serial literature, such as detective fiction, spy stories, and sci-fi.) The methodologies of German *Rezeptionkritik* and American reader-response criticism, although they are oriented toward the actual reading of texts, are not in their essence sociological approaches. And yet they do have in some sense a linguistic, semiotic, and hermeneutic quality, since they focus their attention not so much on the audience and its social composition as on the relationship between the text and the audience and on those features of the text that allow them to evoke certain reactions in readers (whence the concepts of the "implicit reader" and the "horizon of expectation"). Here the sociological methodology and language of Pierre Bourdieu have had great influence, both in France and outside of it. Bourdieu proposed a sociology of cultural processes and a concept of "cultural capital," and distinguished between various fields of cultural activity, substituting for the concept of "cultural hegemony" that of "symbolic violence."[38] Several scholars—Pascale Casanova providing perhaps the most authoritative voice among them—have applied the ideas of Bourdieu to literary studies, with fascinating results.[39]

The problem with these various schools of literary sociology is that they have concentrated on individual aspects of literary communication (e.g., the canon, genre, imitation, irony, allegory, the market, center and periphery). Though many of these different dimensions are of some importance, in focusing on them, these approaches have all so far failed to construct actual literal histories of any completeness.

There is another type of history, and that is the history of ideas or of ideologies. This has often been approximated, especially in France and Italy, and particularly by Gramscians, to the history of intellectuals and their role in society. The history of ideas, it must be admitted, no doubt has a role to play in any more general social or cultural history. Its main interest is in movements within society, in the hegemonic or contested ideas within them, in the rise and fall of new ideas and projects, and in the role intellectuals and writers play in different societies in the formation and diffusion of these ideas. The problem of what role to attribute to intellectuals has arisen in various periods of history in many nation-states. Was their role granted to them or seized by them? At various points their position has been seen to be organic, critical, or challenging (to use Gramsci's terms). It is a key aspect of Italian history, and may be similarly central in all those countries in which national unification came late and by unusual means, since in such places, in the absence of well-defined interests and in the presence of excessively weak political structures, a particularly central role was given to intellectuals in propping up those in power, intervening on behalf of the people, or simply in radical contestation.[40] And yet the identification of intellectuals and literary figures, though it is not unjustified in the history of many nations, has ended too often in eliding the uniqueness of literature and in reducing literary history to the history of ideologies. Literary history has become the history of intellectuals and their role, of their explicit and implicit connections with the world of ideas, of movements, of the great trends.

Yet another sort of literary history of considerable interest is that which focuses on writers and their lives. This is a type of history that has its own particular problems, problems of legitimacy and of methodology. For example, is it really possible to reconstruct and interpret the course of a life, assembling its details into an orderly and meaningful narrative? What are the interpretive tools to which one can legitimately have recourse in doing so? What narrative choices should one make among the many that have been tried in this particular literary genre? And does a writer's life have its own particular characteristics that make it different from the lives of other people? Moreover, this sort of history raises delicate questions about the relationship between literature and biography, between social history and the history of individuals. The relationship between a writer's life and work is, as is well recognized, very complex and problematic, and the tendency to interpret, or even psychoanalyze, a writer on the basis of hidden themes or recurring metaphors in his work was quite widespread among twentieth-century biographers. On the other hand, nobody is inclined to deny absolutely either the inherent interest or the theoretical legitimacy of the biography as history and narrative. Indeed, it is a curious fact that not a few of the leading lights of the Russian formalist movement (Šklovskij, Eichenbaum, Tynianov), after falling victim to political repression, turned to writing literary biographies, thus making a prudent retreat from the world of expressive text to the past world of single authors' lives. A further problem that should not go unnoticed is that the organic development of a writer's life cannot always be schematized and inserted into the broader historical development of a society. An individual life may trace an arc that departs significantly from the arc traced by social structures, with their internal dynamics of organization, transformation, and stabilization. There are writers who found themselves in a reasonably harmonious relationship with their time and others whose lives had a developmental rhythm that contrasted greatly with the surrounding rate of social development, either because their lives anticipated society's future course too soon or because they remained attached to old ways and old values. There are writers whose lives have straddled some great social transformation, and who lived half in one historical period and half in another. Here again arises the problem, to which I made reference at the beginning of this essay, of the relationship between the individual and the general. The material and existential circumstances of a writer's life stand in a relationship to his work that is complex and problematic, yet at the same time concrete and particular; but the relationship that such circumstances have with the historical context of the writer's lived experience is instead abstract and generalized. To emphasize the particular circumstances of individual lives and works can confer a certain thickness and authenticity to a literary history, but it risks shattering any more general design, thus reducing history to a series of portraits or busts of individual writers.

The types of literary history that I have discussed so far tend to consider the literary work as a document, not a monument, interest themselves more in contexts than in texts themselves, and take their points of departure from individual elements of the historical context: institutions, language, ideas, intellectuals, and so on.

But what of types of literary history that concentrate more directly on texts themselves and tend to treat them as monuments instead of documents? As representative examples of this category, we will consider now two other approaches, both of which have been tried many times and ended in failure; because of this, their viability remains open to question. I am talking about the history of literary forms and that of literary themes.

The idea of doing literary history as a history of literary forms was the great dream of the Russian formalists, and later of the Prague structuralists. It is an idea that has been taken up several times, perhaps never so bravely as in the 1960s and '70s, when a school of thought that had emerged in the first decades of the century was relaunched in a quite different intellectual atmosphere. At the roots of this project (initiated by Tynianov and taken up later in Prague by Mukařovský[41]) is the idea that literary forms have their own existence and agency. Conjoined with this is the notion that there is an evolution of forms through time (in language, genres, meters, structures) along their own particular line of development (the "series"), which runs parallel to—if sometimes slightly out of sync with—other series following their own evolving paths (e.g., ways of living, *mentalités*, cultural representations, imaginaries, ideologies).

I believe there is a subtle point here calling for deeper exploration. Literary forms can certainly be said to have their own histories. One could imagine, for example, a history of the octave, or a history of *terza rima* from Dante through Machiavelli to the modern era, or a history of *poesia barbara* (modern accented poetry that imitates classical quantitative meters), of prose poetry, of free verse. Each of these literary forms appeared at a certain moment in the development of literature and not before or after; each had an originator and went through transformations and innovations. And yet, after all the great work done on one aspect of the history of literary forms or another, the realization has been that it is not possible to construct a proper literary history on this basis, since a literary history that takes forms as its point of departure will never escape those forms into the broader landscape of literary production. And the precise reason for this impasse is that literary forms have in themselves no meaning: the individual formal characteristics of a work (rhetorical, metrical, or linguistic) only have a role in the structure of a work if they are placed in some relationship with elements of that work's thematic content.

Less frequent have been attempts to write literary histories focusing on literary themes. There is the recent and ambitious essay by Francesco Orlando, who dedicates a whole book to certain images that recur in Western literature through all the many centuries of its evolution, images of what he calls "obsolete objects": the landscape with ruins, the deconsecrated church, the desiccated flower, the necromantic relic, the buried treasure, the antiquarian's paraphernalia, the fraying habit, the dilapidated house, the haunted castle, the city swallowed up by the desert, the tacky souvenir.[42] We are dealing with recurring or widely employed images or thematic elements, very often organized in "chaotic enumeration" as studied by Leo Spitzer, which are for the first time in Orlando's book put systematically at the center of our attention, defined and scrutinized in all their specificity and difference. Moreover, the images are placed in connection with a larger and more meaningful system, with the broader cultural or literary imaginary, and even with a generalizing history of the relationship between humankind and things, culture and nature.

But even with such an enthralling instance of this type of work, the question nevertheless arises of whether it is really possible to write satisfying literary history by beginning from a single theme or even an entire network of themes. The question remains even in cases where a scholar departs from a single element or network and connects it to a more general and comprehensive thematic structure that constituted—so he may claim—the imaginary of an entire historical era. A work like that of Ernst Robert Curtius, on a quite broad series of themes that recur in classical and medieval literature,[43] though having some of the features I am talking about, is in the final analysis rather partial. The themes (or topoi) that it takes as its purview are appealed to in order to support or collaborate a historical thesis that is quite subjective and clearly ideologically motivated: that of the continuity of the classical Christian tradition and medieval literature.[44] Thematic reconstruction can too often degenerate into a kind of historical taking of sides, an almost obsessive reference back to past traditions, all within a generalizing and universalizing drift that more often than not ends up occluding the particular characteristics of individual periods or works. Examples of successful thematic research do exist, made possible by a certain compactness of the themes in question in particular historical periods, or by the particular density of certain thematic strands,[45] which thus collected around themselves whole sections of the imaginary in a consistent way through various periods of history.[46] And yet even when we move on to works dedicated to single genres or styles (Bakhtin's epics and novels,[47] for example, or Moretti's *Bildungsroman*,[48] Bakhtin's carnivalesque, Frye's romances and comedies, or Leo Marx's pastoral[49]), this approach, which at different times privileges an entire tradition in its thematic consistency, or its incarnation in particular works of art, tends to partiality. And departing from partial reconstructions, it is difficult to attain the ideal of a generalized and comprehensive literary history. Whenever one finishes reading a work of this nature, the same question always arises: are these literary genres and styles best defined and described in terms of the thematic structures that characterize them or in terms of their formal and rhetorical features?

The real achievement would be to provide at the same time a history of literary themes and literary forms, with the two aspects linked closely together. But I am not sure whether even this, once it was attained, would be enough. Indeed, I have the impression that to the question "What is literary history a history *of*?" it is possible to give, at present, only a provisional and unsatisfactory answer. One thing, in any case, is certain: whoever takes it upon himself to write a literary history should be aware that he has in front of him a choice, a necessity to take an explicit stand in terms of his point of view and his aims. This is what David Perkins means when he writes that a literary history must be written from a specific point of view.[50] The same idea, expressed in a bolder and more imaginative way, appears in a dense passage by Walter Benjamin: "Just as flowers turn their heads towards the sun, so, in the power of a secret heliotropism, does all that has been tend to turn itself towards the sun which is rising in the sky of history."[51] According to this idea the past, even the past of literary imagination, presents itself to us as we watch the sky of history in a certain perspective, and we who contemplate and try to understand it have inevitably our own viewing-place, our own perspective.

Bearing this principle in mind, we can add that the most useful and convincing literary histories are those that combine more than one of the approaches I have surveyed, thus avoiding the limitations of any single approach. Avoiding a simple identification of literary history as a whole with one type of literary history is particularly important for those who focus on context and risk thereby making a history of literary works into a history of documents. If we are really serious about constructing an image of the flower that turns to us from the past and lifts itself into the sky of history, we have to embrace multiple perspectives, triangulating contrasting approaches and insisting on maintaining and exploring the relationship between texts and contexts.

We come now to the second question I wanted to ask: *how* does one do literary history? Well, how are literary histories done? If one looks at the formal structures of literary history, one can observe that two approaches are preeminent, two approaches that alternate and contrast with each other within the single peculiar genre of literary history, a peculiarly *narrative* genre. These approaches are narrating and describing. There is a continual oscillation between these two modes of writing in the works that we call literary histories. Often an author halts his or her narrative to begin a description of individual works of art; he contemplates and analyzes them, describing them in all their specificity, letting us understand how they are constructed. Then, knowing well, like any good storyteller, that audiences do not like excessively long descriptions, he or she returns to the dominant mode, to the rhetorical and structural principle at the foundation of all literary histories, that is, to narrative.

The circumstances of the production of texts, the events of authors' lives, the main features of their works, their reception by the public, the place their formal and thematic choices earn them within a tradition and a system of genres, the place they occupy in some aesthetically defined canon . . . In literary histories, all these elements are integrated and organized into a narrative that conforms to the conventions of logical and linear development, makes use of effects such as complication as denouement, and pays attention to the devices of suspense and surprise.[52]

Of course, there is more than one way of organizing a narrative. There is the classic model of the *Bildungsroman*. There is the foregrounding and placing in relief of a few exemplary characters of literary history in a manner reminiscent of the historical novel. There is the exciting journey between texts encountered almost by chance in a narrative that is like nothing so much as an adventure novel. There is the dense cataloging of dates, lives, genres, and texts in a literary history that approaches the nineteenth-century novel in its overfed vastness. There is the imitation of the experimental novel, aiming to provide a deliberately fragmented account of the literature of the past. And finally there is the ambitious attempt at creating a literary history that is consonant with the modern or postmodern sensibility, with multiple plotlines and perspectives, intersections and superimpositions, and a few pregnant moments in which the *longue durée* breaks into the present, revealing the existential timelessness of the human condition. Perhaps the greatest example of this kind of narrative is Erich Auerbach's masterpiece, *Mimesis*,[53] which closes—and this is no accident—with discussions of James Joyce and Virginia Woolf.

NOTES

1. Stephen Jay Gould, "So Near and yet So Far," *New York Review of Books* XLI, 17 (October 20, 1994): 26.

2. D. Perkins, *Is Literary History Possible?* (Baltimore: Johns Hopkins University Press, 1992).

3. H. Taine, *Histoire de la littérature anglaise*, 2nd ed. (Paris: 1866), I: xlvii: "si elles fournissent des documents, c'est qu'elle sont des monuments."

4. The interpretation of the two concepts of *documents* and *monuments* among historians has varied substantially. See the very clear survey in the entry "Documento/Monumento" contributed by Jacques LeGoff to *Enciclopedia* (Turin: Einaudi, 1978), V: 38–48. LeGoff recalls the antipositivist criticisms leveled by the *Annales* school against the very concept of *documents*, and appeals to the reflections of literary historians such as Paul Zumthor and philosophers such as Michel Foucault to support his argument that modern historiography, or "total history," is leading to the overcoming of any distinction between documents and monuments, to the broadening of the concept of document (to include literary, iconographic, and archaeological types of evidence among others), and to the wholesale attribution of the status of monument to virtually any significant document of the past.

5. R. Wellek, review of C. Guillen, *Literature as System: Essays towards a Theory of Literary History*, in *Yale Review* LXI (Winter 1972), 258.

6. R. Wellek, "The Fall of Literary History," in *The Attack on Literature and Other Essays* (Chapel Hill: University of North Carolina Press, 1982), 75.

7. P. Szondi, "On Textual Understanding" [1962], in *On Textual Understanding and Other Essays*, ed. H. Mendelsohn (Minneapolis: University of Minnesota Press, 1986), 13–14.

8. R. Ceserani, *Raccontare la letteratura* (Turin: Bollati Boringhieri, 1990).

9. D. Perkins, ed. *Theoretical Issues in Literary History*, Harvard English Studies XVI (Cambridge: Harvard University Press, 1991).

10. "Littérature et histoire," ed. C. Jouhaud, special issue, *Annales: Histoire, Sciences Sociales* XLIX (March–April 1994).

11. "On Writing Histories of Literature," ed. R. Cohen, special issue, *New Literary History* XVI (Spring 1985); "On Writing Histories of Literature," ed. J. Schmidt, special issue, *Poetics* XIV (Spring 1985).

12. R. Barthes, "Histoire ou littérature?" in *Annales* (1960), later collected in *Sur Racine* (1964) and in *Oeuvres complètes*, ed. E. Marti (Paris: Seuil, 1993), I: 1087–1103.

13. L. Febvre, "Littérature et vie sociale: De Lanson à Daniel Mornet un renoncement?" *Combat pour l'histoire* (Paris: A. Colin, 1953), 264: "une histoire historienne de la littérature."

14. Ibid.

15. Jouhaud, "Présentation," in *Annales* (1994), 271.

16. Ceserani, *Raccontare la letteratura*, 33–63.

17. Perkins, *Is Literary History Possible?*, 9.

18. For an introduction to reception theory, see H. R. Jauss, *Literatur als Provokation* (Frankfurt: Suhrkamp, 1970); H. Weinrich, *Literatur für Leser* (Stuttgart: Kohlhammer, 1971); J. P. Tompkins, ed., *Reader-Response Criticism* (Baltimore: Johns Hopkins University Press, 1980); H. R. Jauss, *Toward an Aesthetic of Reception* (Minneapolis: University of Minnesota Press, 1981); R. C. Holub, ed., *Reception Theory: A Critical Introduction* (London: Methuen, 1984); U. Eco, *The Role of the Reader* (Bloomington: Indiana University Press, 1984); R. Warning, ed., *Rezeptionästhetik* (Munich: Fink, 1994). For an introduction to the New Historicism, see S. Greenblatt, *Renaissance Self-Fashioning* (Chicago: University of Chicago Press, 1980); H. A. Veeser, ed., *The New Historicism* (New York: Routledge, 1989); R. Wilson and R. Dutton, eds., *New Historicism and Renaissance Drama* (London: Longman, 1992); Jurgen Pieters, ed., *Critical Self-Fashioning: S. Greenblatt and the New Historicism* (Frankfurt: Lang, 1999); C. Colebrook, *New Literary Histories: New Historicism and Contemporary Criticism* (Manchester, UK: Manchester University Press, 1997); C. Callagher, *Practicing New Historicism* (Chicago: University of Chicago Press, 2000); M. Payne, ed., *The Greenblatt Reader* (Malden, MA: Blackwell, 2005).

19. L. Febvre and H.-J. Martin, *The Coming of the Book: The Impact of Printing, 1450–1800* [1971] (London: Verso, 2010); H.-J. Martin, *The History and Power of Writing* [1988] (Chicago: University of Chicago Press, 1994); F. Furet and J. Ozouf, *Reading and Writing: Literacy in France from Calvin to Jules Ferry* [1977] (Cambridge: Cambridge University Press, 1982).

20. H. R. Jauss, *Aesthetic Experience and Literary Hermeneutics* [1982] (Minneapolis: University of Minnesota Press, 1992); W. Iser, *The Fictive and the Imaginary: Charting Literary Anthropology* [1991] (Baltimore: Johns Hopkins University Press, 1993).

21. Published by Winter (Heidelberg) beginning in 1962.

22. E. Köhler, *Ideal und Wirklichkeit in der höfischen Epik: Studien zur Form der frühen Artus- und Graldichtung* (Tübingen: Max Niemeyer, 1970); *Der literarische Zufall* (Munich: Fink), 1973; *Literatursoziologische Perspektiven* (Heidelberg: Winter, 1982).

23. H. R. Jauss, *Alterität und Modernität der mittelalterischen Literatur* (Munich: Fink, 1977).

24. J. McGann, "Canonade," *New Literary History* XXV (Summer 1994): 487–504; see J. Guillory, *Cultural Capital: The Problem of Literary Canon Formation* (Chicago: University of Chicago Press, 1993).

25. F. de Sanctis, *History of Italian Literature* [1870–71] (New York: Basic Books, 1959).

26. G. G. Gervinus, *Geschichte der poetischen Nationalliteratur der Deutschen* (Leipzig: Engelmann, 1835–42); L. Stephen, *History of English Thought in the Eighteenth Century* [1876] (New York: Harcourt Brace, 1962); G. Brandes, *Main Currents in Nineteenth Century Literature*

[1872–90] (London: Heinemann, 1906); É. Legouis and L. Cazamian, *Histoire de la littérature anglaise* [1924] (Paris: Hachette, 1933).

27. The distinction between *Kultur* and *Zivilisation* is very neat in German: by *Kultur* is understood the original, hereditary patrimony of a people, the totality of its traditions, customs, and characteristics; by *Zivilisation* is meant a process of cultural, intellectual, and spiritual refinement. See R. Eckhert, *Kultur, Zivilisation und Gesellschaft: Die Geschichtstheorie Alfred Webers* (Basel: Kyklos, 1970).

28. H. Blumenberg, *The Legitimacy of the Modern Age* [1972] (Cambridge: MIT Press, 1983).

29. Of interest in this regard (even in the title) is H. K. Bhabha, *Nation and Narration* (London: Routledge, 1990).

30. For Wölfflin's central ideas, see *Principles of Art History* [1915] (New York: Dover, 1950); and *Gedanken zur Kunstgeschichte* (Basel: Schwabe, 1940); for those of Focillon, see *The Life of Forms in Art* [1934] (New Haven: Yale University Press, 1942).

31. It is a curious fact that Wellek, for all his doubts about the legitimacy of literary history, dedicated some of his most important studies to stylistic periodization: for example, his essays on the concepts of the baroque, classicism, romanticism, realism, naturalism, and symbolism collected in *Concepts of Criticism* (New Haven: Yale University Press, 1963) and *Discriminations: Further Concepts of Criticism* (New Haven: Yale University Press, 1970).

32. A. Hauser, *The Social History of Art* [1951] (New York: Routledge, 1999); *Mannerism: The Crisis of the Renaissance and the Origin of Modern Art* [1965] (New York: Knopf, 1965). Along the same lines, with particular attention to literature: G. R. Hocke, *Die Welt als Labyrinth: Manierismus in der europäischen Kunst und Literatur* (Hamburg: Rowohlt, 1987). Italian scholars working in the same tradition include Mario Praz, Walter Binni, and Ricardo Scrivano.

33. J. Rousset, *La littérature de l'âge baroque en France* (Paris: Corti, 1954).

34. A. Gramsci: "Every time the question of the language surfaces [in Italian history], in one way or another, it means that a series of other problems are coming to the fore: the formation and enlargement of the governing class, the need to establish a more intimate and secure relationship between the governing groups and the national-popular mass, in other words to reorganize the cultural hegemony": from *An Antonio Gramsci Reader: Selected Writings, 1916–1935*, ed. D. Forgacs (New York: Schocken Books, 1988), 357 (from the Italian original: *Quaderni dal carcere*, ed. V. Gerratana (Turin: Einaudi, 1975), 2346). See C. Dionisotti, *Geografia e storia della letteratura italiana* (Turin: Einaudi, 1967).

35. In Italy, there has been a huge surge in linguistic history, often involving sophisticated methodologies and always diverging from simple linguistic analysis to larger historical structures and events. Recently several new histories of the Italian language, arranged by theme or by region of Italy, have been published, and they often employ novel

interpretive approaches and present us with syntheses of some originality and interest. See, in particular, F. Bruni, ed., *L'italiano nelle regioni: Lingua nazionale e identità regionali* (Turin: Utet, 1992–97); *Storia della lingua italiana*, with volumes addressed to each successive century and written by a team of scholars under the direction of F. Bruni (Bologna: Il Mulino, 1989–2006); and A. Asor Rosa, ed., *Storia della lingua italiana* (Turin: Einaudi, 1993–94).

36. V. Branca, *Tradizione delle opere di G. Boccaccio* (Rome: Edizioni di storia e letteratura, 1958); *Boccaccio medievale* (Florence: Sansoni, 1970).

37. I discuss these issues at some length in my *Raccontare la letteratura*, pp. 102–6. Fuller references: R. Engelsing, *Der Bürger als Leser: Lesergeschichte in Deutschland, 1500–1800* (Stuttgart: Metzler, 1974); R. Escarpit et al., *Atlas de la lecture à Bordeaux* (Bordeaux: Faculté de Lettres, 1963); R. Escarpit, ed., *La lecture populaire en France du Moyen Âge à nos jours* (Bordeaux: Faculté de Lettres, 1965); R. Darnton, "Readers Respond to Rousseau: The Fabrication of Romantic Sensitivity," *The Great Cat Massacre and Other Episodes in French Cultural History* (New York: Basic Books, 1984), 115–63.

38. P. Bourdieu, *The Field of Cultural Production: Essays on Art and Literature* (New York: Columbia University Press, 1993), and *The Rules of Art: Genesis and Structure of the Literary Field* [1992] (Stanford, CA: Stanford University Press, 1996).

39. P. Casanova, *The World Republic of Letters* [1999] (Cambridge: Harvard University Press, 2004). See, for applications, A. Boschetti, ed., *L'Espace culturel transnational* (Paris: Nouveau Monde Editions, 2010), and for critical objections, C. Prendergast, ed., *Debating World Literature* (London: Verso, 2004).

40. To this strand of inquiry belong the studies in Florentine humanism of Hans Baron (*In Search of Florentine Civic Humanism: Essays on the Transition from Medieval to Modern Thought*, Princeton, NJ: Princeton University Press, 1988) and of Eugenio Garin (*Italian Humanism: Philosophy and Civic Life in the Renaissance*, New York: Harper & Row, 1965), many studies on Machiavelli, Bruno, Campanella, those of Franco Venturi on the Italian illuminati, and so on. An exemplary collection of such material can be found in *Intellettuali e potere*, edited by C. Vivanti, vol. 4 of *Storia d'Italia: Annali* (Turin: Einaudi, 1981).

41. J. Tynianov, *Archaisty i novatory* (Leningrad, 1929); Italian translation: *Avanguardia e tradizione* (Bari: Dedalo, 1968); J. Tynianov, *Poetika / Istorija literatuřry / Kino* (Moscow: Nauka, 1977); J. Mukařovský, *Aesthetic Function, Norm and Value as Social Facts* (Ann Arbor: University of Michigan Press, 1979).

42. F. Orlando, *Obsolete Objects in the Literary Imagination: Ruins, Relics, Rarities, Rubbish, Uninhabited Places, and Hidden Treasures* [1993] (New Haven: Yale University Press, 2006).

43. L. Spitzer, *La enumeración caótica de la poesía moderna* (Buenos Aires: Instituto de Filologia, 1945).

44. E. R. Curtius, *European Literature and the Latin Middle Ages* [1948] (New York: Pantheon Books, 1953).

45. Exemplary in this connection are J. Rousset's studies of seventeenth-century France, among which is the already cited *La littérature de l'âge baroque en France.*

46. This is the case, for example, for a theme like shipwreck, present in literature from Homer to the postmodernists: see L. Sannia Nowé and M. Virdis, eds., *Naufragi: Atti del Convegno di Studi Cagliari 8–9-10 aprile 1992* (Rome: Bulzoni, 1993); M. di Maio, ed., *Naufragi: Storia di un'avventurosa metafora* (Milan: Guerini e Associati, 1994). On thematic criticism in general, see W. Sollors, ed., *The Return of Thematic Criticism* (Cambridge: Harvard University Press, 1993).

47. M. Bakhtin, *The Dialogic Imagination* (Austin: University of Texas Press, 1981).

48. F. Moretti, *The Way of the World: The Bildungsroman in European Culture* [1986] (London: Verso, 1987).

49. M. Bakhtin, *Problems of Dostoevsky's Poetics* [1929] (Minneapolis: University of Minnesota Press, 1984), and *Rabelais and His World* [1941, 1965] (Bloomington: Indiana University Press, 1993); N. Frye, *Anatomy of Criticism: Four Essays* (Princeton, NJ: Princeton University Press, 1959); L. Marx, *The Machine in the Garden: Technology and the Pastoral Ideal in America* (New York: Oxford University Press, 1964).

50. Perkins, *Is Literary History Possible?*, 13.

51. W. Benjamin, *On the Concept of History*, http://members.efn.org/~dredmond/Theses_on_History.html.

52. All these aspects receive a thorough analysis in the chapter "La storia letteraria come genere narrativo," in my *Raccontare la letteratura*, 17–32 (cited earlier).

53. E. Auerbach, *Mimesis: The Representation of Reality in Western Literature* [1946] (Princeton, NJ: Princeton University Press, 2003).

WORKS CITED

Asor Rosa, A., ed. *Storia della lingua italiana.* Turin: Einaudi, 1993–94.

Auerbach, E. *Mimesis: The Representation of Reality in Western Literature* [1946]. Princeton, NJ: Princeton University Press, 2003.

Bakhtin, M. *The Dialogic Imagination.* Austin: University of Texas Press, 1981.

———. *Problems of Dostoevsky's Poetics* [1929]. Minneapolis: University of Minnesota Press, 1984.

———. *Rabelais and His World* [1941, 1965]. Bloomington: Indiana University Press, 1993.

Baron, H. *In Search of Florentine Civic Humanism: Essays on the Transition from Medieval to Modern Thought.* Princeton, NJ: Princeton University Press, 1988.

Barthes, R. "Histoire ou littérature?" In Vol. 1 of *Oeuvres complètes*, edited by E. Marti. Paris: Seuil, 1993: 1087–1103.

Benjamin, W. *On the Concept of History.* http://members.efn.org/~dredmond/Theses_on_History.html.

Bhabha, H. K. *Nation and Narration*. London: Routledge, 1990.

Blumenberg, H. *The Legitimacy of the Modern Age* [1972]. Cambridge: MIT Press, 1983.

Boschetti, A., ed. *L'Espace culturel transnational*. Paris: Nouveau Monde Editions, 2010.

Bourdieu, P. *The Field of Cultural Production: Essays on Art and Literature*. New York: Columbia University Press, 1993.

———. *The Rules of Art: Genesis and Structure of the Literary Field* [1992]. Stanford, CA: Stanford University Press, 1996.

Branca, V. *Tradizione delle opere di G. Boccaccio*. Rome: Edizioni di storia e letteratura, 1958.

———. *Boccaccio medievale*. Florence: Sansoni, 1970.

Brandes, G. *Main Currents in Nineteenth Century Literature* [1872–90]. London: Heinemann, 1906.

Bruni, F., ed. *Storia della lingua italiana*. Bologna: Il Mulino, 1989–2006.

———. *L'italiano nelle regioni: Lingua nazionale e identità regionali*. Turin: Utet, 1992–97.

Callagher, C. *Practicing New Historicism*. Chicago: University of Chicago Press, 2000.

Casanova, P. *The World Republic of Letters* [1999]. Cambridge: Harvard University Press, 2004.

Ceserani, R. *Raccontare la letteratura*. Turin: Bollati Boringhieri, 1990.

Cohen, R., ed. "On Writing Histories of Literature." Special issue, *New Literary History* XVI (Spring 1985).

Colebrook, C. *New Literary Histories: New Historicism and Contemporary Criticism*. Manchester, UK: Manchester University Press, 1997.

Curtius, E. R. *European Literature and the Latin Middle Ages* [1948]. New York: Pantheon Books, 1953.

Darnton, R. "Readers Respond to Rousseau: The Fabrication of Romantic Sensitivity." *The Great Cat Massacre and Other Episodes in French Cultural History*. New York: Basic Books, 1984: 115–63.

Dionisotti, C. *Geografia e storia della letteratura italiana*. Turin: Einaudi, 1967.

Eckhert, R. *Kultur, Zivilisation und Gesellschaft: Die Geschichtstheorie Alfred Webers*. Basel: Kyklos, 1970.

Eco, U. *The Role of the Reader*. Bloomington: Indiana University Press, 1984.

Engelsing, R. *Der Bürger als Leser: Lesergeschichte in Deutschland, 1500–1800*. Stuttgart: Metzler, 1974.

Escarpit, R., ed. *La lecture populaire en France du Moyen Âge à nos jours*. Bordeaux: Faculté de Lettres, 1965.

Escarpit, R., et al. *Atlas de la lecture à Bordeaux*. Bordeaux: Faculté de Lettres, 1963.

Febvre, L. "Littérature et vie sociale: De Lanson à Daniel Mornet un renoncement?" *Combat pour l'histoire*. Paris: A. Colin, 1953: 264.

Febvre, L., and H.-J. Martin. *The Coming of the Book: The Impact of Printing, 1450–1800* [1971]. London: Verso, 2010.

Focillon, H. *The Life of Forms in Art* [1934]. New Haven: Yale University Press, 1942.

Frye, N. *Anatomy of Criticism: Four Essays*. Princeton, NJ: Princeton University Press, 1959.

Furet, F., and J. Ozouf. *Reading and Writing: Literacy in France from Calvin to Jules Ferry* [1977]. Cambridge: Cambridge University Press, 1982.

Garin, E. *Italian Humanism: Philosophy and Civic Life in the Renaissance*. New York: Harper & Row, 1965.

Gervinus, G. G. *Geschichte der poetischen Nationalliteratur der Deutschen*. Leipzig: Engelmann, 1835–42.

Gould, Stephen Jay. "So Near and yet So Far." *New York Review of Books* XLI, 17 (October 20, 1994): 26.

Gramsci, A. *Quaderni dal carcere*, edited by V. Gerratana. Turin: Einaudi, 1975: 2346.

———. *An Antonio Gramsci Reader: Selected Writings, 1916–1935*, edited by D. Forgacs. New York: Schocken Books, 1988: 357.

Greenblatt, S. *Renaissance Self-Fashioning*. Chicago: University of Chicago Press, 1980.

Guillory, J. *Cultural Capital: The Problem of Literary Canon Formation*. Chicago: University of Chicago Press, 1993.

Hauser, A. *Mannerism: The Crisis of the Renaissance and the Origin of Modern Art* [1965]. New York: Knopf, 1965.

———. *The Social History of Art* [1951]. New York: Routledge, 1999.

Hocke, G. R. *Die Welt als Labyrinth: Manierismus in der europäischen Kunst und Literatur*. Hamburg: Rowohlt, 1987.

Holub, R. C., ed. *Reception Theory: A Critical Introduction*. London: Methuen, 1984.

Iser, W. *The Fictive and the Imaginary: Charting Literary Anthropology* [1991]. Baltimore: Johns Hopkins University Press, 1993.

Jauss, H. R. *Literatur als Provokation*. Frankfurt: Suhrkamp, 1970.

———. *Alterität und Modernität der mittelalterischen Literatur*. Munich: Fink, 1977.

———. *Toward an Aesthetic of Reception*. Minneapolis: University of Minnesota Press, 1981.

———. *Aesthetic Experience and Literary Hermeneutics* [1982]. Minneapolis: University of Minnesota Press, 1992.

Jouhaud, C., ed. "Littérature et histoire." Special issue, *Annales: Histoire, Sciences Sociales* XLIX (March–April 1994).

Köhler, E. *Ideal und Wirklichkeit in der höfischen Epik: Studien zur Form der frühen Artus- und Graldichtung*. Tübingen: Max Niemeyer, 1970.

———. *Der literarische Zufall*. Munich: Fink, 1973.

———. *Literatursoziologische Perspektiven*. Heidelberg: Winter, 1982.

LeGoff, Jacques. "Documento/Monumento." *Enciclopedia* (Turin: Einaudi, 1978), V: 38–48.

Legouis, É., and L. Cazamian. *Histoire de la literature anglaise* [1924]. Paris: Hachette, 1933.

Maio, M. di, ed. *Naufragi: Storia di un'avventurosa metafora*. Milan: Guerini e Associati, 1994.

Martin, H.-J. *The History and Power of Writing* [1988]. Chicago: University of Chicago Press, 1994.

Marx, L. *The Machine in the Garden: Technology and the Pastoral Ideal in America*. New York: Oxford University Press, 1964.

McGann, J. "Canonade." *New Literary History* XXV (Summer 1994): 487–504.

Moretti, F. *The Way of the World: The Bildungsroman in European Culture* [1986]. London: Verso, 1987.

Mukařovský, J. *Aesthetic Function, Norm and Value as Social Facts*. Ann Arbor: University of Michigan Press, 1979.

Orlando, F. *Obsolete Objects in the Literary Imagination: Ruins, Relics, Rarities, Rubbish, Uninhabited Places, and Hidden Treasures* [1993]. New Haven: Yale University Press, 2006.

Payne, M., ed. *The Greenblatt Reader*. Malden, MA: Blackwell, 2005.

Perkins, David, ed. *Theoretical Issues in Literary History*. Harvard English Studies XVI. Cambridge: Harvard University Press, 1991.

———. *Is Literary History Possible?* Baltimore: Johns Hopkins University Press, 1992.

Pieters, J., ed. *Critical Self-Fashioning: S. Greenblatt and the New Historicism*. Frankfurt: Lang, 1999.

Prendergast, C., ed. *Debating World Literature*. London: Verso, 2004.

Rousset, J. *La littérature de l'âge baroque en France*. Paris: Corti, 1954.

Sanctis, F de. *History of Italian Literature* [1870–71]. New York: Basic Books, 1959.

Sannia Nowé, L., and M. Virdis, eds. *Naufragi: Atti del Convegno di Studi Cagliari 8–9-10 aprile 1992*. Rome: Bulzoni, 1993.

Schmidt, J. "On Writing Histories of Literature." Special issue, *Poetics* XIV (Spring 1985).

Sollors, W., ed. *The Return of Thematic Criticism*. Cambridge: Harvard University Press, 1993.

Spitzer, L. *La enumeración caótica de la poesía moderna*. Buenos Aires: Instituto de Filologia, 1945.

Stephen, L. *History of English Thought in the Eighteenth Century* [1876]. New York: Harcourt Brace, 1962.

Szondi, P. "On Textual Understanding" [1962]. In *On Textual Understanding and Other Essays*, edited by H. Mendelsohn. Minneapolis: University of Minnesota Press, 1986: 13–14.

Taine, H. Vol. 1 of *Histoire de la littérature anglaise*, 2nd ed. Paris, 1866: xlvii.

Tynianov, J. *Archaisty i novatory*. Leningrad, 1929.

———. *Avanguardia e tradizione*. Bari: Dedalo, 1968.

———. *Poetika / Istorija literatuřry / Kino*. Moscow: Nauka, 1977.

Veeser, H. A., ed. *The New Historicism*. New York: Routledge, 1989.
Vivanti, C., ed. *Intellettuali e potere*. Vol. 4 of *Storia d'Italia: Annali*. Turin: Einaudi, 1981.
Warning, R., ed. *Rezeptionästhetik*. Munich: Fink, 1994.
Weinrich, H. *Literatur für Leser*. Stuttgart: Kohlhammer, 1971.
Wellek, R. *Concepts of Criticism*. New Haven: Yale University Press, 1963.
———. *Discriminations: Further Concepts of Criticism*. New Haven: Yale University Press, 1970.
———. Review of *Literature as System: Essays towards a Theory of Literary History*, by C. Guillen. *Yale Review* LXI (Winter 1972), 258.
———. "The Fall of Literary History." *The Attack on Literature and Other Essays*. Chapel Hill: University of North Carolina Press, 1982: 75.
Wilson, R., and R. Dutton, eds. *New Historicism and Renaissance Drama*. London: Longman, 1992.
Wölfflin, H. *Gedanken zur Kunstgeschichte*. Basel: Schwabe, 1940.
———. *Principles of Art History* [1915]. New York: Dover, 1950.

REMO CESERANI was a professor of comparative literature at the University of Bologna until November 2006. Since then, he has taught courses as a visiting professor at ETH Zurich, the University of São Paulo, and Stanford. Among his recent books are *Convergenze* (2010), on the relationship between literature and the other disciplines (2010); *L'occhio della Medusa*, on photography and literature (2011); *Letteratura nell'età globale* (2012; with Giuliana Benvenuti); and *Gli uomini, i libri e gli altri animali* (2013; with Danilo Mainardi). He was a coeditor of the *Dizionario dei temi letterari* (2007) and, with Umberto Eco, of an anthology of texts on fog, *Nebbia* (2010). In 2012, he received the Feltrinelli Prize for European Literature from the Accademia dei Lincei, Rome. His website is www.ceserani.com, and he may be reached at puckee123@gmail.com.

CARLOS M. F. DA CUNHA

The Center and the Margins

ABSTRACT: In this article, we propose a reflection about two recent histories of literature, the *Comparative History of Literatures in the Iberian Peninsula* (2010) and the *Critical History of Portuguese Literature* (1993–2010). In the first, which is spatially/topographically oriented and has a revisionist purpose, Portuguese literature emerges as (geographically) decentered and (temporally) fragmented. The second offers, from a critical standpoint, a summary of all the knowledge accumulated through the historiography of Portuguese literature. Apropos of both, we question the possibilities of connection among space, history, and literature.

KEYWORDS: literary geography, lusophone literatures, the center and the margins.

Literary history has been experiencing a process of critical review in recent decades, with renewing trends originating from various sectors. In one of the latest issues of the electronic journal *Acta fabula*,[1] there is an intense reflection about the renovation projects of literary history in France, in particular about *The French Global: A New Approach to Literary History* (McDonald and Suleiman), wherein the rereading of the history of French literature is suggested from a world/global perspective, taking into consideration its interaction with other international cultures from the Middle Ages until the contemporary world of "francophony." It is a revolutionary history that breaks away from the nationalist logic and the idea of continuity that constitute the background of traditional literary histories, thus emphasizing circulation and exchange across the planet.[2]

This tendency toward reading and interpreting literary works in a transnational/global perspective is one of the major guidelines of literary historiography in the United States. For instance, Wai Chee Dimock and Lawrence Buell, editors of *Shades of the Planet: American Literature as World Literature* (2007), claim that American literature is transnational, something that is visible in the multiculturalism of a presumed homogeneous American canon. Additionally, they assume that one cannot justifiably study American literature in isolation in the era of globalization. Bearing this perspective in mind, they root their analysis in its connections with West Africa, Eastern Europe, Iran, Iraq, India, China, Mexico, and Australia.

These new histories fit into the *transnational turn*, which characterizes the main reforming guideline of present-day literary historiography. On the other hand, the debasement of the "great narratives" of modern times (Jean-François Lyotard) and the spatialization of time and of historiography in postmodernism (as mentioned by Fredric Jameson) have been reflected in the primacy conferred to the spatial dimension, particularly in the fields of postcolonial studies and comparative literature. It is in fact legitimate to speak about a (re)invention of "literary geography," resulting from the shift of literary studies from a temporal framework (i.e., literary history) toward a spatial model whose scale has become worldwide/global.

This connection, which relegates to a secondary position the traditional temporal/chronological perspective, has a productive effect, as observed by Moretti: "Geography is . . . an active force that pervades the literary field and shapes it in depth" (3). Upon this assumption lies his proposal to create a "literary geography": "Making the connection between geography and literature explicit, then—mapping it: because a map is precisely that, a connection made visible—will allow us to see some significant relationships that have so far escaped us" (3).

To some extent, this proposal corresponds to the "production of space" (2000), as theorized by Henri Lefebvre. Literary history, inasmuch as it is linked to the representations of space, which are coded practices bound to knowledge and power (political, economic, and epistemological), plays a key role in the production of literary spaces and the corresponding representations. Indeed, romantic geopoetics and historical poetics used to link literary production to the national spaces and even came to establish a literary cartography for Europe that opposed northern literatures to southern literatures. The recent reappearance of the concept of world/global literature is connected with the process of globalization, and in particular with the internationalization of the literary market.

The *Comparative History of Literatures in the Iberian Peninsula*,[3] an innovative exercise of literary historiography, fits mostly into this framework, starting with its revisionist purpose, which is accomplished through the use of a geographic/topographic model.[4] In this work, the Iberian Peninsula is conceived as a(n) (arranged) literary space, with a complex plurality of cultures, languages, identities, nationalities, and populations (including nomadic, refugee, and migratory), in its connections with other spaces such as the American, European, African, Mediterranean, and Atlantic.[5] The result is a kind of map of the *literary space* of the Iberian Peninsula:

- Cities, cultural centers, and enclaves:
  in Castille, (metonymy for) Spain;
  in the "historical nationalities" (enclaves) and in their cultural centers: Basque Country, Catalonia, and Galicia.
- Cities, cultural centers, and peripheries (*extrapeninsular and insular*):
  the construction of the literary city in lusophone Africa;
  the south of Spain;
  the Canary Islands;
  the Atlantic lusophone islands: Cape Verde, Madeira, and the Azores.

As stated in the introduction, the goal of this comparative history is not as much "to trace a thorough itinerary of the different literatures" as it is to provide an understanding of the Iberian Peninsula as a complex and dynamic network of interrelations (2010, xi). Hence, great relevance is assigned to the issues of multilingualism and spoken language, to the connections between the time frames and the literary intersystems: "a decentralized and 'multipolar' approximation to the question being elaborated, resulting in the configuration of a literary map with defined contours by the end of six chapters" (xii).

It is nonetheless necessary to observe that the histories of national literatures, focused on a narrative (more or less teleological) ranging from the Middle Ages to the contemporary era, with their representative authors and their national canon, are deliberately absent from this work. That is the case of the Portuguese literature discussed, for instance. The geographical map has thus taken over history and replaced it. History can only be found in fragments, apropos of some themes, without the possibility of being arranged into an organic unity. Nothing here allows for a "history of Portuguese literature," except for its absence. This changes everything, because it leaves a clear path for an "unthought" itinerary through Portuguese literature, in a transnational framework.

In this comparative history of the Iberian Peninsula, the choice for the primacy of geography involves the will to cross national boundaries. Therefore, it focuses on the study of the cultural centers (cities, enclaves, or peripheries), enabling a detour from the perspective of national territories and relegating "national literatures" to a secondary position. On the other hand, the nineteenth and twentieth centuries are assigned far less relevance than the earlier periods (i.e., the Middle Ages) and the transnational perspective[6] that preceded the forging of nation-states.

The innovative aspect of this work thus lies in its choice of a spatial explanatory model (geographic/topographic) over the chronological time of the traditional narrative (causal, organicist, and teleological), relying on a hypertextual-type discourse organization.[7] The collective authorship of this new literary history underscores its heterogeneity, privileging multiplicity and microhistory to the detriment of the entirety of "great narratives." It thus comes close to what David Perkins has coined "postmodern" literary history: "Because it aspires to reflect the past in its multiplicity and heterogeneity, it does not organize the past, and in this sense, it is not history" (60).

Indeed, the new comparative literary histories avoid a unified history and seek to associate the literary cultures with heterogeneous spaces, which is why they could be accused of not producing *history*. According to Perkins, this is a central issue concerning the possibility of literary history as a discipline and the great dilemma faced by every literary historian: "We must perceive a past age as relatively unified if we are to write literary history; we must perceive it as highly diverse if what we write is to represent it plausibly" (27).

In a famous study, Roland Barthes wondered about the feasibility of connecting history and literature ("Histoire ou littérature?"), and René Wellek went as far as to question the possibility of literary history as a discipline.[8] Now, considering the new spatial models of literary historiography, we can redirect the question: to what extent is it possible to reconcile geography and literature; or, is literary geography possible? In other words, can literature be conceived without history?[9]

The examples of postmodern literary history to which Perkins refers[10] are further characterized by a national framework of reference, identifiable for the connoisseur of the traditional literary histories. However, in the spatial model, the "nation" (the center) is deliberately marginalized in the name of the attention devoted to the "margins." In the Portuguese case, central attention is paid to the extrapeninsular peripheries (the national islands and Cape Verde; lusophone Africa). We are thus deprived of the temporal and national references that underlie the constitution of the history of Portuguese literature.

Without downgrading the merit of the spatial perspective, we must keep in mind that literature has traditionally organized itself historically and on the discourse plane of literary history (national). Indeed, the matrix of literary history, of eighteenth-century origin, is linked to the "national literature" and structured around the idea of nation and national history. Literature itself emerged in connection with the European nation-states. Portuguese writers, like writers in other countries, have since Romanticism embraced the patriotic mission of founding a literature and a culture focused on the nation. Thereafter, and until approximately two decades ago, Portuguese history would become the central topic of Portuguese literature, which is particularly visible in a vast set of literary groups and movements that attempted to portray Portugal and offered solutions to regenerate the country from the decadence with which it was diagnosed (in particular, since Herculano). In recalling Romanticism, suffice it to mention the Geração de 70 (group of rebellious Portuguese intellectuals committed to social and artistic reform), the Neogarretismo (literary revival inspired by author Almeida Garrett), the Saudosismo (literary movement inspired by nostalgia), the Portuguese Renaissance, the Lusitanian Integralism, and so forth.

Most of the time, these groups reacted sharply in periods of political sensitivity and played significant roles in widespread movements (often leading them) associated with political and economic crises and threats posed by foreign powers. In the 1890s, for example, formative events included the Ultimatum, the Republican revolution of 1891, and the crisis of the liberal state and its public finances. Aftershocks of such events and their effects on the literary community extended into the first decades of the twentieth century. Likewise, the First World War and the crises of the First Republic, among other factors, explain the increasing strength of the nationalism propagated by such literary figures.

In turn, modern literary studies, dominated by the discourse of literary history, became institutionalized in higher education and secondary education under the banner of the romantic concept of national literature, connecting itself in its origin and evolution with the concept of national identity, and in its ideological commitments with the modern nation-states. Literary history has thus contributed toward the modeling of the "awareness of national identity" (Moisan 1990, 66) in terms of ideology, ethics, civism, and morality. Therefore, the teaching system became harmonized with the nationalization of literature and intensified it. In Portugal, from 1895 to 1974, the syllabi and textbooks of secondary teaching reveal increasing nationalism and patriotism, as education was deemed a factor in national regeneration. In this view, national literature, with its literary canon of great authors, proved to be a powerful instrument of socialization and training of young citizens according to the official image of the nation. From that perspective, literary history presented itself as a narrative that offered a kind of self-portrait of the nation (Neubauer). It was the connection established between literary history and national identity that defined the discipline's purpose throughout the nineteenth and twentieth centuries.[11] Thus, despite the successive attempts at renewal, leaning more toward either literature or history, the model of literary history remained stable (national, based on a chronology and on a canon).

The culmination of these efforts is present in the recent *Critical History of Portuguese Literature* (expected to include nine volumes), edited by Carlos Reis and with specific editors for each volume.[12] The work is not intended, as claimed by the editor, to replace the traditional literary histories but rather to "undertake anthological-type collections" in order to provide the reader with "contact with different critical approaches on authors, works, periods and generations" so as to produce a "polyphony of critical voices that will stimulate the readers-students to utter their own critical discourse."[13] This work is characterized by a spirit of remarkable openness while at the same time retaining the traditional periods, with their canonical authors. Therefore, it affords, within its own parameters, the range of critical thinking about the history of the literature produced over a century and a half.

The distance between *Critical History of Portuguese Literature* and *Comparative History of Literatures in the Iberian Peninsula* is immeasurable. The absence of Portuguese literature from the latter work contrasts with its tridimensional presence in *Critical History*. These polar examples attempt to illustrate the (im)possibilities of literary history and of the comparative geography of literatures. The spatial/topographic model of *Comparative History* shows us what "literature" (in a broad sense) might have been, but in a different political framework, implying the existence of a "literature" independent of nation-states. In reality, however, that was not the case. Despite its weaknesses, it is in literary history (with its diversity) that literature and Portuguese literature in particular find their space. We are left to ponder that a combination of the two models, geography with history, might offer an account of the unity and diversity, the identity and plurality, the continuities and ruptures, the national/local specificities as well as their interaction with other literatures, with other ages and spaces—indeed, a model that would provide an account of the margins without transforming them into a new center.

NOTES

1. *Acta fabula*, January 13, 2012, http://www.fabula.org/revue.

2. See Jean-Louis Jeannelle, "Le global, le national & le planétaire," *Acta fabula*, Dossier critique: "Histoires littéraires," http://www.fabula.org/revue/document6741.php.

3. Edited by Fernando Cabo, Anxo Abuín González, and César Domínguez, 2010, vol. I.

4. This work is part of the comparative histories of the International Comparative Literary Association, the first of which was published in 1967; nearly thirty volumes have been published since (http://www.benjamins.com/cgi-bin/t_seriesview.cgi?series=CHLEL; accessed September 3, 2011). Its main goal is to create a transnational perspective for the literary cultures of vast regions. Its spatial orientation emerged in 1986 and characterized the latter volumes.

5. See Feldman 134–5.

6. In his review of this work, David Gies stresses this preference for prenational eras: "Is this volume weighed more heavily on premodern languages and literatures than on more modern issues (which seem to leak in near the end)? Perhaps, but this might be a result of the fact that there existed more cross-fertilization of linguistic systems, more natural comparativist writing during a time when political and geographical borders were more fungible" (55).

7. The spatial/topographic model of this history is inspired by Mario Valdés and the work *Literary Cultures of Latin America: The Comparative History* (3 vols.), edited by Valdés and Djelal Kadir, which postulates the possibility of creating new literary and cultural spaces.

8. "Is it possible to write literary history, that is, something that is simultaneously literary and a history?" (Wellek 315).

9. "Is it conceivable to think of university scholarly study (*Wissenschaft*) of literature 'after history'?" (Bahti 1992, 292).

10. *Columbia Literary History of the United States* (Emory Elliott et al., 1987) and *New History of French Literature* (Denis Hollier, ed., 1989).

11. In the transition period from the nineteenth to the twentieth century, Gustave Lanson maintained a belief in the scientific renewal of the humanities and the application of scientific rigor to literary history but further emphasized its civic, moral, and national dimension (1965, 56).

12. Vol. 1: *The Middle Ages*, by Aida Fernanda Dias; Vol. 2: *Humanism and Renaissance*, by José Augusto Cardoso Bernardes; Vol. 3: *Mannerism and Baroque*, by Maria Lucília Gon-

çalves Pires and José Adriano de Carvalho; Vol. 4: *Neoclassicism and pre-Romanticism*, by Rita Marnoto; Vol. 5: *Romanticism*, by Carlos Reis and Maria da Natividade Pires; Vol. 6: *Realism and Naturalism*, by Maria Aparecida Ribeiro; Vol. 7: *From the End of the Century to Modernism*, by José Carlos Seabra Pereira; Vol. 8: *Modernism* (unpublished); Vol. 9: *From neo-Realism to Postmodernism*, by Carlos Reis.

13. These quotes are taken from the "Introduction" by Carlos Reis, included at the beginning of each volume.

WORKS CITED

Bahti, Timothy. *Allegories of History: Literary Historiography after Hegel*. Baltimore: Johns Hopkins University Press, 1992.

Barthes, Roland. "Histoire ou littérature?" *Sur Racine*. Paris: Seuil, 1979 [1960], pp. 137–57.

Cabo Aseguinolaza, Fernando, Anxo Abuín González, and César Domínguez, eds. *A Comparative History of Literatures in the Iberian Peninsula*. Vol. 1. Amsterdam: John Benjamins, 2010.

Dimock, Wai Chee, and Lawrence Buell, eds. *Shades of the Planet: American Literature as World Literature*. Princeton, NJ: Princeton University Press, 2007.

Feldman, Sharon. "Introduction: The Iberian Peninsula as a Literary Space." In *A Comparative History of Literatures in the Iberian Peninsula*. Vol. 1, 133–37. Amsterdam: John Benjamins, 2010.

Gies, David T. Review of *Comparative History of Literatures in the Iberian Peninsula*. In *Recherche Littéraire/Literary Research* 27 (Summer 2011): 51–55.

González, Anxo Abuín, and Anxo Tarrío Varela, eds. *Bases metodolóxicas para unha historia comparada das literaturas na Península Ibérica*. University of Santiago de Compostela, 2004.

Lanson, Gustave. *Essais de méthode, de critique et d'histoire littéraire*, edited by Henri Peyre. Paris: Hachette, 1965.

Lefebvre, Henri. *La production de l'espace*. 4th edition. Paris: Anthropos, 2000 [1974].

McDonald, Christie, and Susan Suleiman, eds. *The French Global: A New Approach to Literary History*. New York: Columbia University Press, 2010.

Moisan, Clément. *L'histoire littéraire*. Paris: P.U.F., 1990.

Moretti, Franco. *Atlas of the European Novel: 1800–1900*. London: Verso, 1999 [1998].

Perkins, David. *Is Literary History Possible?* Baltimore: Johns Hopkins University Press, 1992.

Reis, Carlos, ed. *História crítica da literatura portuguesa*. 8 vols. Lisbon: Verbo, 1993–2010.

Valdés, Mario, and Djelal Kadir, eds. *Literary Cultures of Latin America: A Comparative History*. 3 vols. New York: Oxford University Press, 2004.

Wellek, René. *Teoria da literatura*. Lisbon: Edições Europa-América, no date.

CARLOS M. F. DA CUNHA is an associate professor at the University of Minho (Braga, Portugal; carmel@ilch.uminho.pt), where he teaches Theory of Literature and Cultural Studies; some of his publications include: *The (Im)possible Worlds of Vergílio Ferreira* (Lisbon: Difel, 2000), *The Construction of Literary History Discourse in 19th Century Portuguese Literature* (Braga: Centro de Estudos Humanísticos/Universidade do Minho, 2002), and *The Geography(ies) of Literature: From National toward Global* (Guimarães: Opera Omnia, 2011). He is currently studying the issue of world literature and preparing a critical study of literary history in twentieth-century Portugal. He may be reached at carmel@ilch.uminho.pt.

FRANS WEISER

"Internal" Literary History
Rubem Fonseca's "Intestino Grosso"

ABSTRACT: The term literary history has been understood in diverging contexts in the twentieth century, although, as Eduardo Coutinho points out, its practice in Latin America is increasingly subject to interrogations of the concepts that have traditionally defined critical interpretation. Building on Wendell Harris's distinction between external and internal literary history, this paper argues that Rubem Fonseca's short story "Intestino Grosso" (Large Intestine) rather than being only a textual artifact that critics utilize to impose their external readings upon literary events, also acts as a form of internal literary history as produced from within fiction to comment upon the state of contemporary Brazilian literary criticism.

KEYWORDS: Rubem Fonseca, internal literary history, mock interview, literary criticism.

Eduardo Coutinho argues in "Rewriting Latin American Literary History" that if "one can no longer limit the field of literature to fictional or poetic written production, the corpuses which formed the basis of traditional literary histories lose their rigidity and become multiple and dynamic, giving way to the coexistence of distinct canons within the same context" (2003, 105). One of the challenges to establishing the parameters of literary history has been the wide variety of ends served by the term, having denoted anything from pure history to literary theory and even the sociology of literature, depending upon the practitioner (Pelc, quoted in Harris 1994, 436).[1] Roberto Schwarz's use of Machado de Assis's fiction as a lens through which to link contemporary and historical Brazilian culture in effect fuses such literary historical definitions. Equally concerned with the consequences of Latin American cultural imitation of foreign models, Silviano Santiago bridges the linguistic divide in Latin America by employing Borges's "Pierre Menard, autor del Quijote" to serve as a model for his manifesto of scholarly and critical, as opposed to purely cultural, anthropophagy.[2] Schwarz and Santiago exemplify less traditional historical interpretations of literature, conceiving of fiction as a prism through which to elucidate contemporary critical concerns, yet they reiterate the interdependent text-critic relationship that Gilberto Teles claims literary history requires, namely the intervention of scholars in order to analyze elements both internal and external to historical works (2002, 13). Is the progress of the varied forms of literary history, then, the purview of critics and scholars alone who read history, theory, and sociology through literature, or can literary texts themselves transform from objects of study into cultural artifacts that enter into the historical dialogue on their own terms?

Harris suggests that diachronic literary histories that stress temporal sequences over authorial intention can be classified based on two tendencies: their focus upon relational influences that are either *internal* to the succession of texts (in other words, between author and author, text and text) or *external* (i.e., based on shifting historical contexts of production) (441–42). Yet self-reflexive texts that comment upon literary events might be considered to constitute a form of internal literary history in a different sense, as being organically generated from within literature rather than as narratives imposed upon the past from external positions. Rubem Fonseca's 1975 "Intestino Grosso" is one such text, and although its title alone playfully suggests that it details internal movements, it is Fonseca's attempt to critique the extraliterary from within the realm of fiction that attests to this story's status as internal literary history.

Less a short story than a dialogue that purposefully eschews plot development, the narrative consists of an interview between a first-person journalist and an Author, who, despite being nameless, would appear to share a similar philosophy to that of Fonseca, while the fictional references made to the Author's work parallel Fonseca's previous collections.[3] Biographical criticism is of limited value in this case, however, as Fonseca's fictional Author makes clear from the start that this is no realist, journalistic, or innocent confrontation; far from modestly agreeing to an interview, the Author requests to be paid per word. In fact, he wastes no time in mocking the debate on what constitutes the core attributes of Brazilian national identity, the same issues that preoccupy Schwarz and Santiago. He highlights the reluctance of literary criticism to embrace change, claiming to have struggled for years to be published because of market expectations imposed by critics constructing in the present supposedly historical national attributes: "Demorou. Eles queriam que eu escrevesse igual ao Machado de Assis, e eu não queria, e não sabia . . . Os caras que editavam os livros, os suplementos literários, os jornais de letras. Eles queriam os negrinhos do pastoreio, os guaranis, os sertões da vida. Eu morava num edifício de apartamentos no centro da cidade" (1994, 461). That the farce of a simulated interview is approached through fiction is all the more ironic because at the time Fonseca explicitly refused to provide interviews, maintaining that "everything he has to say is in his books" (Lowe 1982, 110), and which he proves via his Author's textual deconstruction of public codes of morality.

While the other stories that constitute Fonseca's third collection of short stories, *Feliz ano novo* (1975), bear the writer's trademark mixture of violence and ironic understatement,[4] the ironic gaze of "Intestino Grosso" is leveled at the factors informing the institutionalization of social codes rather than social confrontation.[5] As the short story ends, the first-person journalist complains to his editor, "Esta entrevista parece um Dialogue des Morts do classicismo francês, de cabeça para baixo" (469), and this experience of defamiliarization parallels the reader's own frustration of expectations in a story that appears to better fit the genre of literary criticism, although the diegetic Author's critique is leveled not at nineteenth-century France but rather at the state of contemporary Brazilian scholarship and the publishing market. Indeed, while "Intestino Grosso" is not one of the five stories that caused the collection to be banned in 1976,[6] it metafictionally comments upon the very issues of morality and censorship that were directed against the book, almost as if in anticipation of those charges, or, as Lowe suggests, an "ironic rebuttal" against the censors who had previously accused Fonseca of being pornographic (1982, 110). Indeed, the fictional Author discusses the pornography in his work, although the end result is not that the short story is pornographic but rather that it transforms into a dialogue about theories of pornography (Sá 146).

Can a short story, then, intrude upon the territory of the essay? Most essays about literature ultimately touch upon literary history whether it is their primary intention to do so or not (Harris 436), although David Perkins has a different kind of definition in mind when he poses a provocative question in the title of his monograph *Is Literary History Possible?* (1992).[7] While the field has evolved from traditional narrative history of the nineteenth century to what he terms the "postmodern encyclopedia"—a series of separate essays on distinct authors or works—the former mode lacks complexity while the latter lacks coherence. For Perkins, the act of writing literary history presumes that the past is relatively unified, while to accurately represent that past, scholars must perceive it as extremely diverse (1992, 27). This conundrum leads him to a conclusion whose paradox he suggests is symptomatic of contemporary debates regarding knowledge: "we cannot write literary history with intellectual conviction, but we must read it" (17). Yet, by creating parameters based on conceptions of totality and coherence, Perkins presupposes certain formal constraints about the practice of reading and writing about the past, for the critique of flawed attempts at totalization need not itself be either totalizing or book-length in order to constitute literary history.

As Hayden White has argued in texts such as *Metahistory*, the internal critique of conventional discursive practices forms an essential part of the exercise of the discipline of historiography. Perkins may well not agree with such a stance, for he takes issue with White's suggestion that the emplotment and narrativity inherent in historiography borrow from literary tropes, arguing instead that "narrative history differs fundamentally from fiction because, in constructing a novel, the 'plot' takes precedence over the 'story' . . . That we can make many different narratives out of the same events does not mean that the structure of events in our narrative is not true of the past" (34–35). Despite his rebuttal of White, however, it is noteworthy that the objections Perkins raises against the possibility of literary history, namely the inherent distortion and partiality of any narrative about the past, in addition to the subjectivity of the author, discrediting any pretense to scientific objectivity, in fact rehearse the very same concerns being concomitantly discussed in new or postmodern historical fiction in North and Latin America.[8]

In contrast to Perkins, Coutinho notes that within the last two decades, Latin American literary history has become characterized by its disassociation from the European models and values upon which it has historically been predicated, a process of interrogation that has included anything from challenging the viability of the terms *literary* and *history* to deconstructing the traditionally defining concepts of historical linearity, evolution as progress, and the nation as the default unit of measure. This shift has, in turn, led to a rethinking of the ability of umbrella terms such as *Latin America* to account for the Americas' regional varieties of culture as well as the issues of inclusion of historically marginalized groups, leading to a new, unavoidably comparative form of literary history, which quite simply entails "the narrativization of literary events" (103). Indeed, it is within "this complex net of relationships [that] two distinct temporal and spatial instances are confronted, and it is in the intercourse between these two instances of production and reception of texts that the discourse of literary history is woven, no longer as a supposedly objective report of facts, but as story, as fiction" (104). "Intestino Grosso" is emblematic of this shift from facts to fiction as a strategy to narrativize Latin American literary events. If, as Coutinho suggests, the notion of linearity in literary history has been replaced by an emphasis upon dialogue (103), then a dialogue—which does not allow plot to take precedence over story, as Perkins fears—is precisely what Fonseca offers as a method to critique the very same issues of Western values and national metanarratives that Coutinho identifies.

The artificiality of internalizing outdated European logic in a Brazilian context is made evident when the Author explains that he doesn't write exclusively about marginal individuals attempting to enter bourgeois society through violence, summarizing a novel, *O anão*, of his own that was written in the style of Proust. Although discussed in serious terms, the satire is an absurd amalgam of dukes and duchesses who marginalize a newly married wife because her family tree is inferior, leading the woman to seek psychoanalytic help as the story develops into tragedy. In leading up to the discussion of the European-influenced novel, the Author's equally absurd initial definition of pornography in literature is that it contains individuals without any teeth. The young duchess keeps most of hers in the book, which the Author explains via a parodic reference to the excess of authorial allusions made to foreign canonical texts, in this case T. S. Eliot's modernist poetry: "Bem, alguns são postiços. Mas isso não é dito muito claramente . . . Apenas, numa passagem, eu me refiro à dificuldade que ela tem de comer um pêssego, uma citação poética—do I dare, etc.—para bons entendedores" (Fonseca 462).

In fact, these jabs at literary criticism form the central means of understanding the text's metacritical scope in relation to pornography. The Author's book *O anão* has been criticized for being pornographic, but as the Author points out, the book doesn't actually feature a midget in its pages, although "mesmo assim alguns críticos afirmam que ele simboliza Deus, outros que ele representa o ideal de beleza eterna, outros ainda que é um brado de revolta contra a iniqüidade do terceiro mundo" (465). In the same fashion, Fonseca's short story does not provide pornography, nor does it actually feature the large intestine promised by the title. Instead, Fonseca's Author utilizes these subjects as points of departure to reverse the traditional focus of the critic upon the artist to that of the artist upon the critic's sense of aesthetics: "Ao atribuir à arte uma função moralizante, ou, no mínimo, entretenedora, essa gente acaba justificando o poder coativo da censura, exercido sob alegações de segurança ou bem-estar público" (466).

The story's title provides the two keys to breaking down the narrative, already signaling the subversive attitude of the text by pointing to "a dissolução das antíteses alto/baixo, sublime/grotesco, aludindo à dimensão corporal inferior quando se aborda um tema 'elevado' como a literatura" (Figueiredo 2003, 26). Without implying profanity, the image of the large intestine invites association with human feces, deployed cynically in the story. Similarly, the Author's comments about literature and the publishing market are tongue in cheek in calling out the manner in which euphemism has itself become a dominant discourse in the name of good taste. Additionally, it turns out that "Intestino Grosso" is not only the name of the story the reader experiences but also one of the Author's previous novels. Pornography, the Author explains, is linked to the organs of excretion and reproduction, but in "meu livro Intestino Grosso eu digo que, para entender a natureza humana, é preciso que todos os artistas desexcomunguem o corpo, investiguem, da maneira que só nós sabemos fazer, ao contrário dos cientistas, as ainda secretas e obscuras relações entre o corpo e a mente" (466). If literary history has been conceived as the privileged space of critics, Fonseca understands the exploration of the relationship between mind and body as being accessible by art alone.

The Author demonstrates that pornography is not neatly quantifiable when the journalist shifts the theme of the discussion. The Author simply repeats the fairy tale of "Hansel and Gretel" (João e Maria), a narrative taught to children the world over. Yet, with its celebration of thievery and murder, it is "uma história indecente, desonesta, vergonhosa, obscena, despudorada, suja e sórdida. . . . Mas quando os defensores da decência acusam alguma coisa de pornográfica é porque ela descreve ou representa funções sexuais ou funções excretoras" (463).

In other words, the judgment of pornography does not reflect a social norm but a construct imposed upon the public, and as the example of the fairy tale illustrates, its exercise is hypocritical at best. In fact, based on arguments of morality, life itself would be pornographic, since it is dependent upon reproduction and excretion. Yet it is not only artists who are pornographic but also those critics who attempt to control the artist, and this is perhaps the most critical claim of Fonseca's Author. His fear is that as world populations rise, a lack of resources will turn communities into cannibals, an issue that Jonathan Swift brought up in satirical context centuries ago, and which the Author wishes to capitalize upon in order to propose "mystic cannibalism" as a new religion. The reference to anthropophagy is no accident, of course, given its foundational importance as a national trope in twentieth-century literature, film, and criticism. Exercised in any of these modes of production, the celebrated activity of cannibalizing foreign models is a pornographic behavior of which both writers and critics are guilty, whether established as a Brazilian or a farther-reaching Latin American critical strategy.

The Author scoffs when the journalist asks whether a Latin American literature exists, echoing Coutinho's critique of the influence that European models have maintained upon Brazil. The author quips in response to the notion of a regional literature, "Só se for na cabeça do Knopf" (468), a reference to the North American publishing house and the role that English translation has had in inventing a Latin American canon for international export. Yet in addition to drawing such attention he criticizes the tendency of intellectuals to conform to foreign ideals, continuing, "Não me faça rir. Não existe nem mesmo uma literatura brasileira com semelhanças de estrutura, estilo, caracterização, ou lá o que seja. . . . Passamos anos e anos preocupados com o que alguns cientistas cretinos ingleses e alemães (Humboldt?) disseram sobre a impossibilidade de se criar uma civilização abaixo do Equador" (468).

"Intestino Grosso" is certainly not a far-reaching historical study. If anything, as a fragmented and uneven diatribe against critical tendencies, it is more akin to an essay in Perkins's "postmodern encyclopedia." The story is not superior to traditional forms of literary history but rather, as an alternative, demands to be read in a different context. It is firmly rooted in the present as a journalistic activity of interviewing, yet as Coutinho maintains, "Literary History is, thus, the history of both the production and the reception of texts, and for the historiographer these texts are at the same time documents of the past and experiences of the present time" (104). Fonseca's Author is a product of those processes, and in addition to being aware of the processes that have formed his trajectory and shaped the reception of his work, he is extremely interested in opening the debate on how these practices control society.[9] Far from constructing a linear or narrative progression, Fonseca attempts to offer no conclusion to the Author and journalist's dialogue—the latter simply turns off the recorder when he can stand to listen no longer—nor is the social realist writer portrayed as a privileged defender of public justice. The editor's response to the journalist's dismay may prove analogous to the story's relation to critical theory:

> "Esses escritores pensam que sabem tudo," eu disse, irritado.
> "É por isso que são perigosos," disse o Editor. (469)

Despite offending the elements of good writing, or perhaps precisely because of its offenses, "Intestino Grosso" reaffirms the role of the literary in "literary history." At the same time, its overt self-reflexivity calls attention to the conventions that have historically structured critical approaches, as Fonseca's mock interview illustrates one approach to the "rewriting" of literary history (in the sense that Coutinho details), one that shifts away from universal frameworks to analyze the confluences of overlapping approaches to literary renewal.

NOTES

1. Gilberto Mendonça Teles, for example, refers to the subtle distinction among "história literária," "história de literatura," and "historiografia literária," as the field of critical theory continually develops new methods and practices (2002, 11).

2. See, for example, Schwarz's *Que horas são?* and Santiago's "O entre-lugar no discurso latino-americano."

3. The fictional author discusses the degree of pornography in a supposed book of his entitled *O anão que era negro, padre, corcunda e míope*, which, as Vidal points out, forms an echo of Fonseca's "Os graus" from his second collection of short stories, in 1965, *A coleira do cão* (1994, 68).

4. Silva explores this dynamic in great detail in *O caso Rubem Fonseca: Violência e erotismo em* Feliz ano novo.

5. As Sá notes, Fonseca has returned to the device of reflexive writers-as-characters in a variety of later stories and novels at various points in his trajectory, including *Bufo & Spallanzani* (1985) and *E do meio do mundo prostituto só amores guardei ao meu charuto* (1997).

6. For a thorough discussion and critical interrogation of the processes surrounding the censorship of *Feliz ano novo*, see "A proibição: Os bastidores da censura" in Silva's *Rubem Fonseca: Proibido e consagrado*. In *The Muffled Cries*, Baden provides a more cursory look at the ban, but he helpfully explores it in relation to the larger rubric of artistic censorship during the military dictatorship.

7. René Wellek first asked the same question in *Theory of Literature* (1956), noting the difficulty in creating a product that is both literary and historical at once. Perkins revisits the question in the context of what he sees as the recent revival of literary history determined by quite distinct concerns about production (1992, 9–12).

8. Early examples include Linda Hutcheon's *A Poetics of Postmodernism* (1988), Fernando Aínsa's "La reescritura de la historia en la nueva novela histórica" (1991), and Seymour Menton's *Latin America's New Historical Novel* (1992).

9. Although the expression "Feliz ano novo" later became a protest slogan against the regime of Ernesto Geisel, Fonseca's concern regarding censorship of ideas is not necessarily directed at the dictatorship under which he wrote the piece but rather at the gatekeepers of art. Baden suggests that Fonseca had supported the regime in its early years and, thus, that the banning of the book came as a surprise (1999, 104, 107).

WORKS CITED

Baden, Nancy T. *The Muffled Cries: The Writer and Literature in Authoritarian Brazil, 1964–1985*. Lanham, MD: University Press of America, 1999.

Coutinho, Eduardo de Faria. "Rewriting Latin American Literary History." *Neohelicon* 30, 1 (2003): 103–8.

Figueiredo, Vera Lúcia Follain de. *Os crimes do texto: Rubem Fonseca e a ficção contemporânea*. Belo Horizonte: Editora UFMG, 2003.

Fonseca, Rubem. *Contos reunidos*. São Paulo: Companhia das Letras, 1994.

Harris, Wendell V. "What Is Literary History?" *College English* 56, 4 (April 1994): 434–51.

Lowe, Elizabeth. *The City in Brazilian Literature*. East Brunswick, NJ: Associated University Press, 1982.

Perkins, David. *Is Literary History Possible?* Baltimore, MD: Johns Hopkins University Press, 1992.

Sá, Sérgio de. *A reinvenção do escritor: Literatura e "mass media."* Belo Horizonte: Editora UFMG, 2010.

Silva, Deonísio da. *O caso Rubem Fonseca: Violência e erotismo em "Feliz no novo."* São Paulo: Editora Alfa-Omega, 1983.

———. *Rubem Fonseca: Proibido e consagrado*. Rio de Janeiro: Relume-Dumará, 1996.

Teles, Gilberto Mendonça. *Contramargem: Estudos de literatura*. Rio de Janeiro: Editora PUC-Rio, 2002.

Vidal, Ariovaldo José. *Roteiro para um narrador: Uma leitura dos contos de Rubem Fonseca*. Cotia: Ateliê Editorial, 2000.

FRANS WEISER is a visiting professor at the University of Georgia. He has published journal articles on contemporary Luso-Hispanic historical fiction, metafiction, and theory. His current research interests include American intellectual history and reflexive film. He may be reached at frweiser@uga.edu.

ISAAC LOURIDO
Translated by Manus O'Duibhir

The Crisis of Literary History and Disciplinary Renovation
The Alternative of Systemic Theories

ABSTRACT: This article reviews the principal debates and challenges to literary history after the critical revision of the discipline in the last third of the twentieth century. More specifically, the article evaluates the possibility of constructing a historiographical model founded on systemic theories, with the capacity to contribute to the renovation of the discipline of literary history. Alternative historiographical methods, based on polysystem theory, theory of literary field, and the theorization of literature as institution, are examined with the intention of showing the advantages that these approaches can bring to the study of literature, but also their failings, and the debates they have provoked that have yet to be resolved. Finally, the article proposes possible applications of these alternative approaches to literary history to the lusophone literary systems.

KEYWORDS: crisis of literary history, systemic theories, lusophone literary systems.

Constitution and Crisis of Literary History: Challenges and Possibilities for the Discipline

A synthetic study of the constitution of literary history (LH) as discipline and discourse should attend to a series of fundamental factors. The first of these has to do with the fact that LH is, essentially, a European discipline. That is to say, LH is epistemologically configured in accordance with the localized rhythms and functionalities of specific European cultural centers. The second factor has to do with the chronological development of LH in the passage from the eighteenth to the nineteenth century, and therefore is linked to the decay of classical and neoclassical poetics, and the reaction against the principles of universality and rationality of the Enlightenment. Finally, it is necessary to analyze the trajectory of the discipline in terms of tensions that are manifest at different levels: between different epistemological and philosophical models, between national and geocultural spaces and schools, between differently assumed roles and functions, and also between different disciplines and fields of knowledge.

This article attempts to create a dialectical comprehension of the processes that not only allowed for the emergence of LH as discipline and discourse but also its legitimization and institutionalization. This dialectic should include a mapping of the emergence of national identity, linked to the nation-state, at the ideological, ethical, civic, and moral levels, the assumption of some type of historicist paradigm, as well as an understanding of the emergence of LH as civil history and its progressive scientific legitimization (Cunha 2002, 25–38). The emergence of LH reinforced the abandonment of the classical and humanistic thought of the Renaissance and involved a chronotopic reorientation from the cosmopolitan to the national, and a correlative understanding of an autonomous and diverse development of various "national organisms."

In *The Rise of English Literary History* (1941), René Wellek argued that the constitution of LH involved, on the one hand, the fusion of biography and criticism and, on the other, the importation of the narrative structures of political historiography. This capacity to assimilate not only practices from the field of knowledge but also programs initially defined in terms of philosophical and ideological intent forms part of the configuration of the two principal literary historiographical models of the first half of the nineteenth century. As opposed to the German Romantic model, which is marked with Hegelian historicism and a Herderian genetic historicism, it is important to take into account the models that are informed by Enlightenment values, connected to the processes of social reform derived from the French Revolution and representative of the political-cultural hegemony of France in the first half of the nineteenth century. These approaches are related in some ways to the philosophical innovations of Francis Bacon at the start of the seventeenth century and also to what would be known in the following century as *philosophical history*, concerned with offering a unified vision of the object of study, determining its temporal development in terms of determinate categories (origin, progress, advance, decadence), and attempting to find a causal explanation for the succession of different phases (Equipo Glifo 2003).

Typical of the protean character of the discipline was the development of the positivist LH, based on the investigation of the facts (literary, in this case), conditioned by the methodology and scientific objectives imported from the natural sciences, and—a fundamental point—linked to the Darwinian and Spenserian conception of nature and evolution that was to become hegemonic in the second half of the nineteenth century. Equally reflective of the dialectic development of LH is the historiographic criticism of Gustave Lanson, the basic elements of which were the adaptation of an epistemology that would later be recognized as *sociological*, and which entailed the rejection of a mechanistic positivism that diminished the importance of observation and reflection as intellectual faculties, and likewise diminished the consideration of the civic, moral, and national functions of literature.

In this revision of the constitution of the discipline, the pragmatic and performative functions of LH are vital points of interest in the construction of national literatures, both in the phase of their "invention" and in the social institutionalization of systems of symbolic capital and naturalized cultural habitus, an operation that was efficiently enforced through formalized education systems. These matters have been studied in the now classic works of Benedict Anderson, Eric Hobsbawm, Terence Ranger, and Anne-Marie Thiesse, works that tend not only to discredit the idea of a natural national identity but also to dissect the mechanisms through which collective adhesion to such an identity is achieved. In this regard, Cunha (129–60) queries the ways in which LH can function as a "história profunda da nação" (deep history of the nation), encouraging an understanding of LH as a discursive-rhetorical construct with a relevance to the political-ideological spheres, a path that was explored as well in the classic works of Hayden White and David Perkins.

Precisely this involvement in the pragmatic-ideological spheres has been the main basis for objections to LH's status as a scientific discipline. The revision of the positivist model, and reconfigurations of the discipline such as those of Lanson, or Wilhelm Dilthey's *Literaturwissenschaft*, or even the French comparatism of the first half of the twentieth century, reflects a desire to achieve scientific status that is a real leitmotif of LH. In this development, it is worthwhile to pay attention to the dialectic of history and criticism, moving from the simplistic understanding of literary criticism as a subjective discourse, as well as the limiting of its role to the field of autonomous action as opposed to literary and general history.

The use of teleological principles in any historiographical model marks specific limits with regard to the standards of scientific objectivity deemed necessary in the natural sciences. Taking on board the thought of Siegfried J. Schmidt on these matters, it is necessary to point out that the scientific value of LH tended to be related to the supposed objectivity of its results, with this objectivity deemed as correlative to truth. The extreme exigencies imposed by these standards were a central factor in the delegitimization of the discipline, a process already visible in the first half of the twentieth century, reflecting the fact that for some paradigms the construction of a scientifically valid LH was an impossibility.

In this synthetic reconstruction of the development of LH, one must consider the mid-twentieth-century work of René Wellek. As José Antonio Escrig notes, Wellek defined (in a report written for the Modern Language Association in 1952) a tripartite division within literary research consisting of the complementary fields of textual criticism, literary history, and literary criticism, with a notable interdependency between the last two. Within LH itself, Wellek distinguished between two approaches: those oriented toward a broad cultural history on the one hand and those closer to art history, with a greater dependence on aesthetic theory and the consideration of the work of art as *monument*, on the other. In a paper presented at the congress of the International Comparative Literature Association in 1970, and which would form part of the much-cited article "The Fall of Literary History," however, Wellek identifies an "atomistic factualism," a sterile archeologism, the insufficiency of causal explanations derived from social sciences, and the submission of LH to the political history of nations as basic factors that hindered the articulation of LH as an autonomous discipline. He suggested three models for its renovation. The first would be based on the negation of historical causalism in the study of literature, and would take as its paradigm work such as that of Benedetto Croce, which understood the work of art as a unique and immediately present phenomenon. As against this antihistoricist model, Wellek identified a model that took account of historical factors, its origin in Marxist and positivist thought, which was most visible in the postulates of sociologically informed LH. The third model had to do with approaches that attempted to trace an internal evolution in literature, as exemplified in the work of the Russian formalists and Czech structuralists but also in some elements of the approaches of reception theory, sociology of literature, and Gadamerian-inspired hermeneutics.

Though LH underwent a long process of criticism in the twentieth century, it is also important to note the central role that the idea of *crisis* would acquire in the 1970s. Cunha (457–63) notes the persistence of LH as a university discipline, as compared to its gradual exhaustion as a *discursive formation*. But he also puts this decadence of the discipline in the context of the broader crisis of concepts such as *history* (and the weakening of ideas of historical reason and concomitant myths), *modernity* (and the goals of progress and improvement that it would supposedly involve), as well as the concepts that LH had served (nation, national identity, and civic-moral conscience). The emergence, since the nineteenth century, of a new idea of literature, based on the aesthetic autonomy of the literary and the incompatibility of literature and history, was central to the weakening of these concepts. This is manifest in the contrast between the growing theorization of literary history and the scarcity of historiographical works that take account of this thought, perhaps a symptom of the lack of spaces within which the complementarity between literary theory and LH could be developed.

A range of factors that were important in the debates of the 1960s and '70s, and that were developed in the following years, should take into account the following positions:

- The removal of the opposition between objective and subjective forms in literary studies, as reflected in the recognition of the interpretative and necessarily partial discursivity of LH.
- An idea of *literature* that does not depend on essentialized categories and is open to relational and functional thought.
- The assimilation of the "linguistic turn" in the social and human sciences (with the rhetorical and pragmatic implications that this turn implies) and its influence in the critique of the hegemonic models of historiography in works such as those by Hayden White.
- The definition as a theoretical object of study, under non-normative parameters, of the social functions of both LH and literature itself.
- The broadening of the field of study and the consequent decentralization of literature, which is now seen as part of a wider field of cultural systems. This broader approach has had different expressions in cultural studies, New Historicism, and polysystem theory.
- The assumption of the general principles of poststructuralism, with the significant presence of Michel Foucault: the questioning of the figure of the author and an increasing disinterest in the reconstruction of the biographical context of creation; the linking of discursive practices (among these LH), *episteme*, and power; the recognition of new subjectivities, legitimacies, and discursivities that are important in the development of counterhistories.

- The emergence of paradigms that, like the sociological model of Robert Escarpit or those derived from the French Annales school of history, reject historiography as a narrative of events. The Annales school, specifically, gave special attention to the methodological debates between general and cultural history and focused on broad historical processes and structures of *longue durée.* They also encouraged interdisciplinarity and explicative rather than interpretative discursivity.
- On an institutional level, the public interrogation of the epistemological basis of LH and its pertinence and viability. René Wellek's presentation of 1970, which could be said to symbolically begin the process of disciplinary self-questioning, was accompanied by another important event, the founding, in the same year, of the journal *New Literary History,* whose second issue questioned the continuing relevance of LH. Another important event in this history was the publication of David Perkins's *Is Literary History Possible?* (1992) and the discussion prompted by the journal *Neohelicon* in 1993.[1]
- The emergence of decolonizing paradigms, such as that promoted by Walter Mignolo, which highlighted LH's status as a European discipline, and the challenge posed to it by the field of postcolonial and subaltern studies.

In this context, the challenges that contemporary LH must face can be organized in three large areas, defined by their heuristic, methodological-discursive, and institutional bases. By *heuristic* I mean that which concerns the selection of principles that should orient historiographical work before its elaboration, and this involves the systematization of an object of study for LH. This, in accord with the cultural turn already mentioned, the spatial turn in the social sciences, or the systemic turn that this article assimilates, could include *literature* (implicitly this means national literature), *culture, system* or *field,* or even *literary zone.* It is also absolutely necessary to clarify the links between historiographical discourses and specific identitary constructs. Finally, it would be necessary to adopt thought-out approaches toward the representation of time, which is traditionally central to the discipline, and toward the representation of space.

Methodology and *discursivity* are the problems most frequently related to the disciplinary definition of LH. Pertinent here are the debates on the periodization and organization of the materials of historical-literary discourse and the search for discursive and periodological models not bound to totalizing or teleological schemes. Also important is the reconsideration of synchronic as well as diachronic levels of historiography, the attempt to connect narrative formulas and hermeneutic paradigms, and the reevaluation of notions of authorship and authority. This group would likewise include a reflection on the importance of methodological and procedural innovation, with a focus on the necessity, or not (in terms of scientific value/objectivity), of the use of empirical methods.

On the *institutional* level, it would be important to reflect upon the ways in which LH attempts to retain its prestige through a renewed positioning within the disciplinary and academic field. The proposals of the last four decades, of course, have also been part of a redefinition of the functional and performative attributes developed by LH on ethical, ideological, social, and political levels. Relevant in this regard is the reflection on the possibility of including historiographical work in long-term plans for public intervention, on the relationship between performativity and literary emergence, or, finally, on the need for a constant, dynamic, and nonconditioned validation of the discipline.

Systemic Epistemology and Historiographical Models

In the context of not just LH but the contemporary renovation of the study of literature as a whole, the bases upon which we can speak of *systemic theories*, or a *systemic epistemology*, are related to a group of theoretic paradigms that comprehend cultural systems, to a greater or lesser degree, as entities ruled by relational and functional principles of a communicative nature and tending to create autopoietic and autoreferential realities (Tötösy de Zepetnek 1992). This group of theoretical paradigms would include, in accordance with the loose criteria defined by the Hungarian-Canadian researcher, the polysystem theory of Itamar Even-Zohar and researchers at Tel Aviv University, the empirical science of literature, founded by Siegfried J. Schmidt and developed by the NIKOL group, the various theories propagated by literary scholars, such as those devised by Jacques Dubois and Peter Uwe Hohendahl, and the various sociologically based paradigms that use the notions of *system* and *field*, with special importance given to the work of Pierre Bourdieu and his disciples.

In all of these systemic theories, there is a desire to move past the schemes of analysis that had already shown signs of exhaustion by the mid-1970s, and whose lineage could be traced to elements of Romanticism and positivism on the one hand, and the structuralist tradition on the other. Systemic theories aspire, to varying degrees within any given approach, to levels of scientific value and objectivity in their analyses and deny the criteria of taste, canonical status, or a priori interest in the definition of their object of study.

None of the systemic paradigms here mentioned corresponded to an explicit interest in the disciplinary reconfiguration of LH, and it is difficult to reconstitute from the theoretical-methodological corpus traits that would allow us to speak of a systemic historical-literary epistemology. However, despite the unstable relationship that these theoretical approaches have with LH, it is possible to undertake a critical review of systemic theories and methodologies and explore the ways in which their innovations are relevant to LH as a discipline.

Thus, in order to create a historiographical model based on *polysystem theory*, it is necessary to attend to the way in which it comprises literary and cultural systems that are interlinked and internally complex, and thereby dynamic and contingent. As opposed to the centrality of notions such as *change* and *diachrony* as the bases of historical research, dynamic functionalism values stability and synchrony as historiographical categories.[2] The first of these terms is understood in relation to the analysis of the struggles between centers and peripheries, and to the functions assumed by canonized models. Synchrony becomes the basis for a new perspective: *dynamic polychrony*, the comparison of synchronic sections of given systems. Polysystem theory, then, opts to consider literary systems in terms of their links with adjacent systems or structures, whether these are cultural, political, or economic.

Of interest here is the work of Even-Zohar and the members of the Unit of Cultural Research at Tel Aviv University, who focus on the Hebrew-Israeli cultural system, which comprises a series of elements (territorial dispersion, an indefinite community) that problematize conventional LH. This means that the group works with an alternative concept of *history*, oriented toward the analysis of change in a diachronic perspective but renouncing the chronological schemes traditionally accepted in LH. The incorporation of a synchronic dimension should be understood in terms of a questioning of the links between LH and long-term historical periods on the one hand, and LH and a totalized referent (e.g., literary system, national literature) on the other.

This refusal of the existence of a unique model of historiographical application, or a conception of a (complete) LH of a determined system (linked to a national referent), allows us to advance in the formation of methodology for a polysystemic LH. In the first place, the idea of *system* obliges us to overcome the study of a determinate textual tradition situated "in context"; it also allows us to decenter canonized works as privileged objects of study. The vital point here is the incorporation of systemic categories that have been elided in historical research, such as production, consumption, institutions, market, and repertoire, and also the inclusion of intersystemic relations and transfers, with obvious repercussions in terms of the ideas of tradition, continuity, and territoriality, which constitute the foundations of the historiographical model that has been hegemonic since the nineteenth century. This would mean the possibility of an LH that attends to more than literary or philological factors, extends beyond the national, and is more attentive to the planned, constructed, and institutional nature of cultural systems, elements that are especially visible in emerging systems (such as the Angolan, Mozambican, or Galician, in the lusophone world) but never absent in the stronger, more stable systems (such as the Portuguese or Brazilian).

In the work of the Belgian researcher José Lambert, we can find other elements of interest for the application of polysystem theory to LH. Lambert ("In Quest of Literary World Maps") proposes a merging of systemic and "alternational" principles with a spatialized analytic gaze. Lambert conceives, then, LH as the study of literary practices and processes within a given geocultural space; a particular example could be presented as *The Literary History of [a given place]*. Lambert structures a historiographical model based on the dynamic, nonunivocal relationship among linguistic, literary, and political maps that attempts, ultimately, to attend to the heterogeneity and dynamism of social systems (e.g., linguistic and cultural competition, the definition of boundaries, relations of exportation and importation, deterritorializations, intercultural hierarchies) as opposed to the homogenizing approaches often associated with centers of power (Lambert 1999, "Aproximaciones sistémicas y la literatura").

Siegfried J. Schmidt defines the basic problems for a definition of LH from a *constructivist and empirical* viewpoint: (a) the necessity of establishing concrete definitions for the concepts of literature, history, literary history, study of literature, theory, method, and so on; (b) the consideration of the data of LH as able to be interpreted and evaluated; (c) the linking of data for the construction of coherent units (periods, epochs, genres), but with the understanding of history as a retrospective construction; (d) a reflection on the nature of historical representation that should account for certain preliminary considerations—every LH is partial; narrative conventions provoke an order that depends on the activity of the author; the opposition to the conventional narrative model allows for accusations of arbitrariness and relativism; (e) the placing of the scientific value of LH in its aspects that make our experience accessible and understandable, on the one hand, and in terms of plausibility, acceptability, and social intersubjectivity, on the other; (f) the articulation of LH as a complex history of the relations among systems of social life; (g) the critical assimilation of the intellectual tradition that puts into question the concepts of *text*, *subject*, and *sense*; (h) the consideration of LH as a social and political institution and as a legitimizing science; (i) the reconsideration of the role of interpretation in LHs.

A central question for the concretization of a historiographical model in accordance with the postulates of the empirical science of literature is the difficult harmonization of constructivism and empiricism in the area of LH. In the words of Schmidt (266), "the constructive 'nature' of our cognition excludes the possibility of an empirical literature—it is not possible to demonstrate the descriptivity of our historiographical affirmations," a circumstance that causes the author to propose, synthetically, the elaboration of an "empirical mentality," with the construction of intersubjective bases, coherent in their argumentation and with sufficient factual guarantees. It would also be necessary to consider different levels of empiricality, especially those that could be applied to literary texts as material resources; this last approach would be inevitable in the moments when these are the only elements within a given period but would only be valid at those moments when the ("current") reading of literary texts corresponds intersubjectively with the reading of nonliterary texts from the same period.

Demonstrating that the most direct link between the systems theory of Niklas Luhmann and literary studies passes precisely through Schmidt's empirical science, Manuel Maldonado Alemán also reflects upon systems theory's importance for LH. For Maldonado Alemán, the study of LH is based, first of all, on intra-, extra- (relationships between a system and its environment), and inter- (relationships between systems) systemic relations. At the same time, Maldonado Alemán identifies as the principal challenges for the establishment of a historiographical model the problems of integrating the evolutionary character of LH with the understanding of system not as process but as state, best approached with the concepts of autopoiesis, autoreference, and autonomy. He also recognizes the difficulties of understanding extra- and intersystemic relations and their functioning as indicators of systemic limits.

The proposed solution is provided by the notion of *structural coupling*, "which emphasizes the influence of the environment on the system, and is complementary to the notion of autopoiesis and indicates the relationships of dependence, adaptation, and compatibility that are established between a systemic unit and its environment" (Maldonado Alemán 31), and moves the focus of study to the continuous process of coupling that is dynamic and evolutionary. Overall, Maldonado Alemán's approach seeks to understand LH as a complex process of evolution, with stages of variation, selection, and stabilization, and with a double focus of observation that also involves the functioning of the literary system as an environment for other social systems.

In the development of a model for LH based on the *theory of literary field* (Bourdieu), an important methodological question arises involving the tension between the synchronic and diachronic planes. The comparison between *literary history* and the *history of a given field* should be understood as a history of struggles with different types of capital at stake and for which the reconstruction of an internal logic (or habitus), which regulates behaviors and positions within the field, should be undertaken. On the other hand, Bourdieu defines a field as a "synchronization of discordant times" (Bourdieu and Wacquant 1992, 66–70; Bourdieu 1992, 238–40), alluding to the necessity of recognizing in this concrete state of the field the preceding historical development and, in his words, the dynamic of "permanent change" that guarantees the field's continuity and that, for the agents and groups involved in the struggle for capital and institutional control, constitutes the main index of its pertinence to the same.

The French sociologist proposed a *genetic analysis* of the constitution of, and tensions within, a given field as well as the study of the relationship between the field studied and other fields, especially the field of power (Bourdieu and Wacquant, 67). Both the conceptualization of the literary field and its applications to literary historiography have been frequently criticized because of their subjection to a particular period of French literature. This has led to the recognition of a type of conceptual a priori in the thought of Bourdieu: the history of an artistic field is the history of the struggle for the achievement and conservation of its autonomy.

However, it is important to recognize two distinct uses of the theory of field in its application to historiographical programs. The first, linked to authors such as Anna Boschetti, Gisèle Sapiro, and Fabrice Thumerel in the French context, and Patricia Cabrera in the Mexican, is the analysis of consolidated literary fields, with recognized autonomy and localized origins and, because of this, suitable for the development of genetic analysis. The second use is the application of Bourdieu's theories to those literary fields with less autonomy, or whose existence has been put in question (such as the Galician, or those of African countries with Portuguese as an official language), and it is obvious that processes of constitution, autonomization, and legitimization of the literary field (with regard to other cultural fields, other literary fields within the same social space, and the broader field of power) should be of special interest for historiographical work, normally undertaken in relation to the processes of identity formation, which is nearly always conceived in national terms.

One application of the theory of cultural fields to the study of literature is that based on the prosopographic method, the most dynamic branch of which is a political history of the elites. Prosopography, in a wider sense, is the interpretation of internal relations among collective subjects, including political, economic, and social powers (Carasa Soto 1994, 41–51). This is the elaboration of collective biographies through the compilation and cross-referencing of a series of data that would delimit the positions and trajectories of the agents selected, with the ultimate aim of identifying the field's historic structure. This perspective allowed researchers, such as Gisèle Sapiro and Rémy Ponton in the French context, to study writers in concrete moments and showed the special productivity of the theory of literary field as a literary theory of authors.

Despite the epistemological difference between the Bourdian approach and those approaches that consider *literature as an institution*, many practitioners of the latter chose to establish analogies between the two models, based on their interest in the study of the material and symbolical conditions of literary activity and, also, in the sociological grounding of their proposals. The most well-known cases are those of Jacques Dubois, Cees van Rees, Alain Viala, and Peter Bürger. Bürger, however, and unlike the others mentioned, proposed an institutional LH, based on a critique of the traditional narrative model and giving a decisive importance to the processes of the avant-garde, with these seen as moments of crisis in which institutional mechanisms are questioned and identified with greater clarity and therefore open to a more precise study.

Of more importance for the creation of an LH is the methodological approach suggested by Peter Uwe Hohendahl in his theory of the literary institution. The German author thus identifies four indispensable areas of study for the development of a literary history: (1) the conditions of emergence for the practices of reading and writing; (2) the systems of norms and conventions that dominate the institution; (3) the relations between the literary institution and other cultural and political institutions; and (4) the processes of change within literary institutions (Hohendahl 1989, 34). This is a program that, although absolutely aware of the importance of the national in historiographical construction, assimilates the notion of *public space* and demonstrates an explicit interest in the performative function of LH, literary theory, and criticism in conforming their objects of study.

Xoán González-Millán moved away from some of these orientations in his definition of a historiographical model that would suit marginal literatures or, in general, literatures in societies where the institutionalization of discursive production is controlled from an exogenous political space. His program could be applied to peripheral or minority literatures (such as Galician literature) in the European context, as to literatures in a colonial setting or in the process of emergence (the African literatures in Portuguese), and was based on four areas of basic interest: the material and institutional conditions of the production and reception of literary discourse; the reception of literary texts, with all the particularities associated with marginalized experience; the identification of systems of codification on linguistic, aesthetic, and ideological levels; the dynamics of intertextuality (González-Millán 1992, 451–52).

A comparative analysis of the approaches related to a systemic epistemology and their (not very numerous) historiographical applications shows the range of functions that each of these could fulfill. It is clear that the theory of literary field has more potential for the study of literary agents and producers; the theories of literary institution have greater applicability in the study of material conditions and infrastructures and the conditions of readership, diffusion, and market. Polysystem theory, on the other hand, was used with greater frequency for the study of texts and their literary and sociocultural function, making use of the suggestive notion of *repertoire*.

From another perspective, the incorporation of notions such as *autonomy* and *legitimization* in the methodological frameworks with a sociological basis (such as the theory of literary field or the literary institution) allowed for a greater linking of systemic-empiric theories and the pragmatic and teleological processes of national construction. This circumstance explains the success of studies of literary institution or field in peripheral or emerging cultural systems such as the Galician.[3] On the other hand, and from a pragmatic-performative perspective, the polysystem theory was the preferred basis for those approaches that, far from a national pragmatics, were interested in describing and analyzing the interferences and the conflicts derived from the dynamic relationships between systems.

In the same way, some relationship should be formed between epistemological renovation in the academic sphere and the greater or lesser centrality of literary or cultural areas. In this sense, the perspectives and methodologies of systemic theories seem able to take on the challenges posed by peripheral or emergent literary systems to literary theory and history, especially in terms of the processes of institutionalization and social legitimization inherent in the emergence of these new literary systems; the representative case in the lusophone world would be the literatures in Portuguese language of Africa (Salinas Portugal 1999). If the definition of new objects and horizons for research necessarily demands the articulation of renewed conceptual tools, the principal obstacles for their effective application should be located in the use of pragmatic strategies based on the repetition of hegemonic models, which have as their aim the international recognition of a literary system. This piece argues, in turn, that the (symbolic) struggle between center and periphery in a "cultural intersystem" (Torres Feijó 2000) can also take place in the literary (Mata 2004, 231) and in the academic sphere, and that the constitution of a renewed epistemology for LH (like that here situated within the systemic theories) can only occur from positions and spaces removed from the romantic epistemological model of the nation, a model still hegemonic in the cultural and academic centers of the lusophone world.

NOTES

1. The inquiry promoted by *Neohelicon* contained the following questions: (1) Is the methodology of literary history, elaborated in the nineteenth century, still valid? (2) Can the work of literary history be absolutely restricted? Is it possible that the questions it addresses can be resolved by linguistics, cultural anthropology and sociology, or even philosophy? Does literary history have a justification and space for its existence? Does literary history have any status outside the academy? Does it create public interest? Does the role and justification of literature diminish because of mass culture and its media? (3) What place does comparatism, in the broad sense of the word, have in comparative literary history and world history? (*Neohelicon* XX, 2: 9–10).

2. Even-Zohar (*Polysystem Studies*) defines dynamic functionalism in terms of the con-

nections established among Russian formalism, Czech structuralism, the semiotics of culture of the Tartu school, and polysystem theory. The basic shared principles of these approaches are the understanding of literature as a dynamic phenomenon, the recognition of conflict as the motor for change in the interior of the system, and the integration of literary systems in wider polysystems as an important element in the way they function.

3. Here one could cite the recent work of Antón Figueroa, *Ideoloxía e autonomía no campo literario galego* (Ames: Laiovento, 2010), or Roberto López-Iglésias Samartim, "O processo de construçom do sistema literário galego entre o franquismo e a transiçom (1974–1978): Margens, relaçons, estrutura e estratégias de planificaçom cultural," doctoral thesis, University of Santiago de Compostela, 2010.

WORKS CITED

Bourdieu, Pierre. "Le champ littéraire." *Actes de la Recherche en Sciences Sociales* 89 (1991): 3–46.

———. *Les règles de l'art: Gènese et structure du champ littéraire.* Paris: Seuil, 1992.

Bourdieu, Pierre, and Loïc J. D. Wacquant. *Réponses: Pour une anthropologie réflexive.* Paris: Seuil, 1992.

Bürger, Peter. "On Literary History." *Poetics* 14 (1985): 199–207.

Cabrera López, Patricia. *Una inquietud de amanecer: Literatura y política en México, 1962–1987.* Mexico: Centro de Investigaciones Interdisciplinarias en Ciencias y Humanidades (UNAM) / Plaza y Valdés, 2006.

Carasa Soto, Pedro. *Elites, Prosopografía Contemporánea.* Universidad de Valladolid, 1994.

Cunha, Carlos Manuel Ferreira da. *A construção do discurso da história literária na literatura portuguesa do século XX.* Braga: Centro de Estudos Humanísticos/Universidade do Minho, 2002.

Dubois, Jacques. *L'Institution de la littérature: Introduction à une sociologie* [1978]. Brussels: Editions Labor, 2005.

Equipo Glifo. "Historia literaria." *Diccionario de termos literarios.* Vol. II: E–H. Santiago de Compostela: Centro Ramón Piñeiro para a Investigación en Humanidades, 2003. 619–27.

Escrig, José Antonio. "Escenarios del debate sobre la historia literaria." In *Teorías de la historia literaria*, edited by Luis Beltrán Almería and José Antonio Escrig. Madrid: Arco Libros, 2005. 23–44.

Even-Zohar, Itamar. "Polysystem Studies." *Poetics Today* 11, 1 (1990).

———. *Papers in Culture Research.* Tel Aviv: Porter Chair of Semiotics, Tel Aviv University, 2005. Accessed June 6, 2012, from http://www.even-zohar.com.

González-Millán, Xoán. "A configuración historiográfica dunha literatura marxinal."

Actas do I Congreso Internacional da Cultura Galega. Santiago de Compostela: Dirección Xeral de Cultura, 1992. 444–52.

Hobsbawm, Eric J., and Terence Ranger. *The Invention of Tradition*. Cambridge: Cambridge University Press, 1984.

Hohendahl, Peter Uwe. *Building a National Literature: The Case of Germany (1830–1870)*, translated by Renate Baron Franciscono. Ithaca, NY: Cornell University Press, 1989.

Lambert, José. "In Quest of Literary World Maps." In *Interculturality and the Historical Study of Literary Translations*, edited by Harald Kittel and Armin Paul Frank. Berlin: Erich Schmidt, 1991. 133–44.

———. "Aproximaciones sistémicas y la literatura en las sociedades multilingues." In *Teoría de los polisistemas*, edited and translated by Montserrat Iglesias Santos. Madrid: Arco Libros, 1999. 53–70.

Maldonado Alemán, Manuel. "La historiografía literaria: Una aproximación sistémica." *Revista de Filología Alemana* 14 (2006): 9–40.

Mata, Inocência. "O espaço da Lusofonia literária: Para uma crítica da razão africana." In *Bases metodolóxicas para unha historia comparada das literaturas na península Ibérica*, edited by Anxo Abuín González and Anxo Tarrío Varela. Santiago de Compostela: Universidade de Santiago de Compostela, 2004. 225–34.

Mignolo, Walter. "Rethinking the Colonial Model." In *Rethinking Literary History: A Dialogue on Theory*, edited by Linda Hutcheon and Mario J. Valdés. Oxford: Oxford University Press, 2002. 155–93.

Perkins, David. *Is Literary History Possible?* Baltimore: Johns Hopkins University Press, 1992.

Salinas Portugal, Francisco. *Entre Próspero e Caliban: Literaturas Africanas de Língua Portuguesa*. Santiago de Compostela: Edicións Laiovento, 1999.

Schmidt, Siegfried J. "Escribir historias de la literatura: Algunas observaciones desde un punto de vista constructivista," translated by Nereida Congost Maestre and Milagro García Ramos, adapted by Francisco Chico Rico. *Teoría/Crítica* 2 (1995): 245–69.

Thiesse, Anne-Marie. *La création des identités nationales: Europe XVIIIe–XXe siécle*. Paris: Editions du Seuil, 1999.

Thumerel, Fabrice. *Le champ littéraire française au XXe siècle: Éléments pour une sociologie de la littérature*. Paris: Armand Colin, 2002.

Torres Feijó, Elias J. "Norma linguística e (inter-)sistema cultural: O caso galego." *Actas del Congreso Internacional de Historia y Cultura en la Frontera: I Encuentro de Lusitanistas Españoles*, edited by J. M. Carrasco González et al. Cáceres: Universidad de Extremadura, 2000. Vol. II: 967–96.

Tötösy de Zepetnek, Steven. "Systemic Approaches to Literature—An Introduction with Selected Bibliographies." *Canadian Review of Comparative Literature/Revue Canadienne de Littérature Comparée* 19, 1/2 (1992): 21–93.

Wellek, René. "The Fall of Literary History." *The Attack on Literature and Other Essays.* Chapel Hill: University of North Carolina Press, 1982. 64–77.

White, Hayden. *Metahistoria: La imaginación histórica en la Europa del siglo XX.* México: Fondo de Cultura Económica, 1992.

ISAAC LOURIDO is a member of the Research Group in Literary Theory and Comparative Literature at the University of Santiago de Compostela. In 2011 he presented his doctoral thesis, titled "As alternativas sistémicas da Historia literaria en situación de conflito cultural: Desenvolvimentos teóricos e modelos de renovación nos casos galego e quebequense" (The Systemic Alternatives to Literary History in a Situation of Cultural Conflict: Theoretical Developments and Models of Renovation in the Galician and Québécois Cases). He was the coeditor, with Burghard Baltrusch, of the volume *Non-Lyric Discourses in Contemporary Poetry* (2012), and his most recent publications are "La crítica historiográfica de José Lambert: Hacia una Historia literaria del conflicto cultural" (2012) and "Entre Rosalía 21 y Labregos do tempo dos sputniks: La poesía galega como espectáculo" (2012). His current lines of research include the theoretical and methodological renovation of literary history and the functional and discursive diversification of contemporary poetry. He may be reached at isaac.lourido@usc.es.

JOBST WELGE

The Problem of Particularity in Literary History

ABSTRACT: The present essay offers a series of reflections on the paradoxical relationship between particularity and synthesis in the practice of literary history. The essay begins by discussing the origin of this dynamic during the Romantic period, reviews the privileging of particularizing narrative and spatial locality in recent publications of literary history, and highlights the central role of the modern novel (with its representation of "particular life") for our contemporary epistemological situation, before proceeding to identify the dynamic within the history and historiography of Brazilian modernism.

KEYWORDS: literary history, particularity, theory of the novel, Brazilian modernism.

Friedrich Bouterwek (1766–1828), now recognized as the first proper historian of Portuguese literature, begins his account (in the fourth volume of his monumental *Geschichte der Poesie und Beredsamkeit seit dem Ende des 13 Jahrhunderts* [History of Poetry and Rhetoric from the End of the Thirteenth Century], published in 1805) as follows: "Even a year ago, I still believed that I would not be able to form from all the materials that I had collected on the history of Portuguese poetry and prose anything more than a coherent fragment."[1] Evidently, ideas and concepts of literary historiography have changed considerably since Bouterwek's day, but his apologetic description of his yet unfinished work as a "coherent fragment" (*zusammenhängendes Fragment*) would almost seem to perfectly characterize what we expect and how we conceive of literary history today—namely, as a somewhat paradoxical or contradictory enterprise. Even as Bouterwek admits to the inevitable lacunae in his work, as well as the material and pragmatic difficulties—for instance, he had not yet attained a copy of Garcia de Resende's *Cancioneiro Geral* (1516), but, he writes, had he waited for it to arrive, his multivolume work would have been delayed even more—his conceptual ideal remains a holistic image of "Portuguese literature" *and* its historiographic representation: "Yet in order to carry out this work even in a preliminary way, the dates that it contains were obtained by various, often labyrinthian and fragmentary ways, and initially they had to be recorded in a strange disorder, until, with the help of chronology, whose high value for literary pragmatism I came to understand once more, something whole [*ein Ganzes*] could develop itself" (Bouterwek, vi). The fact that for Bouterwek the object and the practice of history reflect each other in an ideal totality is symptomatic for the incipient historicism at the beginning of the nineteenth century, in which *historia rerum gestarum* and the *res gestae* themselves, the events and their representation, newly come to coincide.[2] In Bouterwek's preface this idea is expressed in terms that associate the concept of national-cultural totality explicitly with the romantic-poetic culture of southern Europe—that is, in contrast to the more "prosaic" tendency of French literature and the "German universal spirit" (Bouterwek, 4): "For Italian, Spanish, and Portuguese form a closed whole [*geschlossenes Ganzes*], from which one may learn what romantic poetry had once been at its maximum height" (Bouterwek, viii). Portugal, like the other southern European countries, then, is distinguished by its immediate "poetical reflection of nature," as well as the absence of universal "philosophical or aesthetic abstractions" (Bouterwek, viii).

Therefore, the literary historian has to devote himself to the "study of the local" (Bouterwek, 411), that is, the irreducible particularity of national/natural poetry. Bouterwek's contrast between classical and romantic varieties of literature, and his positive evaluation of the latter, anticipates the properly romantic historiography as embodied by authors such as Sismonde de Sismondi, Ferdinand Denis, Almeida Garrett, Alexandre Herculano, and Teófilo Braga.[3] As Roberto Dainotto has shown, such early, typically romantic conceptualizations of literary history, influenced by the geocultural musings of J. G. Herder and Madame de Staël, are grounded in the difference between a European North and South, and they substitute a national(ist) for an earlier cosmopolitan paradigm of the European Republic of Letters.[4] However, somewhat in contrast to Teófilo Braga, as well as the cultural geographies sketched by Madame de Staël or August Schlegel, who opposed the modernity of the North to the imitative literatures of southern Europe,[5] Bouterwek repeatedly voices his belief that the most representative Portuguese works of literature, the works by Luís de Camões and Sá de Miranda, are "organically" and poetically felt, despite having been heavily influenced by classical models.

In this context of an emerging discipline of literary history in Europe, then, Bouterwek may precisely be understood as a transitional figure, for his work on Portuguese literature forms only a part of his gigantic multinational, pan-

European project. He may be seen not merely as a precursor of romantic nationalism, but his essentially cosmopolitan, "prenationalist" approach to literary history may also be related to today's post- and transnational sensibility.[6] Yet it is also important to point out that Bouterwek's Kantian cosmopolitanism, which he explicitly expressed in his "Five Cosmopolitan Letters" (1794), has itself a national index, insofar as he sees especially Germany (next to France, England, and Russia) as a country with a "European-universalist" mission, whereas Portugal, Spain, and Italy—whose "poetic" literary history was spread by his work beyond the borders of the respective countries, in a pioneering feat of scholarship—are seen as "too particular" (and Orientalist) for such a role. Bouterwek promotes a European pluralism, as well as the international exchange of ideas, where individual particularities are preserved. Yet through his Enlightenment ideal of a complementary "general Europeanism" runs a line between nations that are more poetic and nations that are more universal than others.[7]

As the quotations just cited indicate, Bouterwek's tentative conceptual approach to literary history, marking a transitional point between Enlightenment encyclopedism and the romantic taste for the locally specific, wavers between the national and the universal, the fragmentary evidence and the ideal of totality. His European cosmopolitanism acknowledges and values national differences, yet the particularity of literary culture cohabits with the ideal of a coherent presentation of its "totality." Although Bouterwek is keen to link the manifestations of literary culture to the political and national history of its time, the concept of literary history is seen as a privileged medium of envisioning totality, be it with respect to the idea of national character, be it as exemplifications of specific stages of a teleologically conceived development of history. As Hans Ulrich Gumbrecht has shown, this kind of literary history was made possible by and depended on the specifically modern notion of a self-reflexive and totalizing History.[8]

While our contemporary approaches to literary history follow Bouterwek in his dedication to the locally particular (and the transnational), they have renounced the idea of a totalizing, "grand" narrative and have developed different methods of particularizing the very mode of historiographical presentation. Especially recently, after a trend of revisionary, postmodern histories, a new awareness has arisen of the need for "nontotalizing" modes of synthesis. In the following section, I want first to briefly survey some recent examples for this particularizing trend in literary historiography. Second, I will address the question of how this historiographical and epistemological question—the impossibility of conceiving grand narratives—is echoed by the history/historiography of the modern novel, as the quintessential genre of particularity. Finally, I want to ask how the interrelation of these two aspects—the particularization of literary history and literature as the expression of local particularity—may apply to the specific case of Brazilian literature.

The Particularization of Literary History

Recent reflections on the possibilities and problems of literary history have stressed the dialectical relation between totality and fragmentation, between the network and the irreducibly particular.[9] Among the most well-known examples for the postmodern revision of literary history under the sign of the multiple and the fragmentary are the "new" literary histories published by Harvard University Press (*A New History of French Literature*, *A New History of German Literature*).[10] These works written by multiple authors are distinguished by their "thick description" of individual moments and events of literary history. The anthologized essays are arranged in chronological order, yet they eschew any clear causal logic and deliberately juxtapose different genres as well as the individual approaches of the different contributors. While the individual essays are undoubtedly conceived as historical contextualizations of the specific texts and authors at hand, the relations between the different essays are programmatically devoid of a clear sequential logic. Instead, a system of indexed names and terms allows the (already reasonably informed) reader to establish multiple, nonhierarchical relations between the different essays. After its initial appearance in 1989, the *New History of French Literature* has been welcomed as a refreshing deconstruction of conventional literary history, yet it has also provoked criticism, especially David Perkins's claim that this work would eschew history altogether: "Encyclopedic form is intellectually deficient. Its explanations of past happenings are piecemeal, may be inconsistent with each other, and are admitted to be inadequate. It precludes a vision of its subject. Because it aspires to reflect the past in its multiplicity and heterogeneity, it does not organize the past, and in this sense, it is not history."[11] While in my opinion Perkins overstates his case—he glosses over the fact that encyclopedically arranged, microhistorical "thick descriptions" are certainly a different kind of history but still provide historical contextualization of individual texts—he is, of course, right in his assertion that such a work makes no attempt to systematize and "organize" the past. Indeed, this "failure" is precisely the revisionary point.[12]

For a more recent revision of literary history, let me mention an interesting example from Italy, a country with a particularly strong tradition of academic historicism (Francesco de Sanctis, Benedetto Croce, Antonio Gramsci) and a venerable tradition of writing literary histories. The three-volume work *Atlante della letteratura italiana* (Atlas of Italian Literature), published by Einaudi, is one of the most ambitious and sophisticated examples of national literary history in recent times. It is symptomatic for a new tendency that, while following in the microhistorical path of the "New Histories," is also highly aware of the necessity and the challenges of what Michel de Certeau has called the "historiographical operation."[13] This *Atlas* tries to counter the idea of a totalizing, Hegelian historicism by combining historical chronology and context with the particularizing category of space or geography, in order to conceive of a different form of temporality. As the editors write in their introduction, this temporality "is capable to pass from the phenomena of long duration in the Italian literary civilization to the small events, only apparently marginal, which through fulminous ignitions, perhaps by way of a sudden encounter or confrontation, end up determining a shift destined to weigh on the subsequent history" (*Atlante* 2010, xvi).[14] Such an approach appears indeed to be suitable for a national tradition that has been unusually polycentric within the European context. Yet, as the quotation indicates, the focus on spatial marginality also entails a microhistorical dimension, whereby apparently contingent "small events" are seen as replacing a "too much ordered gallery of masters and masterworks" (*Atlante*, xviii), so that they may illuminate literary history also by way of the dead ends, roads not taken, losers of evolutionary processes, as well as coincidences, synchronies, and missed encounters. Moreover, given the editors' desire to displace the centrality of single classical texts, the authors of the *Atlas* were also asked to consider aspects of production, reception, performance, or the relations to other media. Nevertheless, all contributions are grounded in a specific "*hic et nunc*, a spatio-temporal point as concrete as possible" (*Atlante*, xx), a point that mediates contingency with historical decisiveness. Yet eschewing the contemporary "fetishism of the fragment," the editors postulate that a literary history that anthologizes discrete events must also confront the question of interrelations: "In any case, these moments are of interest especially in their relation to so many other moments of the same genre: because of their interconnectedness, more than for their (splendid) isolation" (*Atlante*, xx). Concretely, this means that a series of essays are grouped together under a more general, synthetic account, which presents a larger historical curve or structural background of the cultural "system." In this sense, the *Atlas* may be said to follow in the steps of Pierre Nora's *lieux de mémoire* and the "New Histories," yet it complements the idea of the essayistic narration of "loaded" anecdotes with a more systematic presentation of the spatial and temporal frames (called *reti*, or nets), specifically with regard to the contextualization of the modes of authorship—an approach that is in some respects reminiscent of Pierre Bourdieu's sociological theory of the literary field. Moreover, the combination of deliberately marginal literary manifestations with the "hard facts" of cartographic and infographic elements is clearly indebted to Franco Moretti's polemical intervention in favor of statistical research and the (now routinely criticized) practice of "distant reading," as well as the application to literary history of other epistemological models from the social and natural sciences.[15] In contrast to the acknowledged model of Moretti's *Atlas of the European Novel*, which combined the distribution of literary models in space with the representation of space within realist novels, the *Atlas of Italian Literature* is generally not concerned with this latter aspect.

It is also remarkable that this approach, centered on the locally situated social networks of literary production, is ultimately said not to dismantle the canon but to "better appreciate—and better comprehend—the canonical authors of Italian literature" (*Atlante*, xxiii). Evidently, this work's emphasis on geography and topography is related to what has been called the "spatial turn" in the human sciences, and in this sense it also exemplifies the recent tendency to foreground the question of space within the field of literary history. In contrast to the "New Histories," then, this work places literary objects and events in contexts that are more rigorously defined both spatially and temporally. Einaudi, which published both the original Italian version of Moretti's *Atlas* and the *Atlas of Italian Literature*, is also responsible for the multivolume work on the novel edited by Moretti, now (partly) translated into other languages.[16] Although this work is not explicitly framed as a history of the novel, the wide panorama provided—including essays on individual national traditions, subgenres, themes, material aspects, "key works," and so forth—ultimately amounts to an encyclopedic vision of the novel from its earliest beginnings to the present day, with an unprecedented international range. By way of its encyclopedic, anthologizing approach, this work shares in the contemporary preference for spatial, horizontal, serial, self-consciously fragmentary mapping of a given terrain of knowledge, rather than for the sequential and synthetic mode of proper historiography, although some of the individual essays, in contrast to the "New Histories," use synthetic (and even statistical) methods of presentation.

As we have seen with regard to the *Atlas of Italian Literature*, such a revisionary kind of literary history maintains the general framework of the national while at the same time weakening this category in favor of more local frameworks (regions, cities, provinces). Paradoxically, the "spatial turn" may thus be seen as a reterritorialization of literary studies after the demise of the national as the central organizing category.[17] The decentering of the national by the local and subnational is also embodied by another collaborative enterprise of recent times, namely the three-volume *Literary Cultures of Latin America*. This work is, of course, not the first attempt to understand the literatures of Latin America as a common field "beyond the nation-state" (Valdés, xix).[18] Yet this project is remarkable for its attempt to conceive multilayered constellations that negotiate the subnational with the supranational. As the editor puts it in the introduction: "The reader of literary history ought to be given the larger network of cultural relationships that are at play in the particular detail, but how can we describe multiple perspectives and yet maintain a sense of historical narrative discourse?" (Valdés, xix).

The Novel and Particularity

In general, the examples just discussed all share an approach that favors an idea of literary history as nonhierachical, nonconsequential interconnectedness. This tendency is evidently a reflection of our own epistemological present—the "taste for the particular" as the leading stimulus for the human sciences—just as Bouterwek's idea of *das Ganze* was reflective of the historiographic ideas of his time. Let me state it again: Bouterwek's concept of totality was the objective correlative of the *particularity* of national literature. Even as today we no longer accept unproblematically the national telos of literary expression, we cannot but see literature as an embodiment of particularity. Nowhere is this clearer than in the literary genre that, for better or worse, is universally favored today, namely the novel. How and why is the novel the genre of particularity; to what extent may the history of the novel be understood as the emergence and transformation of the particular? While in the study of the novel these questions are not entirely new, they have never been laid out as forcefully as in Guido Mazzoni's remarkable recent book *Teoria del romanzo* (Theory of the Novel; 2011).[19]

In his historical morphology Mazzoni presents the course of the Western novel precisely as the emergence of particularity—and I would like to argue that this book has much to teach us not only about the novel but also about how literary historians may approach literature as the medium of particularity. In fact, in an afterword he reflects on the question of how such a historically informed theory of the novel has to confront the particular and not subsume it too readily into generalizing abstractions. This explains why the book is as much a theory as a history of the novel (and why its title points toward an implicit critical revision of Georg Lukács's "high theory" of the novel). This is to say that Mazzoni establishes a certain parallel between his own methodological approach—sensitive to historical particularities and differences—and his theory of the novel as a narrative about the emergence of particularity.[20] In this regard Mazzoni invokes Peter Szondi's critique of Hegel's misrecognition of particularity: "Because particularity is the *proprium* of our epoch, the figuration of a single entity, in all the restrictedness of its world, may become a representative gesture" (Mazzoni, 377). According to Mazzoni, the anthropological function of reading novels consists in our experience of what it might have been like to live in a particular time and place, and thus to assume a particular point of view (Mazzoni, 373). The fact that we moderns attribute a singular significance to the "ontological region of particularity" (Mazzoni, 376) explains not only our relation to the modern novel (Mazzoni, 381) but also what we might call the particularization of the epistemological landscape and modes of intellectual operation: " . . . historicism and localism introduce, into the very heart of philosophical theories, an ontology of a narrative sort, the same that resides since time immemorial in any kind of story" (Mazzoni, 380). The practice of storytelling is thus equated with the gesture of historicization, which is in turn coterminous with a "relativistic skepticism" distrusting of time-transcending concepts:

> Few disciplines rest on a foundation so thoroughly nihilistic as philology. The image of the world informing its *a priori* sees reality as an agglomeration of particular events and minimal genealogies: the influence of someone on somebody else, of a singular event on another singular event, of a circumscribed milieu on an individual. . . . Philology knows no other metaphysics

> but one, obtuse and minimal, which is inscribed in the method of mechanical causality. Every form of regularity that assembles particular objects into greater connections comes out of it destroyed. In this sense, philology is an extreme example for how the logic of narrative has penetrated the realm of concepts. (Mazzoni, 381)

On the one hand, then, Mazzoni shows how the history of the European novel moves toward and is coterminous with the "discovery of the milieu" (Mazzoni, 268), with the consequence—most visible in Balzac—that the individual appears more or less connected to (if not determined by) the particularities of the local and the historical (Mazzoni, 270). At a later point, during the time of classical modernism, novelistic, interiorized subjectivity affirms itself by its relative independence, yet even here emerges a characteristic conflict between the universal and the particular (Mazzoni, 395–97). Mazzoni provides an extraordinarily detailed account of how what he calls the "book of particular life" gradually comes to emancipate itself from other literary genres, such as epic and tragedy, and previous conceptions of the novel. The development of the modern novel is associated with a series of discursive transformations that are, in turn, responsible for the demotion of universal concepts in Western metaphysics and for the origin of the perspectivism and particularism of the human sciences (Mazzoni, 165): "The birth of the novel as the genre of private life and the first stages of the development of the European human sciences are contemporary phenomena" (Mazzoni, 166). In the last chapter of his study, then, Mazzoni moves toward the present epistemological situation, where he diagnoses the contemporary skepticism toward essentialist portrayals of cultural phenomena and historical epochs: "Today, whoever wants to reflect on linguistic games and historical periods has to abandon certain gestures that are too immediately synthetic, and has to penetrate into the analytical territory of philology. . . . The synthetic power of certain judgments is directly related to the scarcity of details, to the certainty with which many facts are being ignored" (Mazzoni, 385).

Despite the differences in the examples I have surveyed, we notice the insistence on the genuine particularity of literature and, as a consequence for literary historiography, the implicit or explicit critique of gestures that smack of "immediate synthesis." Yet we have also seen that synthesizing gestures and "historiographical operations" are nevertheless unavoidable and necessary. For instance, one need only look at the chapter headings of Mazzoni's study ("The Novel and the Literature of the Ancient Regime," "The Birth of the Modern Novel," "The Nineteenth-Century Paradigm," "The Transition to Modernism") in order to see that his historical morphology is indeed heavily dependent on synthesizing operations. Or, as David Perkins has put it: "We must perceive a past age as relatively unified if we are to write literary history; we must perceive it as highly diverse if what we write is to represent it plausibly" (Perkins 1992, 27).

Particularity and Synthesis in Brazilian Literature

The question, then, is how to write literary history by avoiding the sin of "immediate synthesis," to write a particular history of particularity. It goes without saying that even more caution would be required if one were to deal with very recent, or contemporary, literature. In a recent essay on the problem of how to categorize the contemporary novelistic production in Brazil and Latin America, Pedro Dolabela Chagas argues that these contemporary novels eschew the traditional paradigm and hermeneutics of nation formation (as present in studies by Roberto González Echevarría and Flora Süssekind) and therefore also require a different historiographical approach. Or, rather, a "historiography" appears impossible in this case, for the novels appear as yet only isolated phenomena in formation. Therefore, "the first step has to be precisely the following: to confront the singularity [of the work], to appreciate it without submitting it to generalization, to let it speak before enlisting it into a lineage, into tendencies. . . . This would mean to privilege criticism over historiography, thus reinvigorating the analysis of the particular, in the light of the difficulty to recognize the synchronic historical picture."[21] Moreover, in his survey of contemporary novelistic production (e.g., of Bernardo Carvalho, Roberto Bolaño), the author also recognizes a lessening of, say, the importance of "Brazilian" national identity for the signification of the novel. The author concludes that, in the present time of "universalizing" globalization, literature takes on the task of representing "individual experience," the "singular individual," and the "circumstantially local" (Chagas, 57). In other words, Chagas sees the contemporary Brazilian/Latin American novel distinguished by what, according to Mazzoni, the modern novel has always been about. In this sense, it might be true that the contemporary novel represents a certain change with regard to a former dominance of the "panoramic" novel of *brasilidade*. Yet Chagas appears to forget, first, that his enlisting of contemporary works under this rubric ("the novel of individual experience, of a mitigated frame of nationality") amounts indeed to nothing but a sort of "generalization" and, second, that the idea of individuality is not exactly something new in the history of the novel. The change he is addressing here might also be described as a move from the novel's task of "manufacturing difference" (P. Casanova) on the level of foundational, individual nationality to one of individuality on a sub- or supranational level.[22] In any event, the deployment of such an argument also points to the difference between the history of the European and the Brazilian/Latin American novel.

And indeed, in the past, both Brazilian literature and its historiography have often been heavily determined by narratives about the formation of Brazilian nationhood. It is all the more remarkable that Antonio Candido, in his classic *Formação da literatura brasileira*, already sees this "nationalist" aspect of literature in the context of a dialectical relationship between romantic and neoclassical tendencies, insofar as his book sets out "to study the formation of Brazilian literature as the synthesis of universalist and particularist tendencies."[23] This is to say that Candido sees his own project as distinct from romantic historiography, where *brasilidade* was necessarily seen as a "differential trace and criterion of value" (Candido 1981, 28).

It is also well known that Brazilian modernism echoes Romanticism in its nationalist aspirations and its efforts to conjoin the particular and the universal. In this context the concern with Brazilian nationhood is perhaps most visible in the writings of Mário de Andrade, who is above all concerned with the integration of regional particularities into a national whole, which as such forms the national-as-particular. The complexity of Mário's nationalism is well captured by Tania Franco Carvalhal: "Mário de Andrade understood what had been an intuition for José de Alencar: A national entity would not exist in its totality without the insertion of all its parts into the whole. It is for this reason that Mário de Andrade searches for a break with geography (*desgeografização*); he wanted to neutralize the emphasis placed on local particularities in order to be able to discover an underlying unity of identity, extending beyond regional differences."[24] In his search for such a strategy of making Brazilian literature at once more particular and more universal, Mario was inspired by the affinities he saw with the similarly "peripheral" and romantic culture of Germany, where music and the popular were seen as distinctive traits. As he proposes in his essay *Teutos mas músicos* (1939), his personal conversion from the "classical" French to the "romantic" German paradigm could mark the way to a properly Brazilian culture: "The fact was that I felt excessively frenchified (*anfrancesado*) in my spirit. . . . I realized that in order to become really Brazilian in my sensibility and in my work, I first had to detoxicate myself from the exaggerated Frenchness of my being."[25] Characteristically, in talking about himself, Mário also talks about Brazil, in this case the formation of Brazilian literature as an emancipation from a universalist model. Similar to Eça de Queirós's renunciation of *his* French past in 1889,[26] for Mário an imported universalism calls up the specter of imitation.

The case of Brazilian modernism, as should have become clear, has a somewhat complex relation to the terms *particular* and *universal*. Therefore, a history of this movement faces unique challenges to integrate this tension—arguably, distinctive of literature tout court—into its own mode of narrative presentation. A very interesting and persuasive attempt has been made in a recent book by Ivan Marques, *Cenas de um modernismo de província* (Scenes of a Provincial Modernism; 2011), This is a self-reflexive attempt to write the literary history of a distinctive inflection of Brazilian modernism, as embodied by a specific group, or generation, of writers from Minas Gerais.[27] Let me conclude this essay, then, by pointing out the ways in which Marques addresses questions of particularity/difference, as well as achieves synthesis/unity.

1. *Local Difference.* The category of peripheral or "provincial" modernism addresses the question of cultural geography—that is, how the "peripheral modernism" of Brazil, despite its unifying and universalizing traits, must in fact be seen as heterogeneous, as a unity made up of different parts. The modernist writers from Minas (the book contains long, detailed chapters on Carlos Drummond de Andrade, Emílio Moura, João Alphonsus, and Cyro dos Anjos) provide thus a kind of alternative modernism to the more "central" and "cosmopolitan" version associated with São Paulo (Oswald de Andrade, Mário de Andrade). The importance of space, the rootedness in a local context ("particular expressions in every historical reality," 9), is associated with the particular cultural situation of the provincial capital of Belo Horizonte.[28] The introductory chapter is dedicated to the local particularities of this regional modernism, and here Marques criticizes previous studies of a strictly sociohistorical bent for having neglected to "investigate the reasons for this singularity" (Marques, 23).
2. *Time/Distinctive Commonalities.* The subtitle of the book ("Drummond and Other Boys from Belo Horizonte") links the idea of the locally distinctive

to the time-bound phenomenon of a literary group, or generation of writers—which is, of course, a traditional concept of literary history. Since the French Revolution, the concept of the generation has served to designate a specific "age cohort" defined by its difference from the values of the past and shaped by common experiences.[29] In other words, the term *generation* gathers historical significance through its designation of an irreducible, chronologically situated span of experience, while it also is constitutionally synthetic in its reduction of many individuals under a single, general rubric (think, say, of the Portuguese generation of 1870). The modernist generation of Minas Gerais, according to Marques, was united by a strong sense of "literary sociability," by the participation in a common journal (*A Revista*) and other editorial projects, by similar social backgrounds, a dislocation within modernity, and trajectories leading from the "private" to the "public" domain (birth in the interior, in traditional families; the sense of social decline; work as public functionaries in the city, as well as a close connection to journalism; later, an affinity with the educational projects of Getúlio Vargas). Common experiences and activities also led to a shared intellectual and literary style or rhetoric, such as the characteristic blending of tradition and modernity, as reflected in the specific urban history of Belo Horizonte (Marques, 20). These commonalities also were linked to a deepened concern with local roots and psychological interiority, "a greater preference for particular beings than for the national myth" (Marques, 22)—yet also, paradoxically, a French-influenced "spirit of classicism" and "universalism" (Marques, 35), which was precisely what Mário de Andrade criticized in them (Marques, 38). All of these traces are designated by Marques as being "particular" to the "character of Minas Gerais" *in general* (Marques, 35). Yet about the group of writers Marques has chosen to study, he also writes: "However, in our search for an identity that we already know to exist among them, we should not exaggerate to the point of neglecting the configuration of the parts. It is in variety that unity is found, as wrote Mário de Andrade, while he observed that in the group of Belo Horizonte, behind the appearance of the most 'harmonious intellectual movement' there was a sum of solipsistic snails [*caramujos ensimesmados*], with everyone preserving his own traits" (Marques, 45–46). Marques moves from Mario's comment about the problem of group formation as unity-in-variety to his own methodological declaration that he wants to "always preserve the particularity of every work" against the background of a shared social and historical condition (Marques, 46).

3. *Particularity in Literature.* Marques writes that "the union of the particular with the universal (another 'characteristic' of the epoch in question) in fact defines the very nature of lyric and art" (Marques, 35). This is to say that Marques, just like Mazzoni, sees literature as the realm of the particular, although it is here not restricted to the genre of the novel. The Minas modernists are paradigmatic for a universalism rooted in a decidedly local experience (Marques, 252–53). This means, for example, that the adoption of a radically subjectivist viewpoint in a novel such as Cyro dos Anjos's *O amanuense Belmiro* (The Amanuensis Belmiro, 1937) can transcend the represented solipsism by appearing as representative for an entire generation (namely, the generation studied by Marques). Furthermore, Marques observes that the author "Cyro dos Anjos shares obviously in the small world of his alter ego, yet he also elevates himself above him" (Marques, 249), so that the pseudoautobiographical account comes to represent "the *bovarysme* of the alienated Brazilian intellectual" (Marques, 239), or what the novel itself, on the occasion of the Carnival celebrations, calls Belmiro's "impossibility to fuse with the masses." In contrast to the objectifying and socially engaged novel of the 1930s, *O amanuense Belmiro* continues the Symbolist concern with an "antisocial" withdrawal to an interior self, yet it is precisely this stance through which dos Anjos achieves a portrait of his generation. The resistance to the social is itself socially determined, and even the most "interiorized" novel maintains links with its particular milieu (see Mazzoni), which in turn, we might add, shares features with other spaces of peripheral modernity and the metonymic figure of the alienated employee.[30]

My point here is obviously not that Marques has reinvented literary history. Rather, his study can simply serve as a self-reflexive example from which we can extrapolate what, in my view, essentially remain the principal challenges for literary history: (1) to demarcate a series of literary objects in circumscribed parameters of time and space; (2) to achieve a certain narrative coherence and "flow" that is not exhaustive but rather a "coherent fragment," in Bouterwek's term, which is concentrated on individual episodes, constellations, or "scenes"; and (3) to wrest a certain general significance from the particular case or case study at hand, and hence also to reflect on the myriad ways in which literature itself produces the universal appeal of particularity.

NOTES

1. Friedrich Bouterwek, *Geschichte der Poesie und Beredsamkeit seit dem Ende des dreizehnten Jahrhundert* (Göttingen: J. W. Röwer, 1805), 4: ii. All translations are my own. Bouterwek's foundational role, even with regard to Brazilian literature, is briefly acknowledged in Tania Franco Carvalhal, "The Foundations of Brazilian Literary Culture," in *Literary Cultures of Latin America: A Comparative History*, eds. Mario J. Valdés and Djelal Kadir (New York: Oxford University Press, 2004), 1: 126–132 (128). On Bouterwerk in the context of early Portuguese literary history, see Carlos Manuel Ferreira da Cunha, *A construção da história literária na literatura portuguesa do século XIX* (Polierdo: University of Minho: 2002), 124, 263–66.

2. Reinhart Koselleck, *Vergangene Zukunft: Zur Semantik geschichtlicher Zeiten* (Frankfurt: Suhrkamp, 1989), 262.

3. See Carlos M. F. da Cunha, "A história literária e a 'invenção da tradição,'" *Limite* 2 (2008), 97–114 (105).

4. Roberto M. Dainotto, *Europe (in Theory)* (Durham, NC: Duke University Press, 2007). Dainotto quotes the Italian historian Federico Chabod's comment on the emergence of European nationalism as a reaction against French universalism: "The particular against the general, the individual against the universal. Exactly because the fear is that universality will suffocate individuality, and that the general will suffocate the particular, for this very reason, the promoters of national individuality hold a strong polemical attitude against [Francocentric] Europeanism" (Chabod, *Storia dell'idea d'Europa* [1961], as quoted in Dainotto, 134).

5. See Cunha, "A história literária," 106, and *A construção do discurso da história literária*, 222–25.

6. The twelve volumes of Bouterwek's "universal" literary history, dedicated to Italian, Spanish, Portuguese, French, English, and German literature, appeared between 1801 and 1820. For an excellent discussion of Bouterwek in the context of early nineteenth-century cosmopolitanism, see Andrea Albrecht, *Kosmopolitismus: Weltbürgerdiskurse in Literatur, Philosophie und Publizistik um 1800* (Berlin: Walter de Gruyter, 2005), 170–78, 300. Albrecht points out that Bouterwek's cosmopolitan approach to literary history becomes somewhat more nationalist after the German Wars of Liberation of 1813.

7. This paragraph is adapted from Albrecht's account. See *Kosmopolitismus*, 302–6.

8. Hans Ulrich Gumbrecht, "Literaturgeschichte—Fragment einer geschwundenen

Identität?," in *Fragment und Totalität*, eds. Lucien Dällenbach and Christiaan L. Hart Nibbrig (Frankfurt: Suhrkamp, 1984), 30–45 (33).

9. Gumbrecht, "Literaturgeschichte"; Miltos Pechlivanos, "Literaturgeschichte(n)," in *Einführung in die Literaturwissenschaft*, ed. Miltos Pechlivanos et al. (Stuttgart: Metzler, 1995), 170–81.

10. Denis Hollier, ed., *A New History of French Literature* (Cambridge: Harvard University Press, 1989); David E. Wellbery, ed., *A New History of German Literature* (Cambridge: Harvard University Press, 2004). See my review in *Poetica* 37, 3–4 (2005), 495–99.

11. David Perkins, *Is Literary History Possible?* (Baltimore: Johns Hopkins University Press, 1992), 60.

12. For a reflection on the aporia of revisionism in literary history, see Miguel Tamen, "Ghosts Revisited: An Essay on Literary History," in Miguel Tamen and Helena C. Buescu, eds., *A Revisionary History of Portuguese Literature* (New York: Garland Publishing, 1999), xi–xxi (esp. xiv–xv).

13. Michel de Certeau, *The Writing of History*, trans. Tom Conley (New York: Columbia University Press, 1988), 48.

14. Sergio Luzzatto and Gabriele Pedullà, "Introduzione," *Atlante della letteratura italiana*, vol. I (Turin: Einaudi, 2010). The third and final volume was completed in late 2012.

15. See Franco Moretti, *Graphs, Maps, Trees: Abstract Models for a Literary History* (London: Verso, 2007), and *Atlas of the European Novel, 1800–1900* (London: Verso, 1998).

16. Franco Moretti, *Il romanzo*, vols. I–V (Turin: Einaudi, 2001–2003).

17. For an overview of the spatial turn and the decentering of the nation, see Carlos Manuel Ferreira da Cunha, *A(s) geografia(s) da literatura: Do nacional ao gobal* (Ponte Guimarães: Opera Omnia, 2011), 45: "Não deixa de ser significativo que as principais tendências do comparatismo actual sublinhem a necessidade de desterritorializar a literatura (nacional), para a sua reterritorialização."

18. Mario J. Valdés, "Introduction: Parameters of Literary History," in *Literary Cultures of Latin America*, vol. 1, xvii–xxv.

19. Guido Mazzoni, *Teoria del romanzo* (Bologna: Il Mulino, 2011). Since Mazzoni's study has not yet been translated, I allow myself to quote rather generously from it.

20. Such a correspondence is not uncommon in the historiography of the novel: "Numerous nineteenth- and twentieth-century literary histories assign to the novel just the storylines that novels typically assign to their own protagonists." Deirdre Shauna Lynch, "History of the Novel," in *The Encyclopedia of the Novel*, ed. P. M. Logan (Oxford: Wiley-Blackwell, 2011), 1: 386–98 (387).

21. Pedro Dolabela Chagas, "Após a nacionalidade: História do romance e produção romanesca no Brasil e na América Latina," *Estudos de literatura brasileira contemporânea* 38 (2011), 41–59.

22. Pascale Casanova, *The World Republic of Letters*, trans. M. B. DeBevoise (Cambridge: Harvard University Press, 2004), 220.

23. Antonio Candido, *Formação da literatura brasileira* (Belo Horizonte: Martins Editora, 1981), 1: 23. On the dialectic of the local and the universal in Brazilian literature, see also Candido, "Literatura e cultura de 1900 a 1945," in his *Literatura e sociedade* (São Paulo: Companhia Editora Nacional, 1976).

24. Carvalhal, "The Foundations of Brazilian Literary Culture," 131.

25. Mário de Andrade, *Musica, Doce Musica* (São Paulo: Martins Editora, 1939), 315.

26. Eça de Queirós, "O Francesismo," in *Obras* (Porto: Lello & Irmão, 1947), 2: 813–14.

27. Ivan Marques, *Cenas de um modernismo de provincial: Drummond e outros rapazes de Belo Horizonte* (São Paulo: Editora 34, 2011).

28. See also Maria Zilda Ferreira Cury, "Ouro Preto, Belo Horizonte, Brasília: The Utopia of Modernity," in *Literary Cultures of Latin America*, vol. 2, 597–614.

29. See also Koselleck, *Vergangene Zukunft*, 313.

30. For a transnational comparison of the novel in this sense, see my essay "Unfähigkeit: Die Figur des Angestellten als schwacher Held im Roman der Moderne" (Italo Svevo and Cyro dos Anjos), in *Arcadia* 47 (2012), booklet 2: 401–20.

WORKS CITED

Albrecht, Andrea. *Kosmopolitismus: Weltbügerdiskurse in Literatur, Philosophie und Publizistik um 1800* (Berlin: Walter de Gruyter, 2005).

Andrade, Mário de. *Musica, Doce Musica* (São Paulo: Martins Editora, 1939).

Bouterwek, Friedrich. *Geschichte der Poesie und Beredsamkeit seit dem Ende des dreizehnten Jahrhundert*, vol. IV (Göttingen: J. W. Röwer, 1805).

Candido, Antonio. "Literatura e cultura de 1900 a 1945." In *Literatura e sociedade* (São Paulo: Companhia Editora Nacional, 1976).

———. *Formação da literatura brasileira*, vol. 1 (Belo Hoizonte: Martins Editora, 1981).

Carvalhal, Tania Franco. "The Foundations of Brazilian Literary Culture." In *Literary Cultures of Latin America: A Comparative History*, eds. Mario J. Valdés and Djelal Kadir (New York: Oxford University Press, 2004), 1: 126–32.

Casanova, Pascale. *The World Republic of Letters*, translated by M. B. DeBevoise (Cambridge: Harvard University Press, 2004).

Certeau, Michel de. *The Writing of History*, translated by Tom Conley (New York: Columbia University Press, 1988).

Chagas, Pedro Dolabela. "Após a nacionalidade: História do romance e produção romanesca no Brasil e na América Latina," *Estudos de literatura brasileira contemporânea* 38 (2011), 41–59.

Dainotto, Roberto M. *Europe (in Theory)* (Durham, NC: Duke University Press, 2007).

Ferreira da Cunha, Carlos Manuel. *A construção da história literária na literatura portuguesa do século XIX* (Polierdo: University of Minho, 2002).

———. "A história literária e a 'invenção da tradição.'" *Limite* 2 (2008), 97–114.

———. *A(s) geografia(s) da literatura: Do nacional ao gobal* (Ponte Guimarães: Opera Omnia, 2011).

Ferreira Cury, Maria Zila. "Ouro Preto, Belo Horizonte, Brasília: The Utopia of Modernity." In *Literary Cultures of Latin America: A Comparative History*, eds. Mario J. Valdés and Djelal Kadir (New York: Oxford University Press, 2004), 2: 597–614.

Gumbrecht, Hans Ulrich. "Literaturgeschichte—Fragment einer geschwundenen Identität?" In *Fragment und Totalität*, eds. Lucien Dällenbach and Christiaan L. Hart Nibbrig (Frankfurt: Suhrkamp, 1984), 30–45.

Hollier, Denis, ed. *A New History of French Literature* (Cambridge: Harvard University Press, 1989).

Koselleck, Reinhart. *Vergangene Zukunft: Zur Semantik geschichtlicher Zeiten* (Frankfurt: Suhrkamp, 1989).

Luzzatto, Sergio, and Gabriele Pedullà. "Introduzione." *Atlante della letteratura italiana*, vol. 1 (Torino: Einaudi, 2010).

Lynch, Deirdre Shauna. "History of the Novel." In *The Encyclopedia of the Novel*, ed. P. M. Logan (Oxford: Wiley-Blackwell, 2011), 1: 386–98.

Marques, Ivan. *Cenas de um modernismo de província: Drummond e outros rapazes de Belo Horizonte* (São Paulo: Editora 34, 2011).

Mazzoni, Guido. *Teoria del romanzo* (Bologna: Il Mulino, 2011).

Moretti, Franco. *Atlas of the European Novel, 1800–1900* (London: Verso, 1998).

———. *Il romanzo*, vols. I–V (Turin: Einaudi, 2001–2003).

———. *Graphs, Maps, Trees: Abstract Models for a Literary History* (London: Verso, 2007).

Pechlivanos, Miltos. "Literaturgeschichte(n)." In *Einführung in die Literaturwissenschaft*, eds. Miltos Pechlivanos et al. (Stuttgart: Metzler, 1995), 170–81.

Perkins, David. *Is Literary History Possible?* (Baltimore: Johns Hopkins University Press, 1992).

Queirós, Eça de. "O Francesismo." In *Obras*, vol. 2 (Porto: Lello & Irmão, 1947).

Tamen, Miguel. "Ghosts Revisited: An Essay on Literary History." In *A Revisionary History of Portuguese Literature*, eds. Miguel Tamen and Helena C. Buescu (New York: Garland Publishing, 1999), xi–xxi.

Valdés, Mario J. "Introduction: Parameters of Literary History." In *Literary Cultures of Latin America: A Comparative History*, eds. Mario J. Valdés and Djelal Kadir (New York: Oxford University Press, 2004), 1: xvii–xxv.

Welge, Jobst. "Review of *A New History of German Literature*." *Poetica* 37, nos. 3–4 (2005), 495–99.

———. "Unfähigkeit: Die Figur des Angetellten als schwacher Held im Roman der Moderne" (Italo Svevo/Cyro dos Anjos), *Arcadia* (2012).

Wellbery, David E., ed. *A New History of German Literature* (Cambridge: Harvard University Press, 2004).

JOBST WELGE is currently a visiting professor in Romance literatures/cultural studies at the University of Konstanz. He has published on various aspects of modernity in Italian, Spanish, and Brazilian literature (on authors such as F. T. Marinetti, C. Malaparte, I. Svevo, R. del Valle-Inclán, E. Pardo Bazán, Rubem Braga, and Bernardo Carvalho). His book *Genealogical Fictions: Cultural Periphery and Historical Change in the 19th-Century Novel* is forthcoming. At present he also is involved in a book-length study of "Introspection, Dislocation, Modernity" in the Latin American novel. He may be reached at Jobst.Welge@uni-konstanz.de.

JOSÉ LUÍS JOBIM
Translated by Lisa Shaw

Ways of Seeing the Past in Literary History

ABSTRACT: This article, after presenting one of the perspectives relating to the European derivation of Latin literature and culture, will consider the issue of national affiliation, principally through the categories of "imitation" and "autonomy"/"originality," seeking to highlight certain aspects of the language and circumstances in which the unitary aspiration of the national, in its different manifestations, came into existence.

KEYWORDS: literary history, Latin literature and culture, history of Brazilian literature and culture.

As we all know, there are different ways of seeing the past. Depending on the principle governing the particular way we choose to see it, the results will be different. When we talk about the history of Brazilian literature, we can, among other options, either situate it within a wider selection of texts both temporally and geographically, an approach that characterizes it as one of the manifestations of a legacy dating back to the origins of Latin culture, or situate it within a more restricted selection, beginning in the nineteenth century and relating only to Portugal. In whichever case, the very delineation of what we refer to as Brazilian literature will also follow from the principle used to define it, and history itself, as a form of discourse, is constructed from principles or premises that are not always visible to its producers.

This article, after presenting one of the perspectives relating to the European derivation, will consider the issue of national affiliation, principally through the categories of "imitation" and "autonomy"/"originality," seeking to highlight certain aspects of the language and circumstances in which the unitary aspiration of the national, in its different manifestations, came into existence.

European Derivations in the Americas

If we begin with the wider point of view, temporally and geographically speaking, that is, with the approach that emphasizes the long-term derivation of national literatures in relation to a Latin legacy (and consequently a European one), we inevitably encounter *European Literature and the Latin Middle Ages* by Ernst Robert Curtius, originally published in 1948. In this book Curtius contends that, although no period in the history of European literature has been so little known or studied as Latin literature of the High and Low Middle Ages, a historical vision of Europe makes clear that it is precisely this period, as the link between the decline of antiquity and the slowly emerging Western world, that occupies a key position (Curtius 1996). However, in this article I prefer to follow the example of the Dominican intellectual Pedro Henríquez Ureña (1884–1946), whose approach favors contextualizing literature within a wider selection of texts, both temporally and geographically, and who characterizes literature as one of the manifestations of a Latin legacy.

Ureña was a transnational man, a university professor in Mexico, the United States, and Argentina, who, even during the period of the so-called literary vanguards, published *Seis ensayos em busca de nuestra expresión* (Six Essays in Search of Our Expression) in 1928. In this book, which was contemporaneous with Oswald de Andrade's *Manifesto antropófago* and Mário de Andrade's *Macunaíma*, Ureña defends his thesis of a long-standing Latin affiliation with geographically different European centers:

> Let's accept frankly as inevitable this complex situation: when we express ourselves there will be within us, along with the unique part that is ours, born of our lives, sometimes as an indigenous heritage, another substantial portion, even if it is just the framework that we received from Spain. I will take this further: not only do we write in the language of Castile, but we belong to the Romance group of countries, the Romance linguistic family that still constitutes a community, a cultural unit, descended from that which Rome organized under its power; we belong—according to the much repeated phrase of Sarmiento's—to the Roman Empire. In terms of literature, since the Romance languages gained a full life of their own, the Romance community has never lacked a center, the successor of the Eternal City: from the eleventh to the fourteenth centuries it was France, initially oscillating between the North and South of the country; with the Renaissance it was the turn of Italy; then, for a brief period, the center tended to be situated in Spain; from Louis XIV onward it was located in France again. Many times the Romance community extended its influence to foreign regions, and we know

> how Paris governed Europe, and briefly the two Americas in the eighteenth century, but from the beginning of the nineteenth century rival regions, in open and lasting opposition, emerged; . . . Even politically we were born and grew up in the Romance community. Antonio Caso identifies with effective precision the three events in Europe whose influence on our peoples was decisive: the Discovery, which was a Spanish event; the Renaissance, which was Italian; and the Revolution, which was French. The Renaissance only partially took shape in Spain—in cultural forms that would be transplanted to the New World; the Revolution was the forerunner of our wars of independence. The three events belong to Romance peoples. We do not have a direct relationship with the Reformation, nor with the constitutional evolution of England, and even the independence and the Constitution of the United States gained prestige among us only thanks to the propaganda that they received in France. (Ureña, 1960 [1928], 250)

Of course, we also know that among the long-standing meanings of the term *literature* there is the Latin-language derivation, which goes from *litterae* (letters) to *litteratura* and then to all the corresponding words in Western languages, such as *literatura* (Portuguese and Spanish), *literature* (English), *Literatur* (German), *littérature* (French), and *letteratura* (Italian), among others, giving the term an intrinsic association with the written word. But we also know that, after national adjectives were associated with this term (e.g., *Brazilian* literature, *Portuguese* literature, *French* literature), these adjectives gained an enormous semantic force from the nineteenth century onward.

National Histories

In the June 1993 edition of the magazine *Le genre humain*, dedicated to "L'Ancien et le nouveau," Maurice Olander (1993, 7) writes that in societies with a biblical tradition, the division between the old and the new has a purpose, namely to tell the providential story of humanity, creating a before-and-after narrative whose central pivot is the appearance of Christianity. As regards the histories of Brazilian literature, perhaps we can say that their purpose was often to create a before-and-after narrative whose central pivot was the emergence of the national. Therefore, the recent questioning of the centrality of the national affects the sense of these histories for today's reader and is linked to the emergence of other theories and ways of seeing the past.

If, in the process of forging a sense of nationality, a certain overarching notion of place was created, acquiring a spatial dimension (associated with a territory) and a political dimension (associated with the nation-state), nevertheless the claim to unity inherent in this conceptualization was also contested. Sometimes what was sought was not a national collective consciousness but rather a regional one. As regards regionalisms in Brazil, it is interesting to remember that the very division of Brazil into "states" (and the changing of the names and territories of these "states"), or even the classification by "regions" (southeast, center-west, northeast, north and south) superimposed on those subdivisions, is recent. If today "regions" and "states" invoke their belonging to the national, whether to denote the insertion of local culture or to demand funding and responses to "regional" or "state" demands, this does not cancel out the invoking, in this process, of the specificity of the "state" or "region" in question. Neither should we forget the short historical duration of the terms in which these divisions and classifications are made—and not only in Brazil or the rest of South America. If we turn our attention to the European context, Storm (2003, 252) informs us that the division of France into *départements* dates from the French Revolution, while many German regions were created during the Napoleonic period. Therefore, the corresponding regional identities are, like those of the nation-states, essentially a modern creation—this even applies to the oldest regions, like Catalonia, Brittany, and Saxony.

Storm observes that in Europe the very character of regionalism—a movement that promoted the study and strengthening of regional identity—underwent profound changes around 1890. For most of the nineteenth century, the study of one's own region was almost exclusively the work of members of learned societies or associations. The main themes of research and debate were the historical, archaeological, and geographical features of the region, and its significance within the national context. Although these societies generally professed to have a pedagogical vocation, the texts they produced and the lectures they organized were basically aimed at their members, who were recruited from a small elite of local notables.

Storm thus calls into question whether regionalism was the focus of these associations, because *the region was considered from a national perspective.* In general it was the historical contribution that each region made to the greatness of the motherland that was important, not the particular identity that distinguished the region from the whole. This was only to change at the end of the nineteenth century, when a group of young and well-educated members of the provincial elite wanted to reach a wider public, an objective that demanded other forms of expression and social interaction. Instead of promoting scholarly studies, the new associations tried to mobilize the middle and lower classes, encouraging them to participate in essentially recreational activities. They organized excursions and festivals, creating local museums and celebrating a shared identity that did not draw on a mythical past but principally on a contemporary popular culture (folklore, handicrafts, and architecture). This awakening of the provinces, Storm argues, occurred at more or less the same time in the whole of Europe, transforming regionalism into a mass movement (Storm 2003, 253–54).

In nineteenth-century Brazil, we know that acquiring knowledge about a given region could result from wider national concerns. The proposal for the establishment of the Instituto Histórico e Geográfico Nacional (IHGB—National Historical and Geographical Institute), in the first half of the nineteenth century, was justified by the lack of an institution "responsible for centralizing vast numbers of precious documents, now spread around the provinces, and which can be of service to the history and geography of the empire" (*Revista do* IHGB 1839, 5–6).

The reference to the empire reminds us that, in the Brazilian case, the monarchy was an important element in the consolidation of the postcolonial state. Since the court was situated in the city of Rio de Janeiro, the "centralization" called for in the proposal for the establishment of the IHGB in the imperial period would effectively mean centralizing activities in that city. However, even afterward, at the beginning of the twentieth century, the interview given to João do Rio by Sílvio Romero, by then an esteemed historian and critic, continues to advocate centralizing in the capital city even discussions *from* and *about* the regions: "The function of the provinces, as I prefer to call them, from the north, south, center and east, is to produce variety within unity and to provide the capital with its greatest talents" (cited in João do Rio, 1907).

Of course, that idea of unity formed part of the movement to assert the national in a postindependence context, and various strategies were adopted that today we can examine with a more distanced and critical eye.

National Assertion, Imitation, and Autonomy

As regards the strategies for the assertion of a national identity in postcolonial Brazil, to begin with, as there was no memory of greatness or vision of national destiny, any construct that legitimized itself as an extension of a traditional history was impossible. Since the long-standing memory was that of the colonial power, after independence the need arose to emphasize difference and autonomy, to produce another form of postcolonial historicity, starting from a point of view presented as *national*, which would even reinterpret the past in order to look for the origins of the present-day nation. However, the other side of the coin could not be ignored, namely that Brazil's colonial situation was unique because, in the history of European colonialism, there was no other case of the central power being relocated to the colony, with the latter being transformed into the heart of the empire. The Brazilian court itself, after independence, was successively presided over by monarchs from the Portuguese royal family, who were also responsible, to a certain extent, for the maintenance of territorial integrity in the emerging country, in marked contrast with the fragmentation of Hispanic America. Daniel Parish Kidder (1815–1892), an American Methodist Episcopal theologian and writer who published a book about his stay in Brazil in the nineteenth century, writes: "While the Spanish American republics have been rent asunder with internal strife and while blood, carnage, and revolution have not ceased to be the order of the day within them, Brazil has remained united, and, with comparatively slight exceptions, has pursued her onward course with increasing prosperity." But he also thought that "elements of disorder exist in Brazil, which have the terrible capacity, unless effectually restrained, of starting into action, and, by their ruinous progress, throwing her fairest prospects into gloom, if not crushing forever the power of her now flourishing and almost idolized dynasty" (Kidder 1845, 403).

The formulation of new ideas about the emerging sense of nationality creatively appropriated certain European concepts and ideas, although at the precise moment when nationalist conceptions were being elaborated, in the nineteenth century, this was not clear to those participating in the process. The language and the circumstances in which these ideas and concepts were processed, being shaped by local particularities and interests, gave rise to a distinct direction for the postcolonial nation-state.

Although European post-Enlightenment and universalist ideas marked the national project (not only in Brazil), these "imported" concepts did not have the same meaning in Brazil as in their original context—that is to say, they were transformed in relation to local interests that emphasized certain aspects and chose to eliminate others, thus giving rise to a distinct configuration. In general, the Europe that the colonies and ex-colonies constructed in their imaginary and in relation to which they positioned themselves, whether as heirs or deniers, is also a non-European construction, in which the supposed "originary" concepts and ideas of the Old World could be used both to justify colonialism and to serve as the basis for emancipatory movements.

In the specific case of literature, the postcolonial perspective, aimed at contesting that of the former colonial power, also spawned the view that a supposed literary "imitation" of the latter should be overcome in order to achieve a presumed state of "autonomy." To some extent, this perspective also resulted in attributing to the former colonial power an absolute identity that supposedly gave rise to "imitations" in other colonized territories.

It is common, moreover, for an ex-colony to attribute an absolute identity to the former colonial power, from which, it is presumed, the colony derived its identity in the past, an identity that should be rejected in postcolonial states. But no identity is absolute, impervious to other cultures, complete on its own. Indeed, even the colonial powers (in fact, principally such entities) are melting pots that contain contributions from the colonies. If a certain colonial perspective signified culturally valuing the contribution of the colonial power and devaluing that of the colony, it must be remembered that, beginning with the economy, a continuing relationship of connection and interdependence characterized the two.

In this sense, there are echoes of a line of thinking, even present among Brazilian literary historians in the twentieth century, that is based on the following basic premise: in the colonial period, Brazilian literature allegedly first "imitated" Portuguese literature; then, with independence and the emergence of Romanticism, it began to develop its own voice, "autonomous," "individual," and so on.

Of course, this kind of opinion flourished in different areas of thinking, giving rise, for example, to the notion that there were universally determined and determinable stages that societies must reach in order to become "developed." Societies that did not pass through these stages and thus still had not attained a level of "progress" were accordingly thought to be comparatively less "modern" and to require a period of preparation, transformation, and patience before they could be recognized.[1]

There are, of course, some ingenious variations on this theme, such as that of Roger Bastide, who argued that imitation was a political means to indicate the presence, in the colony, of competent writers capable of creating works in the style of the colonial power:

> To fully understand seventeenth- and eighteenth-century Brazilian literature and the influence that Portuguese literature had upon it, we must begin with the "colonial situation." It is not sufficient to show that the Portuguese "styles," like those of Arcadia, were passed on to the colony from the colonial power, despite the differences between the two societies, the former based on the particularist family, the latter on the patriarchal family. It is necessary to understand that the "internal environment" explains this phenomenon of [cultural] diffusion and that this diffusion is, above all, a political protest. In reality, it takes the form of a "servile copy" mostly when nativism is developing, when economic oppression becomes more difficult to bear, when in every city, in the main square, the governor's palace and the prison are erected. It is therefore a case of showing that the creoles can produce aesthetic works that are as good as or even better than their metropolitan equivalents, that the "natives" are not "barbarians" who must be ruled from outside, but rather have achieved aesthetic maturity and can govern themselves. It is thus not paradoxical that the Tiradentes conspiracy against Portugal recruited its members among the writers who most imitated Portuguese literary styles. We will find in present-day "colonial" literatures, in the English or French languages, the same phenomenon repeating itself both today and in the past. (Bastide, [1957] 2006, 266)

There are some problems inherent in this reading, beginning with the idea of the unique affiliation of Arcadism with Portugal, as the following text will show, but we should remember the larger framework of references to which it belongs (a framework that includes the thesis that, in Brazil, writers moved from the "imitation" phase, in the colonial period, to the "creative" phase, in the post-independence period, beginning with Romanticism). This framework is taken up again by the Brazilian writers of the modernist movement themselves, but from a perspective in which the former colonial power is no longer considered the primordial reference. In 1924, Mário de Andrade writes in a letter to Carlos Drummond de Andrade:

"We, by imitating or repeating French or German civilization, are primitives, because we are still in the mimetic phase. Our ideals cannot be those of France because our needs are entirely different, our people are different, our land is different, and so on. We will only be civilized in relation to civilizations the day that we create the ideal, the Brazilian point of reference. Then we will move from the mimetic phase to the creative one. Then we will be universal, because we will be national" (2002 [1924], 70).

In this way, moving from the "mimetic phase" to the "creative phase" becomes relevant without anyone realizing how much a series of ways of thinking, drawn from previous stages in the history of Brazilian culture and literature, is being reproduced. After Romanticism began to combat the poetics of imitation and emulation (a trend that prevailed not only in the Iberian Peninsula), a poetics that predominated in the seventeenth and eighteenth centuries, and viewed negatively the tradition of choosing a certain group of authors and works as models to be followed (concomitant with an emphasis on the need to create works that reflected not a previous textual paradigm but rather the supposed unique and original personality of the writer and the country to which s/he belonged), there also emerged a regulatory parameter for literary production. Judged according to this parameter, the poems of Arcadism, for example, came to be seen as lacking in creativity, and emphasis was placed on the implicit "mimeticism" in the accommodation of the texts to neoclassical models of writing, from which the rules for producing Arcadian poetry were said to be derived and in the light of which they were approved or rejected in the eighteenth century.

Antonio Candido clearly points out the ambiguity in the attitude of the Romantics in relation to the Arcadians, at the same time condemning them for their subservience to literary models seen as imitations of the colonial power's models to prove the existence of literary activity in Brazil before independence:

> When we consider our Arcadism, we must remember that for the Romantics it was to a large extent a case of subservience in relation to the literature of the colonial power, and the latter was something that immediately following independence it seemed necessary to reject in all fields. But, at the same time, it was taken as proof of the continuation of intellectual life in Brazil, as well as a justification and source for the literary manifestations of the Romantics themselves, awakening in them, contradictorily, a great deal of pride of the genealogical kind. Thus, it functioned in the immediate aftermath, if not as an aesthetic model (except as regards the Indianism of the two epics), then certainly as a positive factor in the sense of autonomy, which then informed the cultural project of the generations contemporary with independence or which immediately followed it. (Candido, 1995, XII)

The concept of mimeticism also serves to create the idea that the former colonies always produced a posteriori, in accordance with models imported from the colonial power, ignoring the fact that a certain synchrony existed in literary production, not only between former colonies and former colonial powers but also between the latter as a whole and other nations in different historical moments.

In any event, moving forward in time, if we examine the thinking of the literary vanguards of the early twentieth century, we can observe that they often recycled and radicalized elements already present in Romanticism.

When dealing with literary movements or periods, it is interesting to note how the context for a writer's poetics projects itself onto his or her very discourse. By invoking or justifying the reasons for producing their art in such and such a way, writers frequently look to referents in relation to which the meaning of what they are producing delineates itself. Consequently, if, on the one hand, in the poetics of imitation and emulation a canon of authors and works clearly served as a model, on the other, principally after Romanticism, a very different notion of artistic production emerged. Whereas the previous poetics gave value to the past, where it looked for an example and model, the Romantics valued the aesthetics of the expression of the authorial "I," the presence of this authorial "I" in the origin of the work, the "presence" of the writer in opposition to the past of his art. This valorization would continue into the following century.

Modernists and Vanguardists

The fight against the neoclassical norms of the Romantic period is waged, among other means, by alleging that the very presupposition of producing a new classicism—with its notions of exemplarity and the use of the classics as a model—was not appropriate, since a new age demanded a new poetics. A poetics of *today* would be "better" than that of *yesterday*, by very definition. This is also a common trait of twentieth-century vanguards, which declare as obsolete all previous literary production and propose a "new" literature—their own—as the only one of value.

To a certain extent, what the artistic vanguards of the early twentieth century did was to produce a certain "description" of aspects of the past in order to deny them. On creating this image of the past, a relationship was also constructed, which could be disputed, first by questioning what was chosen to constitute the "past," then by analyzing the interests that presided over the choices that were made, and finally by establishing the terms of a contrast with or rejection of the artistic production of the past. In some way the vanguards thus also echoed the voice that they disagreed with. Why? Because, when you attribute to any literary paradigm the function of *model*, the latter can be positive *or* negative. *Negative models* are those that we wish to avoid, oppose ourselves to, or be *different* from. However, they do not cease to be models. In other words, if you want to show your difference in relation to a negative model, it continues to be your referent, even if only so that you avoid it, confront it, or fail to repeat it.

If we wanted to find another key to unlock the relationship of early twentieth-century vanguards with the literature that had gone before, perhaps we could, instead of trying to ignore the links between the two, reconsider in this way. In fact, many groups from the early twentieth century still had as their point of reference authors and literary works from the past, but not as examples or models to be followed. Since the self-image of the vanguardist is strongly marked by the idea of his or her alleged autonomy and brilliant individuality, he or she presumably does not feel self-conscious about treating inherited paradigms with respect.

If we wanted to hazard a generalization, we could argue that a large group of twentieth-century artists appropriates "tradition" in a playful and arbitrary way, in accordance with the most momentary interests of the artistic structures they create. In this way, it seems that in replacing what was proposed in Western artistic practice until at least the first half of the eighteenth century—in other words, replacing regularity and the iterative nature of emulation, of the practices of imitation that successively appeared, but brought with them a certain comforting sense of return to an already familiar sphere—a new agenda emerges, in which even the integration of the already familiar aspires to include something of the unforeseen, the random, and the contingent. Can we say that this art of the present, without the guarantee of a regular and stable relationship with the past, loses entirely any pretension to regularity, iterability, or recursiveness? Perhaps it is more appropriate to argue that the incorporation of new elements into the artistic process itself can also constitute a form of regularity, reiteration, recursiveness, or "tradition," even if only for a short duration.

In the Brazilian case, instead of continuing to look to European "origins" for the elements that would later be "imitated," perhaps it would be more productive to study the reception of these elements in Brazil. In other words, if the cultural product configured in the supposed "origins" is not predominantly determined by an *export* preoccupation in its very "place of origin" (Portugal, France, and so on) but by the reasoning, interests, and motivations of the cultural producers who choose what suits, adjusts, or harmonizes with the product's needs and interests in the context of cultural reception in the (ex-)colonies, then greater attention must be given to the latter.

This context of reception is in some way made up of public networks of meaning, in which symbolically mediated interpretations emerge, including interpretations about what the "place of origin" in question signifies. We know that neither the real Portugal nor the real France nor the real Europe corresponds to either the image of the *colonial power* or that of the *absolute origin of emancipatory thought* that served as a basis for the decolonization movements. But it is not a question of Portugal, France, or Europe as such but rather of the meanings attributed to these places in the reception contexts, in the different historical moments in which the appropriation and circulation of cultural elements from abroad took place. Thus, the interests that affected the importation of these elements can be studied. The very context in relation to which writers and readers in Brazil interpret their experiences (and the texts they read), as well as direct their actions, is always in some way derived from locally rooted preconceptions that contribute to the choices made.

To conclude, we can consider yet another alternative, already put forward by Machado de Assis in chapter XXXVII of *Esaú e Jacó* and significantly entitled "About an Inopportune Thought": "Ideas themselves do not always keep the name of their father. Many appear as orphans, born of nothing and of no one. Each one takes them from the next, makes of them what they can, and carries them to the marketplace, where all take them for their own" (Machado de Assis, 81).

NOTE

1. For Asian examples illustrating this point, see Dipesh Chakrabarty, *Provincializing Europe: Postcolonial Thought and Historical Difference* (Princeton, NJ: Princeton University Press, 2000).

WORKS CITED

Andrade, Mário de. Letter 4 (no date, 1924). In *Correspondência de Carlos Drummond de Andrade e Mário de Andrade*. Rio de Janeiro: Bem-te-vi, 2002. 66–72.

Assis, Machado de. *Esaú e Jacó*. In *Obra Completa*. Vol. 1. Rio de Janeiro: Aguilar, 1962.

Bastide, "R. Sociologia e literatura comparada." *Revista Literatura e Sociedade*, São Paulo,

Departamento de Teoria Literária e Literatura Comparada da USP, no. 9 (2006): 264–69. (Originally published in *Cahiers internationaux de sociologie*, no. 17 [July–December 1957].)

"Breve notícia sobre a criação do Instituto Histórico e Geográfico Brasileiro." *Revista do Instituto Histórico e Geográfico do Brasil* 1, no. 1 (1839), Rio de Janeiro: Imprensa Nacional, 1908, 5–8. 3rd ed.

Candido, Antonio. "Preface." In *Arcádia: Tradição e mudança*, edited by Jorge Antonio Ruedas de la Serna. São Paulo: EDUSP, 1995. xi–xvi.

Chakrabarty, Dipesh. *Provincializing Europe: Postcolonial Thought and Historical Difference*. Princeton, NJ: Princeton University Press, 2000.

Curtius, Ernest Robert. *Literatura européia e Idade Média Latina*, translated by Paulo Rónai and Teodoro Cabral. São Paulo: EDUSP, 1996.

Hansen, João Adolfo. *A sátira e o engenho: Gregório de Matos e a Bahia do século XVII*. São Paulo: Companhia das Letras, 1989.

Kidder, Daniel P. *Sketches of Residence and Travels in Brazil Embracing Historical and Geographical Notices of the Empire and Its Several Provinces*. Vol. 2. Philadelphia: Sorin and Ball, 1845.

Machado de Assis, Joaquim Maria. *Esau and Jacob*, translated by Elizabeth Lowe. Oxford: Oxford University Press, 2000.

Olander, Maurice. Introduction. *Le genre humain*, École des hautes études en sciences sociales, Paris, no. 27 (Summer–Autumn 1993), p. 7.

Rio, João do. *O momento literário, inquérito* (1907). http://www.dominiopublico.gov.br/download/texto/bn000134.pdf.

Storm, Eric. "Regionalism in History, 1890–1945: The Cultural Approach." *European History Quarterly* 33, no. 2 (2003), 251–65.

Ureña, Pedro Henríquez. "Seis ensayos em busca de nuestra expression" [1928]. In Pedro Henríquez Ureña, *Obra crítica*. Mexico City: Fondo de Cultura Econômica, 1960. 237–327.

JOSÉ LUÍS JOBIM is a full professor in the Department of Literary Theory, Brazilian Literature and Culture, at the State University of Rio de Janeiro and an associate professor in the Department of Language Sciences at the Universidade Federal Fluminense. He is currently a researcher at the National Council of Research (CNPq) and the Rio de Janeiro State Foundation of Research (FAPERJ). His latest publications include the books *A crítica literária e os críticos criadores no Brasil* (2012) and *Literatura e cultura: Do nacional ao transnacional* (2013). He may be reached at jjobim@id.uff.br.

Essays

GRAÇA ÍNDIAS CORDEIRO

Belongings and Interactions
Negotiating Portuguese-Speaking Identities in Boston

ABSTRACT: This article reflects on an ongoing research project on the current movement for affirmative action on behalf of Portuguese speakers in metropolitan Boston, through a crosscutting perspective combining ethnography and social history within a socioanthropological analysis. The focus is on the interactive relationships among different Portuguese-speaking immigrants and their descendants in the context of the nonprofit Massachusetts Alliance of Portuguese Speakers (MAPS). What makes the "Portuguese-speaking" case so interesting is its encompassing of a very disparate set of populations and identities, including their contrasting migratory history and pathways of incorporation, as well as their different mother tongues (Portuguese and Kriolu—the Cape Verdian mother tongue).

KEYWORDS: Portuguese speakers, social classifications, social movement, Boston, Massachusetts.

Introduction

Portuguese is the second most widely spoken foreign language in Massachusetts, due to an intense and recent influx of Brazilian immigrants that complemented a tradition of Portuguese and Cape Verdean immigration dating to the mid-nineteenth century. Awareness of the extent of the Portuguese-speaking community is high among the media, political and community leaders, and others connected with its realities.

A movement for affirmative action on behalf of Portuguese speakers in metropolitan Boston is now being carried out by representatives of mostly Portuguese, Brazilian, and Cape Verdean immigrants. The group principally responsible for the effort is the nonprofit Massachusetts Alliance of Portuguese Speakers (MAPS), which has engaged in this work with great dynamism and generally provides social support to Portuguese-speaking populations of Brazilian, Cape Verdean, and Portuguese origin in Massachusetts cities in the Boston area, including Lowell to the north and Framingham to the west. The group is thus attempting to establish a sort of *pan-ethnic* Portuguese-speaking category, inspired by the Hispanic/Latino *pan-ethnic* model—and definitely separate from it.

The specific context for this struggle for a Portuguese-speaking category, and the focus of this paper,[1] is U.S. Census 2010. More broadly, this work fits within an ongoing research project aimed at capturing the local social field of Portuguese-speaking populations through a crosscutting perspective combining ethnography and social history within a socioanthropological analysis.[2] The joining of the lenses of an "ethnographical eye" with historical research is aimed at better understanding the local emergence, uses, and representations of the Portuguese-speaking category, which continues to be renewed with the recent wave of Brazilian immigrants to the area.

Portuguese-Speaking Immigration to Massachusetts

Portuguese (mainly Azorean) and Cape Verdean immigration to Massachusetts and Rhode Island in the nineteenth century was driven first by the whaling industry and then by jobs in textile mills and other manufacturers. Fall River and New Bedford saw the greatest surge in such immigrants, with Cambridge and Somerville coming in second. The numbers dipped in the 1920s owing to stricter U.S. immigration policies, but the Immigration and Nationality Act of 1965 opened the gates once again, eliminating quotas and replacing them with a system that gave immigration preference to applications submitted by the spouses, siblings, siblings' spouses, and siblings' children of U.S. residents. By 1975, the number of immigrants to the United States arriving from Portugal exceeded that from every other country in Europe (Pap 1981; Center for Policy Analysis 2005).

In a certain way, Cape Verdean immigration mirrored Portuguese immigration, but with two important differences: the former did not stop at the end of the 1970s, as did the latter, and the so-called "black" Portuguese—until 1975, the Cape Verde Islands were a Portuguese colony—were considered distinct from other Portuguese immigrants. Separate Cape Verdean communities thus emerged—sometimes near other Portuguese communities, sometimes not—in southeastern Massachusetts and Rhode Island (Machado 1981; Halter 1993) as well as in inner-city Boston, especially Roxbury and Dorchester (Halter 2009, 527). Brazilian immigration followed in the 1980s, with immigrants entering mainly service occupations and mostly concentrated in Somerville, Allston, Everett, Framingham, and Cape Cod and the Islands (Lima and Siqueira, 2008). This area is far from what is known as the Portuguese Archipelago, which covers New Bedford, Fall River, and Taunton, a triangle in southeastern Massachusetts.

As Dario Borin, a professor at the University of Massachusetts Dartmouth, said in a 2007 interview with the *Boston Globe*, "There was already a Portuguese language infrastructure here, with businesses, educational programs, and medical professionals who spoke the language."[3] It's reasonable to assume that language attracted Brazilian immigrants. According to the same article, some 800,000 to 1 million Portuguese speakers inhabit Massachusetts, making it the state's largest linguistic minority.

But . . . can we assume that language in and of itself really binds these Portuguese speakers, coming from far-flung countries? Or is this "unity" a political and social construct designed to give diverse people from Europe, Africa, and Latin America a common identity—in order to create a sort of pan-ethnic consensus as powerful as the Hispanic/Latino one within New England?

Despite it being such a large linguistic minority, many in the Brazilian immigrant population are counted as Hispanic/Latino, and those from Portugal, Cape Verde, and African countries are scattered among white, black, and other categories in a country where racial categories often trump ethnic or linguistic ones. As Paulo Pinto, executive director of MAPS, said in the same *Boston Globe* article: "According to U.S. Census data, the Portuguese-speaking community doesn't exist—we are invisible because we are either miscounted or not counted at all. We are not as lucky as our friends in the Hispanic community to have our own category on the forms."

In fact, the "invisibility" of Portuguese-speaking people extends far beyond the situation in southeastern Massachusetts (Adler 1972; Smith 1974; Moniz 2009). They arrive from different continents and span different races, and also have long, complicated colonial and postcolonial historical connections and relationships in other nations. All this poses a challenge for the vigorous movement toward Portuguese-language identification advocated by MAPS, which has enlisted several community partners in social movements and local political action efforts.

MAPS in Place and Time

MAPS, a multiethnic organization with Portuguese-American origins, is based simultaneously on language and place (neighborhoods). As noted, the group serves people with roots in three ancestries, Portugal, Cape Verde, and Brazil, and has been the main advocate and leader of this identity-making process for more than a decade. The perimeter of this field research is drawn around its various "offices" based in ethnically diverse neighborhoods, with an emphasis on the Portuguese/Brazilian axis of Cambridge/Somerville and the Cape Verdean/Latino/Afro-American axis of Roxbury/Dorchester, where we can find Portuguese-speaking places of public conviviality. Focusing on MAPS and its local embeddeness allows a view into the context of today's urban, multiethnic Boston and its surroundings (Fong and Shibuya 2005), which is an intensively professionalized and well-educated milieu that, over the past four decades, has been transformed from a predominantly white to a diverse multicultural community and from a "mill-based to a mind-based economy" (Bluestone and Stevenson 2000, 8). MAPS, and the area where it operates, offers an excellent opportunity—a rich "urban community laboratory"—for an integrated ethnographic and historical approach to studying this broader metropolitan process. Also, MAPS deserves close analysis for its role in the formation of new ethnic and nonethnic linkages and identities (Glick Schiller and Çaglar 2011, 68) among immigrants and descendants of the Portuguese-speaking, or lusophone, world in the United States.

In fact, Portuguese-speaking immigration to the Boston area, especially to East Cambridge, can be understood through MAPS's own early history. This organization arose from the merger of two local associations of Portuguese Americans, created twenty years ago in Cambridge (Cambridge Street) and in Somerville (Union Square). The mission was to help Portuguese immigrants, who were arriving in large numbers, and also Cape Verdean immigrants, even though they were fewer.

The 1990s was the period of Boston's economic transformation, or "renaissance," in Bluestone and Stevenson's language: "Demographically, the Greater Boston Region has moved from a white ethnocentric to a diverse multicultural community. Industrially, it has been transformed from a mill-based to a mind-based economy. And spatially, the central city has shifted in economic influence from being an all-powerful hub to being part of a true metropolitan area" (Bluestone and Stevenson 2000, 8).

This "multicultural community" has been built through the increase of Hispanics/Latinos and Asians, doubling the minority inhabitants in metro Boston between 1970 and 1990, from 270,000 to 580,000 (Bluestone and Stevenson 2000, 12).

As we have seen, the *Portuguese* have been seen as a recurrent omission, the *invisible minority* that never appears either in bibliographies or maps (Rogers 1974). However, this community was "the largest ethnic group in Southeastern Massachusetts [including] those from mainland Portugal, Cape Verdeans, Madeiras and Azoreans. Some are also from Brazil" (Huff 1989, 9). Caroline Brettell details these groups' so-called social invisibility: "The Portuguese were the only southern Europeans who migrated to the United States in large numbers in the later 20th century. . . . [T]hey have settled in and sometimes remade communities from New Jersey to Boston. Yet, despite the so-called 'Portuguese Archipelago' of southeastern Massachusetts, an ethnic enclave in the full sense of the word, the Portuguese have been and . . . remain an 'invisible minority'" (Brettell 2009, 557).

In East Cambridge, however, Portuguese immigrants have been less invisible than elsewhere (Woods and Kennedy 1962, chapter 4). For its part, the Cambridge Organization for Portuguese-Americans (COPA), one of MAPS's predecessors, organized the first Portuguese Congress in America at Harvard University in 1973: "Cambridge is the site of the convention because it holds many of the Portuguese residing in the U.S." The same report continues: "Three hundred Portuguese-Americans will establish the first Congress of the Portuguese in the United States in a three-day convention here this weekend. The congress is intended to provide Portuguese in America with a greater voice in U.S. government affairs, an organizer of the convention said yesterday. Aurelio Torres, director of the Cambridge Organization of Portuguese-Americans (COPA), the organization that is sponsoring the convention . . . [said the event] will publicize Portuguese contributions to American government and culture" (*Harvard Crimson*, June 1, 1973).

Three days later the *Boston Globe* reported, "Recognition of the Portuguese community as a minority by the competent authorities—local, state and federal —was demanded in the key resolution passed yesterday in the concluding session of the First Portuguese Congress in America" (June 4, 1973). However, this decision didn't lead to concrete actions because "not all of those present . . . were enamored with defining the Portuguese as a legal minority group" (Moniz 2009, 408). Francis Rogers, for example, a Harvard professor of Portuguese/

Azorean and Irish descent, "worked to successfully derail Portuguese minority status. Part of the argument made to the Congressional delegation was that the Portuguese should not be considered a minority group because the Portuguese were not Hispanics and, unlike other minority groups, they were white" (Moniz 2009, 410). Thus, the Portuguese would largely remain a "forgotten minority," as a two-part *Harvard Crimson* article of March 1974 detailed.[4]

Along with the 1980s advent of Brazilian immigration, the inflow from Portugal would virtually stop. The 1993 merger of COPA and SPAL to create MAPS indicated—even through the organization's acronym—the area's diversity of Portuguese speakers, as signaled by the Brazilian arrivals into New England, and the Boston area in particular (Martes and Fleisher 2003; Martes and Soares 2006; Sales 2005). The dispersion of Brazilian immigrants transformed awareness of the overall Portuguese-speaking presence in areas such as Somerville, Allston, and East Boston.

In twenty years, MAPS has expanded from two offices, in Cambridge and Somerville, to several—in Boston, Lowell, and Framingham—covering most areas where Portuguese and Kriolu[5] are spoken by large numbers, including Boston enclaves such as Brazilian Allston and Cape Verdean Dorchester[6]: " . . . the key Portuguese community organization is the Massachusetts Alliance of Portuguese Speakers (MAPS). It has offered some citizenship services intermittently in the last five to seven years, but its main focus is on the provision of social and health services, such as counselling and AIDS education. This focus is a direct result of its funding, which comes from Massachusetts State grants tied to specific social-service goals and from agencies such as the United Way" (Bloemraad 1999, 115).

In recent years, as MAPS's clients have grown more diverse, its staff has followed suit, with Cape Verdean and Brazilian professionals mixing in with Portuguese and Americans. The organization's clients are now chiefly Brazilian, even though it still has important programs for mainly elderly Portuguese.[7]

Among its six offices, two zones are particularly interesting: Cambridge/Somerville, traditionally cities with heavy Portuguese populations (Ito-Adler 1980) but today with a higher proportion of Brazilians, and Roxbury/Dorchester, largely segregated sections with a major concentration of African Americans, Latinos, and Cape Verdeans (Sieber and Centeio 2010).

Cambridge Street, also known as Portuguese Boulevard (Morgenroth 2001), includes headquarters of MAPS and its 1970s predecessor organization, COPA.

Key community institutions such as St. Anthony's Roman Catholic Church, schools with bilingual programs, restaurants and other businesses, Azorean clubs and associations, and seasonal festivals offer an excellent point of observation from both the ethnographic and ethnohistorical points of view (Adler 1972; Pap 1981). The adjacent city of Somerville is intensively occupied by Brazilians, whose visibility through commercial establishments forms a kind of line of continuity with Cambridge.

In Dorchester, one of Boston's most stigmatized neighborhoods, MAPS engages in intense outreach to assist local residents, in laundries, retailers, bars, and restaurants. A nearby Catholic church, St. Patrick's, numerous evangelical churches, and the Jeremiah Burke High School, with its unique bilingual education programs in Kriolu and English, are part of the present context of this association (Gibau 2009, 466–70).

One of the most impressive features of this neighborhood is the colorful and moving Cape Verdean community murals (Cordeiro, Ferro, and Sieber 2012). Here Portuguese mingles with Kriolu and Spanish.

The PSCCC 2010 Census: Portuguese Speakers versus Latinos?

On July 23, 2009, MAPS executive director Paulo Pinto emailed an invitation to several Portuguese, Brazilian, and Cape Verdean leaders from around the state to join him at the MAPS Cambridge office to organize the "Portuguese-Speaking Complete Count Committee for the 2010 U.S. Census," or PSCCC; he copied the U.S. Census Bureau on the email and received an answer the next day expressing support for the initiative. Five days later, a notice of convocation was sent to the same recipients and signed by some of them.

This was the beginning of the federal campaign of the 2010 Census, and the PSCCC brought together Brazilian, Cape Verdean, and Portuguese community leaders in Massachusetts around the survey of Portuguese-speaking people.

The PSCCC's inaugural meeting in MAPS's Cambridge office on August 20 had twenty-nine community representatives, mostly from MAPS (eleven) but also from the U.S. Census Bureau (two), Brazilian associations (three), newspapers, a TV channel (four), the MIRA coalition (one), an immigrant assistance center (one), a bank, a school; a photographer also attended. At the meeting, led by Pinto, nine subcommittees were created (media, faith-based, regional [in four areas], youth, resources, and outreach) and a date was discussed for the campaign kickoff at the State House. Also discussed was the census boycott movement led by the director of a local Brazilian association in protest over the situation of undocumented immigrants. Participants also advocated more representation and resources for Portuguese-speaking groups and for the state as a whole. The campaign was launched in three languages: Portuguese, English, and Kriolu. As Paulo Pinto argued: "A 'complete count' is crucial so that Portuguese speakers, and all Massachusetts residents, have full representation in Congress. A full count also has many other benefits, including ensuring that all communities receive enough government funding for vital services and programs that range from highway construction to education, public safety, health and social services."[8]

But the main effort was directed toward informing the community on how to answer the Census questions 8 and 9, referring to race and ethnicity: In order to get a better picture of its communities, the PSCCC was asking Portuguese speakers to answer the race and ethnicity questions as follows (with the following material quoted or paraphrased from the MAPS site): *Question 8* (or Question 5 for persons 2 and beyond in the household): Check "No—not of Hispanic, Latino or Spanish origin." *Question 9* (or Question 6 for persons 2 and beyond in the household): Check *only* "Some other race" and write in your ethnic/ancestral background, such as Brazilian, Cape Verdean, Portuguese, etc. in the boxes below.[9]

"Ten years ago, we had a lot of Portuguese speakers who got counted as Latinos," said Pinto. "The Latino population got a huge increase in the Census, but we still don't have a picture of our community."

On December 18, Pinto wrote to K. Ludgate, director of the Boston Regional Census Center, expressing his concern regarding an incorrect translation in the Portuguese version of Form D-60 of the Census Bureau's Language Assistance Guide. The term *Latino* (person of Hispanic, Latino, or Spanish origin) was translated to "Latin American," which includes Brazilians, who, however, could not be included as Latinos:

> The delineation of the Hispanic/Latino category as Spanish-speaking is quite clear, and matches the Portuguese-speaking community's understanding that we are not "Latino," as the government uses the term. However, Form D-60 (Portuguese) contradicts this settled definition. D-60 asks: "A pessoa no. 1 é de origem hispânica, latino-americana ou espanhola?" (Is person number 1 of Hispanic, Latin-American or Spanish origin?) . . . Latin-American

> is a geographic designation that certainly includes Portuguese-speaking Brazilians. . . . Other translations of the document reflect the original intent and do not replicate the error. D-60 (Spanish) uses *latino* and not *latinoamericano*. . . . (French, Italian, the same) . . .

And as Pinto clearly pointed out: "Members of our community have made representations in the past regarding the creation of new categories to describe accurately the nation's Portuguese-speaking populations. . . . We recognize that such a solution, however desirable, is not possible with respect to the 2010 Census, and we look forward to continuing discussions on that subject in the future. At this time, we are only asking that you and the Bureau consider a very simple revision of Form D-60 to replace '*latino- americana*' with '*latina*' . . ."

Signatories of this letter included representatives of MAPS, the Brazilian Women's Group, the University of Massachusetts Lowell, Deputy Director, City of Boston, and the AC (representatives of Brazilian, Cape Verdean, and Portuguese associations). On January 4, 2010, the language in the guide was changed.

This claim was accepted in Jan 4 and the Guide text changed.

Unfortunately, the counting of the Portuguese speakers was late in getting started, but the seeds were sown, and MAPS pursued the Portuguese-speaking cause as the major broker in Massachusetts on this issue. This is still an open story.

Misunderstandings of the Meaning of *Portuguese*

The Portuguese-speaking case in Massachusetts offers a useful prism for thinking about identity creation, as related to ethnicity, race, and nationhood, in U.S. society (Cornell and Hartmann 1998; Brubaker 2009). The U.S. Census has a crucial role in this fabric (Schor, 2009).

In some ways, it can be difficult to fit Portuguese-speaking communities into one category within standard North American ethnic/racial or national categories. The origins of these Portuguese-speaking people are on three different continents: Europe, Africa, and South America/Latin America, with a contrasting history of waves of settlement in the host society—an early Portuguese and Cape Verdean immigration to a nineteenth- and early-to-mid-twentieth-century industrialized U.S. society, concentrated in some regions (Rhode Island, southeastern Massachusetts, Cambridge and Somerville); and a more recent Brazilian immigration to a postindustrial society, scattered all over metro Boston and beyond. The colonial and migratory history of these populations is represented in still-vivid memories of Portuguese colonialism in Cape Verde, and negative stereotypes of Portuguese immigrants in Brazil stronger than colonial memories. The racial diversity among whites, African Americans, and Latinos seems to explode within the Portuguese-speaking case: Cape Verdeans once fit mainly in Portuguese and European boxes but then in recent decades took on an African identity with Portuguese as an official national language. Brazilians from Latin America fall outside the Latino box because their language is not Spanish. In addition, some Brazilians are of African descent, "black" in the U.S. and sometimes in the Brazilian context. Finally, Portuguese descendants are of European descent even though they are losing their Portuguese-language skills.

In other ways, we are faced with some paradoxical features concerning the uses and representations of Portuguese language on U.S. land. It seems that those who are the most intensive Portuguese speakers have reservations about being identified as such because of the implications of Portuguese culture or ethnicity (Martes 2000, 170–76). The semantic problem that emerges is that Portuguese is both a language and a nationality. Portugal, besides its colonial and postcolonial history, is still a poor, small country, peripheral in Europe, with a deep history of immigration not only to the United States but also to Europe and, nowadays, to Brazil again. Portuguese therefore refers to a people of low profile, an invisible and forgotten minority in U.S. terms—in large part, because of its lack of political skills and capability to create its own positive identity.

Maybe we have to consider the Portuguese language as a sort of bone of contention among various identities and sensibilities. To share one language may be necessary, but it is not sufficient for building cohesiveness. The PSCCC Census 2010 effort proposed a new component for the landscape of Massachusetts ethnic differentiation—leading to an exploration of the interactive relationships between "we" and "others," both inside and outside Portuguese-speaking populations, in order to better understand how different political and ideological positions, representations, opinions, and sensibilities produce remarkable contrasts regarding nationhood, ethnicity, and race on American soil (Brubaker, 2009). These identities are shaped by a complex set of intertwined social structures and circumstances, such as migratory experiences, social mobility, and "pathways of incorporation that reflected the dynamic between locality and hierarchies of power" (Glick Schiller 2005, 61). We need to explore better the context of the city (Rollwagen 1975; Brettell 2003) and how local urban history intermingles with U.S. Census dynamics, which eventually shape new ethnic, nonethnic, or "para-ethnic" identities that emerge by "an interaction between assignment—what others say we are—and assertion—who or what we claim to be" (Cornell and Hartmann 1998, 72: based on Ito-Adler 1980).

Finally, this research seeks to link the following aspects that are present in these somehow "composite realities" but usually not connected in studies related to Portuguese-speaking communities:

1. The role of the language in the drawing of ethnic and racial boundaries —language as communication, with all its varieties, but also as representation. How is this common language perceived? Does it contribute to the making of a sense of community or, on the contrary, do its varieties and disparate cultural heritages build a separation between them? How does each "community" with the Portuguese label fit? Is the label comfortable for Brazilians? Does it work for Cape Verdeans? What kind of role does Kriolu play in this process? Language is identity, and Kriolu is the Cape Verdean mother tongue, so—what representation does the official language of Cape Verde have in Massachusetts?
2. An interactive approach to Portuguese-speaking populations trying to fill the gap between immigration processes from Portugal (mostly from the Azores), the Cape Verde Islands, and Brazil. Studies of Portuguese, Cape Verdean, and Brazilian "communities" are normally separate and seldom have examined the interactions and intersections within and beyond them. The recent struggle for the cultural, ethnic, or linguistic awareness of what *Portuguese* means in American society shows that this academic fragmentation does not help us understand the complexity of these composite social movements.
3. A more nuanced place-based view of the urban context, requiring consideration of two complementary scales, the metropolitan (metro Boston) and the neighborhood/street (East Cambridge, Somerville, Roxbury/Dorchester). These urban contexts offer keys to understanding social mobility in Portuguese-speaking populations and how local identity affects the complex heritage of social representations and stereotypes that make up social classifications and categorizations. The local urban ambiance likewise must be examined as a crucial variable in that ethno-genesis process. In this sense, more than merely

> a place where immigrants arrive, the city is a place of transformation, innovation, and cultural emergence, constantly moving and being reshaped. In this regard, we want to pursue a kind of "urban anthropology of social change," attentive mainly to the dynamics of collaboration and competition that make the city the best place to grasp innovation and sociocultural creativity (Agier 2009; Velho 2010).

I believe MAPS offers a window to understanding the migratory history of Portuguese-speaking peoples and the way it has been shaped by institutional environments and networks of political alliances—in particular, how individuals have shaped and been shaped by social processes, wherein leaders have played a crucial part in building links among nonprofit organizations and community-based organizations, government, political parties, and so on (Donzelot, 2003). The intertwined relations between the political and organizational environment, through community development oriented by small ethnic and immigrant associations as well as other powerful organizations, have been instrumental in the making of that Portuguese-speaking community.

Furthermore, this development should be integrated within more recent internationalization of the Portuguese language, considered today one of the six major world languages, ever closer to the cases of English and Spanish (Reto 2009)—partly due to the demographic and economic growth in Brazil and some African countries. This region, where Portuguese is the second most spoken foreign language and where a new language-based social movement has emerged, is a case that deserves thorough study.

NOTES

1. This article is based on a paper presented at the Thirty-sixth Annual Meeting of the Social Science History Association, held in Boston, Massachusetts, November 17–20, 2011. I am very grateful for Ariel Salzmann's commentaries at the session "Racial Identity, Culture, and Media," at which this paper was presented.

In the field, I am in debt to my colleagues Tim Sieber and James Ito-Adler for the knowledge they generously shared with me, and also to Paulo Pinto at MAPS, for his empathetic support for this research and all the wider collaboration that the organization allowed me. Former versions of this article were presented orally and discussed at three conferences during 2011: SIEF2011, Tenth Congress, Lisbon, April 17–21, 2011, FCSH—Universidade Nova de Lisboa, Panel P103, "Uneasy Places: Shifting Research Boundaries and Displacing Selves" (org. Isabel Fêo Rodrigues and Frédéric Vidal); Journées d'études,

Frontières et mouvements de la ville: Comparaisons internationales en anthropologie urbaine, Paris, May 3–4, 2011, Ecole des Hautes Etudes en Sciences Sociales (org. Michel Agier); Palestra no Programa de Pós-Graduação em Antropologia Social do Museu Nacional, Universidade Federal do Rio de Janeiro, September 6, 2011. I am deeply grateful for the commentaries provided by Isabel Fêo Rodrigues, Frédéric Vidal, Michel Agier, Stephane Dufoix, and Gilberto Velho.

2. The field research took place over two periods since 2009: first, during a six-month period (January–June 2009), supported by an FCT scholarship, and then during a one-month stay in July 2011; this second stay was accompanied by exploratory historical research, conducted by Frederic Vidal. I acknowledge with gratitude FLAD for the financial aid that made that research possible.

3. http://www.boston.com/jobs/diversityfall_07/an_immigration_phenomenon.

4. Peter A. Landry, "Cambridge's Forgotten Minority: The Portuguese Community Walks a Tightrope of Assimilation," *Harvard Crimson*, March 22, 1974.

5. Kriolu, a language composed from older Portuguese and African languages, is, as noted, the Cape Verdian mother tongue; nevertheless, the country's official language is Portuguese.

6. In 1993, offices opened in Cambridge (formerly COPA) and Somerville (formerly SPAL); 1995, Allston (Boston); 1997, Lowell; 2001, Dorchester; 2006, Framingham.

7. "Elder Services," Massachusetts Alliance of Portuguese Speakers (MAPS), accessed October 10, 2011, from http://www.maps-inc.org/services/elder-services/.

8. "Portuguese Speakers Launch Statewide Complete Count Committee for 2010 U.S. Census," Massachusetts Alliance of Portuguese Speakers (MAPS), accessed October 10, 2011, from http://www.maps-inc.org/press-releases/portuguese-speakers-launch-statewide-complete-count-committee-for-2010-us-census/.

9. "Key Facts about the Census and the PSCCC," Massachusetts Alliance of Portuguese Speakers (MAPS), accessed October 10, 2011, from http://www.maps-inc.org/our-community/census2010/key-facts/.

WORKS CITED

Adler, James P. *The Portuguese*. Vol. 1 of *Ethnic Minorities in Cambridge* (unabridged). Cambridge: Planning and Development Department, 1972.

Agier, Michel. *Esquisses d'une anthropologie de la ville: Lieux, situations, mouvements*. Louvaine-la-Neuve: Bruylant-Academia, 2009.

Bloemraad, Iréne. "Portuguese Immigrants and Citizenship in North America." *Lusotopie* (1999): 103–20.

Bluestone, Barry, and Mary Huff Stevenson, eds. "Greater Boston in Transition." In *The Boston Renaissance: Race, Space, and Economic Change in an American Metropolis*. New York: Russell Sage Foundation, 2002. 1–22.

Brettell, Caroline B. "Bringing the City Back." In "Cities as Contexts for Immigrant Incorporation." *American Arrivals: Anthropology Engages the New Immigration*, edited by Nancy Foner. Santa Fe, NM: School of American Research Press 2003, 163–95.

———. "Current Trends and Future Directions in Portuguese-American Studies." In *Community, Culture and the Makings of Identity: Portuguese-Americans along the Eastern Seaboard*, edited by Kimberly DaCosta Holton and Andrea Klimt, 557–68. North Dartmouth, MA: University of Massachusetts Dartmouth, 2009.

Brubaker, Rogers. "Ethnicity, Race, and Nationalism." *Annual Review of Sociology* 35 (2009): 21–42.

Center for Policy Analysis. *Portuguese-Americans in the Massachusetts Power Structure*. Dartmouth, MA: Center for Policy Analysis, University of Massachusetts Dartmouth, 2005.

Cordeiro, Graça Índias, Lígia Ferro, and Tim Sieber. "Art Builds the City: Boston Community Murals and Local Identity." *Ponto Urbe: Revista do Núcleo de Antropologia Urbana da USP* (2012).

Cornell, Stephen, and Douglas Hartmann. *Ethnicity and Race: Making Identities in a Changing World*. Thousand Oaks, CA: Pine Forge Press, 1998.

Donzelot, Jacques. *Faire societé: La politique de la ville aux États-Unis et en France*. Paris: Editions du Seuil, 2003.

Fong, Eric, and Kumiko Shibuya. "Multiethnic Cities in North America." *Annual Review of Sociology* 31 (2005): 285–304.

Gibau, Gina Sánchez. "Contested Identities: Narratives of Race and Ethnicity in the Cape Verdean Diaspora." In *Community, Culture and the Makings of Identity: Portuguese-Americans along the Eastern Seaboard*, edited by Kimberly DaCosta Holton and Andrea Klimt, 461–95. North Dartmouth, MA: University of Massachusetts Dartmouth, 2009.

Glick Schiller, Nina. "Transnational Urbanism as a Way of Life: A Research Topic, Not a Metaphor." *City & Society* 17, no. 1 (2005): 49–64.

Glick Schiller, Nina, and Ayse Çaglar. "Locality and Globality: Building a Comparative Analytical Framework in Migration and Urban Studies." In *Locating Migration: Rescaling Cities and Migrants*, edited by Nina Glick Schiller and Ayse Çaglar, 60–81. Ithaca, NY: Cornell University Press, 2011.

Halter, Marilyn. *Between Race and Ethnicity: Cape Verdean American Immigrants, 1860–1965*. Urbana: University of Illinois Press, 1993.

———. "Diasporic Generations: Distinctions of Race, Nationality and Identity in the Cape Verdean Community, Past and Present." In *Community, Culture and the Makings of Identity: Portuguese-Americans along the Eastern Seaboard*, edited by Kimberly DaCosta Holton and Andrea Klimt, 525–53. North Dartmouth, MA: University of Massachusetts Dartmouth, 2009.

Holton, Kimberly DaCosta, and Andrea Klimt, eds. *Community, Culture and the Makings of Identity: Portuguese-Americans along the Eastern Seaboard*. North Dartmouth, MA: University of Massachusetts Dartmouth, 2009.

Huff, Toby. "Education and Ethnicity in Southeastern Massachusetts." *Issues in Planning and Policymaking*. Boston: New England Board of Higher Education, 1989.

Ito-Adler, James. 1980. *The Portuguese in Cambridge and Somerville*. Cambridge: Department of Planning and Development.

Lima, Alvaro, and Eduardo Siqueira. *Brazilians in the U.S. and Massachusetts: A Demographic and Economic Profile*. Boston: Mauricio Gaston Institute for Latino Community Development and Public Policy, 2008.

Machado, Deirdre Meintel. 1981. "Cape Verdean Americans." *Hidden Minorities: The Persistence of Ethnicity in American Life*, edited by Joan Rollins, 233–56. Washington, DC: University Press of America.

Martes, Ana Cristina, and Soraya Fleisher, eds. *Fronteiras cruzadas: Etnicidade, género e redes sociais*. São Paulo: Paz e Terra, 2003.

Martes, Ana Cristina, and Weber Soares. "Remessas de recursos dos imigrantes." *Estudos avançados* 20, no. 57 (2006): 41–54.

Martes, Cristina Braga. *Brasileiros nos Estados Unidos: Um estudo sobre imigrantes em Massachusetts*. São Paulo: Paz e Terra, 2000.

Moniz, Miguel. "The Shadow Minority: An Ethnohistory of Portuguese and Lusophone Racial and Ethnic Identity in New England." In *Community, Culture and the Makings of Identity: Portuguese-Americans along the Eastern Seaboard*, edited by Kimberly DaCosta Holton and Andrea Klimt, 409–30. North Dartmouth, MA: University of Massachusetts Dartmouth, 2009.

Morgenroth, Lynda, and Carleen Powell. *Boston Neighborhoods: A Food Lover's Walking, Eating, and Shopping Guide to Ethnic Enclaves in and around Boston*. Guilford, CT: Globe Pequot Press, 2001.

Pap, Leo. *The Portuguese-Americans*. Boston: Twayne Publishers, 1981.

Reto, Luis, ed. *Valor económico da língua portuguesa: Contributos metodológicos e empíricos*. Lisbon: Instituto Camões, CIES-ISCTE, 2009.

Rogers, Francis. "The Portuguese of Southeastern New England: Suggestions for Research." *Luso-Brazilian Review* 11, no. 1 (1974): 3–18.

Rollwagen, Jack R. 1975. "Introduction: The City as Context: A Symposium." *Urban Anthropology* 4 (1): 1–4.

Sales, Teresa. 2005. "A organização dos imigrantes brasileiros em Boston, EUA." *São Paulo em perspectiva* 19 (3): 44–54.

Schor, Paul. *Compter et classer: Histoire des recensements américains*. Paris: Editions EHESS, 2009.

Sieber, Tim, and Maria Centeio. "Working across Difference to Build Urban

Community, Democracy, and Immigrant Integration." In "Where Is Home? Immigrants of Color in Massachusetts." Special issue, *Trotter Review* 19, no. 1 (2010): 7–37.

Smith, M. Estellie. "Portuguese Enclaves: The Invisible Minority." In *Social and Cultural Identity: Problems of Persistence and Change*, proceedings of the Southern Anthropological Society, edited by T. K. Fitzgerald, 81–91. Athens: University of Georgia, 1974.

Velho, Gilberto. "Metrópole, cosmopolitismo e mediação." *Horizontes Antropológicos* 16, no. 33 (2010): 15–23.

Woods, Robert, and Albert J. Kennedy. *The Zone of Emergence: Observations of the Lower Middle and Upper Working Class Communities of Boston, 1905–1914*. Cambridge: MIT Press, 1976.

NEWSPAPERS CITED

Boston Globe

Harvard Crimson

GRAÇA ÍNDIAS CORDEIRO (PhD in social anthropology, 1996, ISCTE, Lisbon; graca.cordeiro@iscte.pt) is a professor in the Department of Social Research Methods at the University Institute of Lisbon (ISCTE-IUL) and is affiliated with its Center for Research and Studies in Sociology (CIES-IUL). She is the author of "As cidades fazem-se por dentro: Desafios de etnografia urbana," in *Cidades: Comunidades e Territórios* (2010), and *Um Lugar na Cidade: Quotidiano, Memória e Representação no bairro da Bica* (Dom Quixote, 1997), among other publications. She is coeditor (with Frédéric Vidal) of *A Rua: Espaço, Tempo, Sociabilidade* (Livros Horizonte, 2008) and (with Luís Baptista and António Firmino da Costa) *Etnografias Urbanas* (Celta, 2003). Her current research focuses on the dynamics of "Portuguese-speaking" identities in Massachusetts. She may be reached at gindias@gmail.com.

MONIQUE RODRIGUES BALBUENA

When the Eye Meets the World
Reading Subjectivity in Two Poems by Carlos Drummond de Andrade

ABSTRACT: This essay examines two different models to understand the relationship between subject and object in the lyric—Georg Lukács's (which emphasizes the transformation of the object) and Jonathan Culler's (which emphasizes the self-dramatization of the subjectivity in the object)—and demonstrates how both models are called into question by two poems of Carlos Drummond de Andrade. By means of a stylistic reading of the poems "No meio do caminho" and "Noturno à janela do apartamento," this essay claims that in these poems the object, albeit differently, participates in the construction of the subjectivity of the lyrical "I" and, in so doing, produces meaning.

KEYWORDS: lyric, object, subject, meaning, Georg Lukács, Jonathan Culler, Carlos Drummond de Andrade.

> A poesia (não tires poesia das coisas)
> elide sujeito e objeto.
> —Carlos Drummond de Andrade

"Only in lyric poetry is the subject . . . transformed into the sole carrier of meaning, the only true reality" (1968, 63), affirms Georg Lukács in *The Theory of the Novel*. In chapter 3, "The Epic and the Novel," Lukács discusses how the novel and the lyric overcome the duality of subject and object, viewed by him as essentially "mutually alien worlds" after the epic era. Since then, he claims, "the extensive totality is no longer directly given . . . the immanence of meaning in life has become a problem . . ." (56). In order to acquire eternal meaning, the duality between subject and object, rewritten as soul and nature, has to be transcended. And this transcendence occurs in the *lyrical moment*: "the great moment . . . the moment at which the meaningful unity of nature and soul or their meaningful divorce, the necessary and affirmed loneliness of the soul becomes eternal" (63).

According to Lukács, what he calls "alien, unknowable nature" (63) carries no meaning; it is later described as "dumb, sensuous and yet senseless" (64). Thus, this harbinger of meaning, the "unity of nature and soul," happens only when the lyric subject projects his "essential interiority" onto nature (63). That constitutes the lyrical moment, when the lyrical subject, with its projected interiority, transforms the outside world into a meaningful, *illuminated symbol*: "At the lyrical moment the purest interiority of the soul, set apart from duration without choice, lifted above the obscurely-determined multiplicity of things, solidifies into substance; whilst alien, unknowable nature is driven from within to agglomerate into a symbol that is illuminated throughout" (63).

The idea of the duality of subject and object continues to concern those who study the lyric. In *The Pursuit of Signs*, Jonathan Culler presents a different take on the "lyric moment," as he discusses the trope of the apostrophe. He argues: "If, as we tend to assume, post-enlightenment poetry seeks to overcome the alienation of subject from object, then apostrophe takes the crucial step of constituting the object as another subject with whom the poetic subject might hope to strike a harmonious relationship. Apostrophe would figure this reconciliation of subject and object" (143).

If such a reconciliation occurs, it is only by the power of the trope, "the incalculable force of an event" (152) that only happens textually: "something to be accomplished poetically in the act of apostrophizing" (143). Indeed, this power has immediacy—giving the lyric its own immediacy—because the apostrophe happens in writing, in "a now of discourse, of writing" (152). Apostrophe produces a "discursive event" (153) and becomes "the essence of happening" (148).

It is clear that for Culler the "moment of apostrophe" (140), this "event" or "happening" through which self and other relate, allowing subject and object to transcend their alienation, paradoxically still relies on the interiority and agency of the subject. To work as a trope, the apostrophe depends on the subject who apostrophizes an object: only by its relationship with the subject, only when it becomes a "you" through poetic intervention, does the object "transcend a purely material condition" (145). Culler admits so much as he states that this linguistic process "can be read as an act of radical interiorization and solipsism" (146).

In that sense, Lukács's and Culler's views present a striking similarity. In both Lukács's lyrical moment and Culler's apostrophe, subject and object can only be reconciled at the symbolic level. The materiality of the object does not matter, since the object, or outside world, has no intrinsic meaning, and it is the poetic subjectivity alone that produces meaning in the process of symbolization—the "happening."

Carlos Drummond de Andrade's "No meio do caminho" and "Noturno à janela do apartamento" allow for a discussion of the relationship between the lyrical "I" and the world. However differently, both poems call into question Lukács's and Culler's models of reconciliation of subject and object. "No meio do caminho" and "Noturno à janela do apartamento" are better read in a detailed and structural manner. My readings are indebted to the device-oriented, rhythmic analytical work by Roman Jakobson, and especially the first poem is analyzed under Viktor Shklovsky's premises in "Art as Technique": "Art . . . exists to make one feel things, to make the stone stony" (1989, 58).

The human encounter with the world has been thematized by different lyric poets and often represented by the scene of encounter between the eye and the world. In his essay about the Homeric view of man and the world, Bruno Snell reminds us that the act of seeing could be expressed by several verbs, many of which did not remain in the Greek language. It was not necessarily the function of sight—as we now have it—that determined or gave significance to the verb; rather, in several cases, it was the object seen and the sentiment fostered by that act of seeing that carried significance.[1] Impressionist painters revolutionized the history of art—and had an impact on poetry as well—by centering, in the "impression" formed by an object in the eye that sees, a sensation that precedes any kind of thought. In other words, they privileged in their art the retinal perception of the world. Eyes have also participated in the construction of the traditional model of desire in the Western lyric, that of desire as a gesture of aggression: the subject sees the object of desire and seeks to invade and take hold of it.

Like other lyric poets, Carlos Drummond de Andrade, in several instances, represents the duality of subject and world by the encounter between the subject's eyes and his surrounding environment. Also, in his focus on the contrast between light and shadows, his representation of negativity through darkness, Drummond gives to visual perception—and therefore the eyes—a significant role. In "A máquina do mundo," for example, as the journeying poet refuses the light offered by the machine that opened itself to him, he "baixa os olhos." This lowering of the eyes prevents him from seeing further, and it signals his refusal and his withdrawal from the world.[2] Eyes will be at the center of my reading, as they figure prominently in both "No meio do caminho" and "Noturno à janela do apartamento."

Published in 1928 in the *Revista de Antropofagia*, "No meio do caminho" was later included in Drummond's first published volume, *Alguma poesia* (1930). It is his most famous poem, and perhaps the most famous Brazilian poem in the twentieth century: often cited and always taught, the poem received countless commentaries and infinite interpretations, and amassed a strong team of detractors. Several elements caused a stir: the treatment of a banal, unimportant topic, contrasting the traditional and valued "poetic subjects";[3] the use of colloquial language—in particular the use of *tinha* in lieu of *havia*, until then the poetic norm; the limited vocabulary; and the repetitive structure. Drummond himself collected many of the written reactions to this poem in a book titled *Uma pedra no meio do caminho: Biografia de um poema* (1967). Viewed as a "peça de escândalo," in what was, in José Guilherme Merquior's words, "um dos últimos escândalos da idade heróica do movimento" (4), "No meio do caminho" is, according to the same critic, the poem that defines Drummond's early poetics, when "A poesia surge quando o universo se torna insólito, enigmático, embaraçoso—quando a vida já não é mais evidente" (25).

Antonio Candido, writing about Drummond's early work, identifies a distrust in the poet's treatment of the "I" and the world, even as he writes as if registering "o espetáculo material e espiritual do mundo" and eventually defining "o Eu e o mundo como assunto de poesia."[4] Drummond oscillates between his "subjetividade tirânica" and his desire to know the Other and be in the world, claims Candido, while stating that "O eu é uma espécie de pecado poético inevitável, em que precisa incorrer para criar, mas que o horroriza à medida que o atrai."[5] The obstacle will appear as a motif in Drummond's poetry, as he examines human connections, and ties between humans and the world. For Candido, the obstacle irrupts in a context in which both the individual and the social world are "tortos," twisted and perverted, in a reciprocal relation.[6] My reading, which follows, is situated in this context.

"No meio do caminho" is a circular poem, one that turns upon and returns to itself. If the speaker is "on the road," this same road leads nowhere but to an inevitable return. The first stanza is an insistent repetition of the first verse, in which obsession and circularity are iconically expressed in the placement of its two parts: (x) "no meio do caminho" and (y) "tinha uma pedra.[7] Visually, this is how the parts are organized:

x y
y x
y
x y

The second stanza begins with the explicit advent of the speaker, an event that changes the rhythm of both the walk and the reading. In visual terms, his entrance corresponds to the two verses that are added to the other final four verses, with these being inversely proportional to those of the first stanza:

c d
a
c x
y
y x
x y

The two new verses ("Nunca me esquecerei desse acontecimento/na vida de minhas retinas tão fatigadas") represent the cut of the initial and final rhythmic scheme ("the montage cut") and bring to the center of the reading the "I" of the poem, the lyric subject, and no longer the world, the object, here presented as road and stone. The world is static, stagnant, and, as in many other poems, acts as a motif expressing Drummond's nihilism. Reflecting upon himself from his observation of the stone, the speaker then inserts himself right into the center of the poem, surrounded by the stone, which dominates the eight framing verses.

"No meio do caminho" problematizes the Lukácsian model, for in it there is a different process: it is the stone, that is, the outside world, that projects itself in the retinas of the speaker, and it is far from being "senseless." The stone penetrates the retinas of the speaker who sees it. It is this inanimate, strong, impermeable, and feminine (*pedra* is a feminine noun) object that moves toward the subjectivity of the speaker.

The encounter of stone and retinas will provoke the appearance of the speaker in the poem, and this experience will be marked forever in his life, imprinted in his memory. It is this same ability to remember, though, that reveals in the speaker the possibility of *processing* something internally, of not being a mere passive perceiver. It is when the speaker graphically appears that the poem projects itself into the future: we see a poet in the present time talking about a past (*tinha*) that he will never forget in the future. In a certain way, if the poem presents a circular journey in space, which in principle leads nowhere, we can also see, through the verbal tenses, a course in time.

Irruption of new elements, the surprise verses of the second stanza, however, allows for the establishment of a bridge between themselves and the others, that is, between these and other verses. If this connection in the confrontation of the speaker with the world occurs through the gaze (and this can be seen through the emphasis on the tired retinas), in the material elaboration of the poem it occurs through the recurrence of the vowel *i*.

Nunca me esquecereI desse acontecImento
Na vIda de mInhas retInas tão fatIgadas
Nunca me esquecereI que no meIo do camInho
tInha uma pedra

Here, an assonance creates this direct relationship between the "I" and the world, since it permeates this crucial moment in which the "I" of the speaker (revealed in the pronoun *me* and the possessive adjective *minhas*, and in the ending of the verbs) and the outside world meet for good through the eye. Retinas are the internal ocular membranes that contain the nervous cells which receive the luminous stimuli and upon which are projected the images produced by the ocular optical system. The stone is what is reflected upon the poet's retinas; the same way that it is still, massively stagnant in the middle of the road, so it will be registered internally, in the retinas that get tired of seeing it. Once memory is dominated by the projected image of the stone, the "I" itself will in its turn resemble the inertia and monotonous paralysis that this stone (that is seen) represents.

The fact that the "I" of the speaker, in this fundamental encounter with the world, is represented by the "retinas" points to the objectiveness of the subject, for it is presented synecdochically, in/as parts—body parts—and not seen as a whole. But "retinas," specifically, complicates any argument that establishes a simple opposition between a subjectivist and an objectivist reading of this poem, as José Américo Miranda tries to do.[8] For, of the eyeball, the retina is the innermost part, the one continuous, as we have seen, with the optic nerve, and it contains, among its layers, the one that is sensitive to light. Furthermore, being continuous with a nerve makes the retina a vehicle that also conveys impulses of sensation (light?) between the brain and spinal cord and the eye. As those verses starting the second stanza connect the speaker and the stone, the retina is also the bridge connecting the outside to the brain and the nerves of the "I." All this suggests, therefore, a relative "interiority," a deeper connection between "body part" and "being," somewhat complicating this "objectiveness of the self."[9]

This encounter between the lyric "I" and the surrounding world constitutes what Lukács would call the "lyric moment" of the poem, when one integrates with the other through the action of the speaker's gaze. There is a merging of speaker and stone, subject and object; but if the speaker is the agent of the gaze that he imposes upon the world, the image that he sees will affect him profoundly—it will remain within him and accompany him forever—changing, or helping to define, his own perception of his self. His identity is shaped by the stone that he sees in the middle of the road and that physically surrounds him in the structure of the poem. Therefore, against the Lukácsian model, there is in this poem an object, whose physical existence and particularities are relevant, which has meaning and projects this meaning onto the subjectivity that confronts it.

This pattern seems, anyway, to subscribe to the Western lyrical tradition of starting from the duality represented by the pairs subject/object, speaker/world and then reaching the lyrical moment through the merging or cancellation of this opposition. Indeed, it is this fundamental unification that brings meaning to the poem—it is the great "happening" of the poem ("Nunca me esquecerei desse acontecimento") as posited by Culler (149), which in turn makes the poem a happening in itself. Merquior identifies a theory of "poetry-happening," in which subjectivity loses ground to the surrounding reality, as a feature of the poetry in Drummond's *Alguma poesia*. He writes,

> Desse modo se afirma em *Alguma Poesia* uma teoria da poesia-acontecimento. . . .
>
> Ora, a equação poesia-acontecimento desloca o acento da sacrossanta subjetividade para a realidade: tudo se passa como se o "vivido" escapara ao solipsismo, às ilusões do cogito narcisista. Na poética do vivido-acontecimento, o sentido da complexidade do real se torna mais agudo. O lirismo se abre à consideração crítica do mundo, despede-se da falsa inocência da escrita. (26)

However, even as it follows the Western dualistic lyrical tradition, "No meio do caminho" subverts the traditional model of desire, for in this case it is the object (the stone) that comes to the subject (the speaker). The latter does not necessarily desire the former but is invaded by it: the image and, with it, the reality of the stone penetrate his mind and memory through the apprehension by the retinas. The poet does not call for it, but in his confrontation with the world, he is taken by it. This way, we have not an extension of the self into the object (Culler 150) but rather an object that extends and invades the subject, giving it a new meaning. In this model, the idea of desire as a gesture of aggression is maintained, but directed in a different way. The poet marches round and round—a movement that connotes a process and a distance—but the stone in the middle of the road is all he sees. Such an image keeps returning to his eyes, and it dominates not only his field of vision but also his field of memory. It is significant that the "I" (present in three verses right in the middle of the poem) is surrounded by the stone in almost symmetrical verses and, most important, that it only enters the poem after having already been violated by the stone.

The recurrence of the consonant *n* contributes to an atmosphere of desolation and negation—for it recalls "Não," pointing to the nihilism that Drummond would later retake more clearly in "Noturno à janela do apartamento," when he affirms that "A soma da vida é nula."[10] In a way, it also points to a trend not at all exclusive to Drummond's poetry but very much characteristic of it: an initial and strong desire for death, which sometimes leads to an almost "natural" identification between one's object of desire and death.

"Noturno à janela do apartamento" is from Drummond's third book, *Sentimento do mundo* (1940), a book that, it is generally agreed, introduces more acutely than before the conflict between the self and the surrounding world. Presenting more elements than "No meio do caminho," "Noturno à janela" is one of the occasions in which Drummond takes up the motif of the motionless world. Also in this poem, in the tension between "I" and world, the external elements, or objects, are greatly important in the definition of the subject's individuality or, rather, in the thoughts the poet develops about his own subjectivity.

In this poem, however, unlike "No meio do caminho," never is the "I" directly articulated in the linguistic text. It is as if, to keep the reader's focus on the internal perspective of the speaker, the latter refuses to say "I," which would betray a self-consciousness and would not be psychologically realistic. Furthermore, here it is possible to perceive the subject having a more active role in his interaction with the outer world—an interaction that is established in the title by the word *window*, traditional bridge between inside and outside. In "Noturno à janela" the world still acts upon the subject, but the subject is more than a passive recipient, for he also projects himself onto the image he sees. One could say that the mutual relationship between subject and object is made clearer, and it is this reciprocity that creates the "happening" of the poem.

In "Noturno à janela do apartamento," only in the title do the words *janela* and *apartmento* appear, yet they have an internal function: they reveal the place where the lyric subject thinks—the point of departure of the gaze that projects he who looks onto the image of the object looked at. The relevance of the contact made through the eye and, from this, the identification between subject and object are initially made explicit in the second stanza, in which stasis dominates both the poet and the world.

Nenhum pensamento de infância
Nem saudade nem vão propósito.
Somente a contemplação
De um mundo enorme e parado

The poet, standing at the window, integrates himself (or is integrated?) into the darkness of the night and contemplates a huge world, motionless like him but fitting within his gaze, comprehended within the frame of the window. In the beginning of the poem, the "escuridão absoluta" (third stanza) already imposes itself: it is announced in the title (with "noturno") and appears in the form of "cubo de treva" and "noite." Silence and darkness are here associated with death.

This stanza also founds the structure, built upon oppositions, that is dominant in the poem: the poet, melancholic, at night, at the window, sees in suicide the only possibility of resolving this melancholy and overcoming the conflict between the inner space (inside the apartment) and the outer space (beyond the window, in the world).

Silencioso cubo de treva:
Um salto, e seria a morte.

However, he rejects this option right away—a fact made clear by the use of the adversative *mas*—creating instead a situation in which he integrates himself into the night and the night, somehow, is integrated into him, as if it were an outside that is inside and is part of himself. Unlike "tantos que escolheram / . . .

a dis- / solução" (as Drummond writes in his poem "A Homenagem," referring to ten writers—including Zweig, Benjamin, and Woolf—who committed suicide), the poet here presents another solution: integration.

> Mas é apenas, sob o vento,
> A integração na noite.

The oppositions continue into the other stanzas: there is no disquiet "somente" contemplation in the second stanza. The negatives *nenhum*, *nem*, *nem* are morphologically contrasted with *somente*, which brings an affirmative in the second stanza. However, the images presented in the two sets of two verses constituting the second stanza are less of an opposition than a parallel: there is no thought or movement in the poet, as the world is also still. Such a parallel stillness can also be seen in the palindromic reappearance of NEM in soMENte, as if they complemented and mirrored each other, like the objects to which they refer. This second stanza, though, as a whole, will be in opposition to the following stanza, which, to this generalized stasis, will contrast a powerful life, in movement, circulating.

The third and central stanza presents the peremptory assertion of life's nullity, as well as an admission of life's power. There is a contrast between vIda and nUla, but, as if an announcement of the final synthesis, we can see life penetrating, or circulating, isomorphically in the stanza, fighting in the escurIDão (/vIDa) absoLUta (/nULa), dripping like lÍquIdo (/vIda), until it annuls the opposition vIda/nUla in the word cIrcUla. So, as the poet realizes that "A soma da vida é nula," he immediately repeats the adversative *mas* to admit—as I have pointed out—that life still has power and circulates, construing thus an antinomy with the death presented in the first stanza.

The same life that had just been declared "nula" now is said to have "tal poder." Darkness, which in an earlier moment was associated with death, is gradually impregnated by life. The stagnant world loses some strength facing the might of life, which circulates everywhere: in the world as well as in the poet, for this image brings to mind both the bloodstream inside his veins and the circulating movement of the light in the lighthouse, foreshadowing thus the end of the poem. This is another instance in Drummond's poetry that serves as a refutation of Lukács's concept of a "senseless world" onto which the subjectivity of the poet is projected, conferring meaning to it.

Then comes the fourth stanza with its Mallarmaic enumerational triads: [11] it begins with "Suicídio, riqueza, ciência . . ." and ends with "noite, mar ou distância." The first three elements are connected to human beings, whereas the last three relate to the surrounding natural world, and the two sets establish an oppositional frame comprehending the two internal verses. This opposition occurs in both sound and visual terms with the symmetrical graphic inversion of ALma/cALa and interrOGa/lOGo.

A ALma severa se interrOGa
E lOGo se cALa

At this point the subject is actually doing something: he is thinking, he is interrogating, even if at the end he falls silent again. Unlike "No meio do caminho," in which the subject is overwhelmed by the power of the stone and basically acted upon by it, in "Noturno à janela" it is possible to perceive a subject that, in all his hesitations and ambiguities, manages to be more active in his relationship to the world. He presents his options, "suicídio, riqueza, ciência"; however, following the pattern of opposition found in the poem, he does not answer the question he poses to himself.

Nevertheless, there is the possibility of choice—in the first stanza he exercises this choice and decides not to jump out the window. In the verses " . . . E não sabe/ se é noite, mar ou distância," the subject of the first clause is the "alma severa," which stands for the poet. The presence of such a subject indicates that even if the poet *does not know*, there is a cognitive subject, or one with cognitive capabilities, present in the poem. It could be argued that this parallels the fact that although the speaker does not explicitly say "I," he can still be perceived by the reader and by himself as existing in his full cognitive and perceptual interiority. As for the subject of the second clause, this is totally open and unclear. But some options are presented there as well—"noite, mar ou distância"—even if the poet refrains from choosing an answer from these alternatives.

In his analysis of this poem, Murilo Marcondes de Moura argues that its oppositions are elaborated in a "sistema de relativizações": basically, what is affirmed is denied—"o poema não apresenta um percurso nítido," "e não existe nenhum eixo linear que se posa tomar como guia."[12] Moura claims that both systems of opposition and relativization build a permanent back-and-forth movement that prevents any significant advancement. The things presented annul themselves mutually ("A soma da vida é nula"?) in a great phonic and visual play:

> A atmosfera silenciosa do poema é perpassada pela enorme incidência da fricativa /s/, espécie de representação sonora do vento ou de um monólogo sussurrado, sistematicamente presente em palavras importantes do poema: "silencioso," "suicídio," "ciência." . . . [A]s relativizações ocorrem no detalhe sonoro. Assim, a "mor*te*" retorna naquilo que a está evitando—in*teg*ração na noite." Na segunda estrofe, o som reiterado da ausência de perspectiva temporal""*nen*hum pensamento," "*nem*," "*nem*"—reaparece na atividade presente do eu lírico—"so*men*te," "con*tem*plação." Na terceira, a oposição entre o /i/ de "vida" e o /u/ de "nula" é neutralizada na palavra "circula." Mesmo a estrofe seguinte, de paralisia diante das alternativas excludentes, está balizada pelo som sui*c*ídio, *c*iência, *s*evera, *s*e, *s*e, *s*abe, *s*e . . ." (1997, 95)

This mutual neutralization is the sole, if only a precarious, movement contrasted to the immobility of the lighthouse, observed by the equally "fixed" (i.e., immobilized) poet.

The last stanza, composed of a single verse, "Triste farol da Ilha Rasa," breaks the strophic and phonic scheme and reveals the final end reached by the poet's gaze. Contemplating a nocturnal and static world from his apartment, the poet, who is also motionless, catches sight of a lighthouse on an island. The poet is motionless but has life circulating in him, his blood flows in continuous movement and he chooses not to die. The lighthouse is also motionless, but the light rotates rhythmically to illuminate the sea and the quay to the ships. However paradoxical, both are motionless but "circulating," that is, they combine the circulation that represents life with a steady, still placement in the world.

Through the act of gazing at the lighthouse from the apartment window, the poet achieves an integration of the apartment and the island—two dichotomous poles that grow in importance in Drummond's work, especially after the poet moves from Minas Gerais to Rio de Janeiro.[13] This integration is like a synthesis of all the oppositions and alternatives presented along the poem. It is important to emphasize that the light shed by the lighthouse, more than "enlightening," solidifies the idea of night's darkness (it is this darkness that guarantees its existence and gives it a raison d'être), into which the poet is integrated as well. Furthermore, it is worth observing that this final monostich inscribes itself on the page, and graphically represents the other side of the bridge that links the subject's look to the object he looks at. Physically it could be perceived as the ray of light that alone crosses the page at the end of the poem, linking the eyes of the poet on one side to the eye of the lighthouse on the other. In this process, a mutual reflection is forged by the two poles, by means of the projection of characteristics onto each other. In a way, both become subjects and objects, exercising a certain agency upon each other. The lighthouse is sad because the poet is sad; it is the poet's gaze that construes this image. But the lighthouse, with its eye of light, also contaminates the eyes that are fixed upon it, and has, similar and symmetrical to it, at the other side of the window, a poet who also resists, motionless and silent, darkness. With tired retinas, he goes on.

"No meio do caminho" and "Noturno à janela do apartamento" are two poems that, thematizing the conflicted relationship between the lyrical self and the world, call into question both Georg Lukács's model of a senseless world that acquires meaning through a projection of the subject upon the object and Jonathan Culler's model, which also is based on the premise of a gap between subject and object, where the "happening" of the poem relies on the subject conferring meaning to the object. Different in the way they portray the relationship between subject and object, both poems by Drummond, nevertheless, present an external world that participates in the definition of the speaker's subjectivity, in the establishment of his individuality. "No meio do caminho" has an external world that more clearly acts upon the subject and affects him in his interiority. In "Noturno à janela do apartamento," subject and object strike a more balanced relationship. Lighthouse and man, connected by an imaginary line created by the reciprocal gaze, share not only agency but also qualities.

NOTES

This piece was first conceptualized in weekly dinner discussions with classmates at the University of California, Berkeley. We wrote a longer collaborative work, based on a common theoretical problem, in which each individual part was engaged in dialogue with the other. My acknowledgments go to Julie Anderson, Sharon, and Zou Lin—the coauthors of "The Dinner Papers."

1. Bruno Snell, *The Discovery of the Mind* (Cambridge: Harvard University Press, 1953), 1–22.

2. See Alfredo Bosi, "'A máquina do mundo' entre o símbolo e a alegoria" (1988), 80–95; José Guilherme Merquior, "'A máquina do mundo' de Drummond" (1965); Betina Bischof, "A recusa à máquina" (2005), 103–46.

3. The nonpoeticality of the object of retinal impression (the stone) betrays the resistance to "important," "poetic" objects of desire in this type of modernist poetry.

4. Antonio Candido, "Inquietudes na poesia de Drummond" (1970), 95.

5. Ibid., 97.

6. Ibid., 103: "A deformação [do mundo social] . . . se articula com a deformação do indivíduo, condicionando-a e sendo condicionada por ela." Betina Bischof, studying Drummond's later poems, also speaks of the relevance of the obstacle in the poet's work, as it becomes an element of his poetics: "aquilo que sempre foi central para essa poesia: o obstáculo, o entrave, a negatividade." Bischof (2005), 47–48. Following Merquior's analysis, Bischof also sees a correspondence, or even equivalence, between the "I" of the poem and the surrounding world in her reading of "A máquina do mundo." Bischof (2005), 111.

7. Antonio Candido affirms that "No meio do caminho" is built on a "processo de saturação da palavra-chave." Candido (1970), 104. Haroldo de Campos sees in repetition the basis for the poem's "concreção lingüística" and aesthetic information (à la Max Bense). Campos claims that the "emoção-surpresa" of the poem is built upon repetition. Campos, in Sônia Brayner (1978).

8. See José Américo Miranda, "Fotografia e poesia: Leitura da forma em Carlos Drummond de Andrade," *Inimigo Rumor* 4 (1998): 76–86.

9. Chana Kronfeld writes about the transition from impressionist to expressionist poetry in Hebrew modernism. Commenting on "Be-leylot ha-stav" (On Autumn Nights) by David Fogel, Kronfeld explains that "On first reading, the poem seems to be a paradigmatic example of impressionistic observation," and the images seem to be "retinal imprints." "However," she continues, "the text, in typical expressionist fashion, presents the most subjective, imperceptible internal qualities as if they were objective sense data." See Kronfeld (1996), 192.

10. In a third poem, "Noturno," we find two verses that I consider a strange synthesis of the circular journey of "No meio do caminho"—which is also a journey in time—and the darkness that dominates "Noturno à janela do apartamento"—darkness that, while working as an important element in the atmosphere of stagnation, here creates an immobility in time: "Viajando parado. O escuro me leva / sem nunca chegar. Sem pedir a bença."

11. Some examples from Mallarmé that come to mind are "Rien, cette écume, vierge vers" and "Solitude, récif, étoile," from the poem "Salut," and "Nuit, désespoir, pierrerie," from "Au seul souci de voyager."

12. Murilo Marcondes de Moura, "Noturno à janela do apartamento," *Inimigo Rumor* 1 (1997): 89–97 [94].

13. *Apartment* and *eyes* appear significantly in at least another of Drummond's poems: in "Opaco," from *Claro Enigma* (1951), the apartment building, by blocking his view, denies the poet the desired sight of the moon and the stars in the sky.

WORKS CITED

Andrade, Carlos Drummond de. *Uma pedra no meio do caminho: Biografia de um poema.* Rio de Janeiro: Editôra do Autor, 1967.

———. *Poesia e prosa.* Rio de Janeiro: Nova Aguilar, 1983.

Bischof, Betina. *Razão da Recusa.* São Paulo: Nankim Editorial, 2005.

Bosi, Alfredo. *O ser e o tempo da poesia.* São Paulo: Cultrix/EDUSP, 1977.

———. *Céu, Inferno.* São Paulo: Ática, 1988.

Campos, Haroldo de. "Drummond, Mestre de Coisas." In *Carlos Drummond de Andrade: Fortuna Crítica*, edited by Sônia Brayner. Rio de Janeiro: Civilização Brasileira, 1978. 246–52.

Candido, Antonio. *Vários escritos.* São Paulo: Livraria Duas Cidades, 1970.

Culler, Jonathan. *The Pursuit of Signs: Semiotics, Literature, Deconstruction.* Ithaca, NY: Cornell University Press, 1981.

Jakobson, Roman. *Questions de poétique.* Paris: Seuil, 1973.

Kronfeld, Chana. *In the Margins of Modernism: Decentering Literary Dynamics.* Berkeley, CA: University of California Press, 1996.

Lukács, Georg. *The Theory of the Novel*, translated by Anna Bostock. Cambridge: MIT Press, 1968.

Merquior, José Guilherme. *Razão do poema.* Rio de Janeiro: Civilização Brasileira, 1965.

———. *Verso universo em Drummond.* Rio de Janeiro: Livraria J. Olympio Editora, 1976.

Miranda, José Américo. "Fotografia e poesia: Leitura da forma em Carlos Drummond Andrade." *Inimigo Rumor* 4 (1998): 76–86.

Moura, Murilo Marcondes de. "Noturno à janela do apartamento." *Inimigo Rumor* 1 (1997): 89–97.

Shklovsky, Viktor. "Art as Technique." In *Contemporary Literary Criticism*, edited by Robert Con Davis and Ronald Schleifer, 55–66. New York: Longman, 1989.

MONIQUE RODRIGUES BALBUENA is an associate professor of literature in the Clark Honors College at the University of Oregon. She was a Starr Fellow at Harvard University and a Frankel Fellow at the University of Michigan. Her book *Homeless Tongues: Poetry & Languages of the Sephardic Diaspora* is forthcoming from Stanford University Press. Her new book project is provisionally titled *Sephardic Literary Responses to the Holocaust.* Balbuena is the Modern Literature editor of the *Encyclopedia of Jews in the Islamic World* and the editor of the new Jewish World Literature series at the Academic Studies Press. She may be reached at balbuena@uoregon.edu.

NOELI DUTRA ROSSATTO
MARCUS DE MARTINI

The Utopia of the Divine in Luso-Brazilian Culture

Joachim of Fiore and Ariano Suassuna's *A Pedra do Reino*

ABSTRACT: This article investigates the presence of the utopia of the Divine, originated in the Calabrian abbot Joachim of Fiore's (1135–1202) philosophical work, in the novel *A Pedra do Reino* (The Stone of the Kingdom), by the Brazilian novelist Ariano Suassuna. Joachite thought can be located in two of the novel's characteristic elements. The first regards the use of the same symbolic hermeneutic *per concordiam* (by harmony). The second regards the theory of the three states of the world and the utopia of the Divine, as found in the first and last parts of the novel's plot.

KEYWORDS: Joachim of Fiore, symbolic hermeneutic, utopia of the Divine, Ariano Suassuna.

Published in 1971, *O Romance d'A Pedra do Reino e o príncipe do sangue do vai-e-volta*, a novel by the Brazilian writer Ariano Suassuna (b. 1927), is already in its sixth edition. Recently, the most popular Brazilian television network, Rede Globo, produced and aired the miniseries *A Pedra do Reino*, under the direction of Luiz Fernando Carvalho.[1] In this analysis, despite the spin-offs inspired by the work, we will focus only on Suassuna's text.

Besides its colorful narrative, this novel may surprise those familiar with the thought of the Calabrian abbot Joachim of Fiore, who lived in the twelfth century and established a reformed branch of the Cistercian order, the order of San Giovanni in Fiore, whose members would later be known as the Florensians. Although Suassuna's novel makes no real reference to Fiore, some characteristic aspects of his doctrine, as well as his strategy of symbolical interpretation by harmony, arise at several moments. Above all, the novel contains Joachite thinking by similitude, wherein—reflecting Neoplatonic tendencies—certain images, namely the Holy Trinity, are reproduced at different points over the course of the narrative.

The four senses of the Scriptures from medieval hermeneutics, with a strong Joachite connotation, are also employed in Suassuna's plot. Allegory and typology are used as means to articulate the meanings of the distinct types (characters and events), which are taken from different literary or historical contexts, as well as to give meaning to new types and antitypes. And harmony, as found in Fiore's hermeneutical strategy, is one of the resources—perhaps the main resource—employed in the novel as a common interpretative thread, ultimately serving a unitary role for the plot's fabric.

Moreover, the theory of the three states of the world, an identifying feature of Joachimism, permeates the structure of the novel in a very peculiar way, most clearly in the opening and closing scenes, where one of the main characters, a monk, holds the Banner of the Divine. This event, a key episode of the novel, situates the plot at the threshold where the Age of the Son gives way to the Age of the Holy Spirit. In addition, still attached to the scheme that attributes specific roles for each of the Trinitarian figures within the three states of the world, the same monk reveals the mission of the Envoy of the Divine in a Joachite key: he has come to avenge his Father, to prove himself his Son, and to bring the fire of the Spirit.

Joachim of Fiore in Luso-Brazilian Culture

The doctrine of Joachim of Fiore—and/or that of his followers—reached the Americas very early and lives on even today in iconography and literature, as well as in manifold popular manifestations in Brazil, the United States, and Canada.[2] Whether through the discoverer Christopher Columbus, who read the events of his own time in a prophetic-apocalyptic key, or through the formation, behavior, and mentality of a number of Portuguese and Spanish Jesuits and Franciscans who took part in the new spiritual conquest, these ideas arrived in the New World.[3] Historical records indicate that the cult of the Holy Spirit was spread in Brazil by immigrants from the Portuguese Azores islands, from the eighteenth century on, most notably in the states of Bahia, Pernambuco, Rio de Janeiro, Santa Catarina, and Rio Grande do Sul. In the nineteenth century, the Azorean immigrants would introduce the same cult in the United States (Massachusetts, California, and the future state of Hawaii) and in Canada (Ontario).[4]

That is how Renaissance Joachimism, remarkably prophetic and utopian, seems to have extended its tentacles to the fecund soil of South and North America. The same imaginary certainly also spurred the Venetian editions of Fiore's three main works between 1519 and 1527—*Concordia Novi ac Veteris Testamenti* (Harmony of the Old and New Testaments), *Psalterium Decem Chordarum* (Psaltery of Ten

Strings), and *Expositio in Apocalypsim* (Exposition of the Book of Revelation)—and all sorts of other prophetic and apocalyptic texts attributed to him.[5]

In Portuguese lands, one of the clear connections between Joachim of Fiore's works—whether apocryphal or authentic—and Renaissance imaginary can be found in the well-known Festivals of the Empire of the Divine Holy Spirit (Festas do Império do Divino Espírito Santo). The liaison between the empire and the divine dates to the thirteenth-century seizure of the south of Italy by the Crown of Aragon. In 1292, Isabel (1269–1336), the Holy Queen—the sister of Frederico, who was the son of Pedro III of Aragon, the ruler of Sicily from 1296 to 1337—was married to Don Dinis, king of Portugal. In that same year (1292), Queen Isabel established the Confraternity of the Holy Spirit of Alenquer (Confraria do Espírito Santo de Alenquer) in Portugal. And it was from the Village of Alenquer, then under the queen's domain, that Spiritual Franciscanism, the propeller of Joachite ideas, would be spread in Portuguese lands.[6]

Other historical connections fill out the picture of the encounter between the empire and the divine. Queen Isabel had been educated in Barcelona, then capital of the kingdom of Aragon, where the Spiritual Franciscans would flock and consequently the site of the Joachite doctrine of the new age of the Holy Spirit. It was probably then that Queen Isabel met a notorious Joachite, the Catalan philosopher and physician Arnold of Villanova (1238–1316), chancellor of the queen's two brothers, Frederico II of Sicily and Jaime II of Aragon.

That is also the alloy between the Portuguese Empire and the divine Holy Spirit. The struggle of the Spiritual Franciscans and the Confraternities of the Holy Spirit, with their ideals of evangelical poverty and prophetic preaching on the advent of a new age when the clergy would no longer be necessary as intermediaries between God and men, met the interests of the rising European monarchies. Around the same time, Marsiglio of Padua (1285–1343), who supported the Spiritual Franciscans, blamed the papacy for divisions among Christians, meanwhile viewing the monarchy as *defensor pax*. The promise of a universal empire on earth, an empire of peace, solidarity, and charity, would always be part of the Franciscan worldview. And in Portugal, such an approach would revive the ancient Joachite prophecy of the emperor of the last days (*dux novus*), aiding in the formulation of the messianic theory of the Fifth Universal Empire.[7] Symbolic and theoretical references to such themes, common to both Sebastianism and Joachimism, appear in the works of the Jesuit Antônio Vieira (1608–1694), who preached on the return of the deceased king Don João IV and the advent of the Fifth Empire, along with the poetry of Fernando Pessoa (*Mensagem*), much as these references appeared in the *trovas* of the poet and prophet Antônio Gonçalves Annes Bandarra (1500–1556).[8]

Joachimist echoes in Portugal, despite their richness, are beyond the scope of this piece.[9] Instead, our aim is to draw on our previous work to establish criteria capable of indicating and evaluating the possible presence of Joachimism in Suassuna's novel.

In another text, Rossatto sought to prove the presence of the Joachite tradition in the structure and symbolism of the Festivals of the Empire of the Divine, citing these manifestations as a real Joachite celebration of the Third Age of the World.[10] Rossatto also added a new kind of proof based on comparative analysis that included the works of Joachim of Fiore, along with his followers and other sources.[11] In addition, doctrinal elements akin to Joachite thought reappear in literary fiction and historiography covering events in late nineteenth- and early twentieth-century Brazil, among them *Os Sertões* (Rebellion in the Backlands), by Euclides da Cunha, and *La guerra del fin del mundo* (The War of the End of the World), by Mario Vargas Llosa, and the historiography dedicated to the theme of the "Contestado War."[12]

Among the doctrinal elements that reappear in the symbolism of the Festivals of the Divine, three deserve special attention. The first is that the festival's main ceremony, with rare exceptions, traditionally consists of a triple coronation (one imperial and two royal), in which a boy-emperor, alongside a young and an old king, is the main figure. This feature was encouraged by the ideas surrounding the Contestado War, particularly in the character Joachim, the boy-god. According to the sociologist José de Souza Martins, "In Contestado, one had to die in order to be reborn in the divine army of Saint Sebastian; the elders should become young, wisdom and power were with the children."[13]

The second feature is that the celebration of the third state, as the Age of the Spirit, reappears in the fulfillment of the expectation of a time of complete spiritual freedom, during which children rule the world, property is divided among the people, and prisoners are released. One of Fiore's best-known passages in *Concordia* shows these expectations to be a response to the symbolical representation of the three states of the world (f. 112a): the first state belongs to the elders, the second to the young, and the third to the boys ("Primus senum, secundus iuvenum, tertius puerorum").

The third feature, in accord with the Joachimism of the Portuguese Spiritual

Franciscans, is that the ideal of the divine empire predicted that the domination of one emperor over other kings would owe more to prestige than to power, since such an outcome would reflect a real spiritual empire. According to the same *Concordia* (f. 122a), in the third state, rule would be administered amid a scene of complete friendship, freedom, and peace. Relatedly, recent studies show that some migration movements from northeastern Brazil to the Amazon region are guided by popular prophecies grounded in Joachite doctrine: one of these foresees a mythical place, after the crossing of the big river, named Paradise of the Divine.[14]

Furthermore, the festivities of the divine, which, according to Joachim, mark the crisis of the Age of the Son (or Age of the Church) and the celebration of the Age of the Spirit,[15] were not always well accepted in ecclesiastical environments. Nor were the ideas of Fiore himself. One of the festivities' most polemical aspects, which soon became a prime target for Catholic orthodoxy, involves the nonparticipation of the clergy (*ordo clericorum*), given that the third state would belong to the monks (*ordo monachorum*). Such a practice may have been sustained beginning with radical interpretations of the Joachite tradition by the Spiritual Franciscans in the late thirteenth century. Such an interpretation, censured by the Commission of Anagni,[16] staged a confrontation between the clerical and the monastic life. However, Franciscan radicalism happens to be rooted in the words of Joachim of Fiore himself. The abbot writes in the *Concordia* (f. 56d) that, in the first state, attributed to the Father, the order of the married (*ordo coniugatorum*) shone; in the second, attributed to the Son, the order of the clerics (*ordo clericorum*) shines; and in the third, attributed to the Spirit, the order of the monks (*ordo monachorum*) would shine. This certainly explains why, even today, the direction and organization of the Festivals of the Divine typically elude clerical control.[17]

After having briefly analyzed the main elements concerning the reception of Joachimism in Luso-Brazilian culture, we must now answer the question that motivates this article: what aspects suggest Joachite ideas in Ariano Suassuna's novel *A Pedra do Reino*?

Joachimism and Utopia of the Divine in *A Pedra do Reino*

For our purposes, an analysis of the beginning of the first chapter of Suassuna's novel, as well as the last chapters, which lead to the climax, will suffice. However, a few general remarks about the plot are necessary.

O Romance d'A Pedra do Reino e o príncipe do sangue do vai-e-volta, which takes place between 1935 and 1938, begins with a great "cavalcade" or "Moorish parade" (*desfilada moura*), as the narrator calls it, on the eve of 1935 Pentecost—that is, before a festival dedicated to the Holy Spirit.[18] The narration by various characters, however, takes place in 1939, after the events. One protagonist is Don Pedro Dinis Ferreira-Quaderna, a kind of synthetic character: a left-wing monarchist, representing a "brown Sebastianism" (*sebastianismo castanho*), which incorporates the ideological, moral, and racial synthesis of two other important characters—Dr. Samuel Wandernes, a poet, prosecutor, nobleman, monarchist, and knight, and Professor Clemente, a criminal lawyer, schoolmaster, philosopher, and communist. Like the figures on playing cards or the characters in the "Cavalhadas" or the "Folias do Divino," one character functions as the opposite of the other. Samuel is the white knight and, in the festivals, plays the role of the Christian Crusader of the Blue Cord; Clemente, for his part, is black and parades as the Moorish knight of the Red Cord.

The narrator then highlights two singularities of the cavalcade that opens the novel. The first is that this episode, as if the characters moved freely from literary narratives or popular imaginary to the living stage of history, had already been predicted by an "enlightened" and "visionary" Brazilian, the poet Gonçalves Dias (1823–1864).

The second singularity is that the cavalcade is led by three men: the first sits on a horse and holds a banner with three red jaguars; the second, right behind him, walks carrying a wooden cross with sparrow hawks, or *carcarás*; the third, called Friar Simão, sits on a white horse and is identified as a bandit-friar or a knight-monk. He holds a banner on which a sun's rays beam over a red field and, in the center, a ring circles a flying white dove. According to the narrator, this is the banner of the Divine Holy Spirit of the Backlands (Divino Espírito Santo do Sertão).[19]

In the three men at the head of the cavalcade, we already see a certain proximity with medieval symbology and, in particular, with that spread in Joachite circles. The animals in the scene reference the four senses of the Scriptures that normally compose the Figure of the World in its distinct and manifold medieval reproductions and that, in Fiore's works, is reproduced in the Tavola XV from the *Liber Figurarum*.[20] It is worth remembering that the four senses of the Scriptures are literal or historical, moral, allegorical, and anagogical. In the traditional Figure of the World, which results, among other things, from the comparison between the visions narrated in the revelations of John, Daniel and Ezekiel, and from the relation with the theory of the four elements, with its platonic-pitagoric bias, four animals appear: the eagle, indicating the air; the ox, indicating the earth; the angel or man, indicating water; and the lion, indicating fire. The author consciously substitutes the sparrow hawk, or *carcará*, for the eagle and the jaguar for the lion. As one of the characters explains, the author is making use of animals from the Brazilian backlands, not foreign ones. This sort of adaptation is also commonly found in medieval iconography, where sometimes the lion is replaced by the bear, as in Beatus of Liébena's *Commentary on the Apocalypse*, composed in eleventh-century Spain.[21] As one of the main characters, Pedro Diniz Quaderna, states, "[I]n my language, lions or eagles, foreign animals, are never found, but jaguars and sparrow-hawks are."[22] However, he does use the angel and the ox, according to the standard symbolism.

All the same, it is important to notice here the three main characters in this "*cavalhada* of the world," according to the expression used by the narrator, given their direct referencing to Joachite symbology and doctrine.[23] The first man, like the first state of the world, is symbolized by the jaguar, indicating the Father period, lived under the regime of a *terribilis dominus*, in which violence, wars, atrocities, servitude, and fear prevail. The second man, characterized by the symbols of the cross, the sparrow hawks, indicates the second state, the Son period, ruled by Christ and his church, lived partially under the law, grace, and freedom. And, most clearly, the third state is personified by a monk, or friar, completely in accordance with the third Joachite period, as propagated by the Spiritual Franciscan friars beginning in the thirteenth century and in which monks would be the main figures. In this the direct correlation between *friar* and the Franciscan order is central. According to Joachim of Fiore, in his *Liber Introductorius* (in *Expositio*, f. 5v), the first of the three states was under the law; the second was under the Letter of the Gospels; and the third would be in complete freedom of the spirit. Yet, according to the *Concordia* (f. 112a), the first state was lived in the servitude of the slaves, the second in the servitude of the children, and the third would be lived in complete freedom of the spirit; the first in fear, the second in faith, and the third in charity; the first, the servant's, the second, the free man's, the third, the friend's.

Moreover, and more evidently, the third character holds the Banner of the Divine in its traditional red color, in itself a clear allusion to the Joachite celebration of the Third Age of the World, according to Luso-Brazilian tradition. It is important to stress that, in the different *figurae* presented by Joachim of Fiore throughout his texts, which are gathered in the thirteenth-century *Liber Figurarum*, the first state is always represented in green, the second in blue, and the third in red.[24]

But there is other, no less meaningful evidence. As in the strategies of medieval interpretation, Suassuna draws from world or Brazilian history and literature to reveal meanings through allegory and typology—that is, the spiritual sense is taken from the historical or literal sense (in the tradition of Augustine's *translata signa*). One example is the similitude established between Peri, a character from the novel *The Guarani*, by the Brazilian writer José de Alencar (1829–1877), and Perival or Perseval, a character from the twelfth-century chivalric romance *The Story of the Grail*, by Chrétien de Troyes. Accordingly, there is parity between Don Antônio Mariz, a Portuguese nobleman, and a character of the same name from *The Guarani*, a prior from the city of Crato, in the Brazilian state of Ceará.[25] We may even compare Antônio Villar, the name used by Luiz Carlos Prestes (1898–1990), a Brazilian army lieutenant who later became a communist leader and, nicknamed the Knight of Hope, returned to Brazil disguised as a priest, and another Antônio Villar, a notorious landholder in the novel.[26] On this count, we may recall that Jorge Amado (1912–2001) wrote the fictional narrative *The Knight of Hope* (1942), which is a sort of biography of Luiz Carlos Prestes.

We can highlight still other examples in Suassuna's novel that are closely related to medieval allegorical comprehension (*intellectus allegoricus*), including through peculiarities of character and individual virtues or vices. One such contrasting set of values plays out in different female characters, where animal nature ("beast," "female ass in heat") is placed against the divine ("angelical nature," "chaste"). We may view a similar incarnation of this perception of female qualities in the contrast between the blonde, tender, sweet Ceci and the provocative brunette Isabel, both characters from Alencar's *The Guarani*. In Alencar's homonymous novel, animal and divine nature are in conflict within a single character, Lucíola. In Suassuna's novel, it is Heliana, the new feminine type, who constitutes the dialectical synthesis of these two extremes.[27]

In a very similar way, although with the focus specifically turned to biblical text and the history of mankind, Joachim of Fiore would understand the meaning of an Old Testament figure in terms of a similar figure from the New Testament or from ulterior history. For example, in the *Concordia* (f. 60d), a woman is understood through another woman, a child through another child, a war through another war, an empire through another empire. Thus "the woman dressed with the sun," from the Revelations of John in the New Testament, reprises Judith, a figure from the Old Testament; and the Old Testament story of Abraham, an old man when he expects a son (Isaac) from his previously barren wife, Sarah, is compared to that of Zachariah, also an old man, married to Isabel, also barren, who gives birth to John the Baptist (*Concordia*, f. 118b and 23b). To Joachim, in short, Abraham is the same (*id ipsum*) as Zachariah; John the Baptist is the same as Isaac; likewise, Sarah and Isabel are the same.

The Hermeneutics *Per Concordiam*

According to our analysis, the end of Suassuna's novel contains additional evidence of the Joachite influence. Relevant passages, besides textually suggesting the Joachite theory of the three states of the world, signal the author's use of a hermeneutical resource very similar to that used by Joachim of Fiore.

By means of an interpreter-character, the popular poet Lino Pedra-Verde, Suassuna develops a hermeneutical strategy that perfectly fulfills the basic requisite for the "by harmony" (*per concordiam*) method created by Joachim of Fiore. Moreover, this interpreter-character shows the thread of the entire plot in figurative terms, decoding what seems absurd in the eyes of other characters, who are blindly grounded in the literal sense of the events.

To Joachim of Fiore, the allegorical and typological interpretations help apprehend characters' roles through their similarities, with the sole purpose of setting them in a historical plan. Harmony, in a different way, serves to reduce the multiplicity of these signifiers, apprehended through allegory and typology and scattered in space and time, to one meaning. The general rule of harmony is the following: two signifiers (or even three) hold only one meaning ("duo significantia unum significatum ostendentia," *Concordia*, f. 7c, 18b, 23b, 42d). And this conforms strictly to the Joachite Trinitarian theory, summed up in the following formula from the *Psalterium decem chordarum* (f. 225): "tres sunt unum et unum tres" (three are one and one three).

The following examples of the interpretation by harmony are central in the works of Joachim of Fiore. According to harmony (*Concordia*, f. 7 d–8a and 18a), we have seen that Abraham means the same (*id ipsum significat*) as Zachariah, Isaac the same as John the Baptist. In addition, Jacob is the same as Jesus the man; Jerusalem is the same as the Roman Church; Samaria is Constantinople;

the Babylonian Empire is the Roman Empire; and the twelve Old Testament patriarchs are the twelve apostles of the New Testament, among other cases.

By the end of the novel (Pamphlet LXXXII: "The Quest for the Sangral"), the poet Lino Pedra-Verde gives an interpretation that, besides revealing the symbolical reading of the novel's events, is very similar to the "by harmony" hermeneutic proposed by Joachim of Fiore. He reveals the meaning hidden in the entire plot through likenesses found in different characters, contexts, and episodes. This rereading, which harmonizes characters and episodes, allows for all events up to this point to be ascribed new meanings along with the literal or historical ones. However, what could be here perfectly identified as the spiritual sense (*intellectio spiritualis*) in the tradition of medieval *lectio historiae* seems to gain a purely aesthetic function.

According to the likenesses model, Lino Pedra-Verde relates episodes taken from very different sources. Certain similar events—such as "to cut one's head off" and "to have the throat cut"—and different characters (signifiers) end up having a single meaning. King Herod, who ordered the beheading of John the Baptist in the New Testament, ends up being the same as Colonel Moreira César, who led the nineteenth-century War of Canudos, with the mission of taking Antônio Conselheiro's head to the capital of the republic, who is the same as Caesar, the Roman Emperor who authorized the beheading of Saint Sebastian.[28] A similar system pertains to a number of historical comparisons. Other signifiers, such as a horse's color, serve as unifiers, as the following excerpt shows: "And that's when you really see the reason for their fear: Saint Sebastian is the same as Saint George, on the back of a white horse killing the dragon; and he's the same as Don Sebastião, who releases the brown Jaguar and sets it on the white Pig that comes from abroad! And he's the same as Don Pedro Sebastião, Don Sinésio Sebastião's father, the one who had the throat cut! They're all only one person."[29]

In the same way, regarding the question asked by Lino Pedra-Verde about one of the novel's main characters—"Who did give the white horse to Sinésio Sebastião?"—two conflicting answers are offered. Some say the animal was given by Jorge de Albuquerque Coelho, who lives in a sugar mill in the backlands of Pajeú. Thence comes the following explanation: "Of course, Doctor, it was Saint George who appeared in the Pajeú, who gave the white horse to the King! It's the Saint Sebastian who appeared in the Stone of the Kingdom, who is the same Don Sebastião who appeared in that Troy, in that Africa that was the Empire of Canudos."[30]

The reduction here centers on the names Sebastião (Sebastian) and Jorge (George): Sinésio Sebastião, a character in the novel, Saint George and Saint Sebastian, two popular saints, Don Sebastião, the king of Portugal who disappeared in the Battle of Alcácer Quibir (Morocco, 1578), and Jorge de Albuquerque, another character in the novel.

Moreover, the reduction owes to parallelism created through similar contexts of war and persecution.

The second answer to Lino Pedra-Verde's question assumes the white horse has been given by Don Antônio, prior of Crato. The text illustrates as follows: "One of the kings of the Stone of the Kingdom was called João Antônio, and he ended up going to Crato, in the Ceará backlands. And if this Don Antônio who gave the horse to Don Sebastião was Prior of Crato, who knows if it wasn't him who was in the Battle of Africa—our King of the Stone of the Kingdom, João Antônio, Prior of Crato! And that's what it is, because they're all the same person—Don Sebastião Barbosa, Saint Sebastian, Don Antônio Galarraz, Don João Quaderna, Don Antônio Conselheiro, Don Pedro I—all these holy and warlike people . . ."[31]

The text elaborates: "Every time that he [the man in the white horse] appears, he adopts a different name, according to the necessities and perils of the War of the Kingdom! He's Don Sebastião, he's Don Pedro, he's Don Pedro Sebastião, he's Don Antônio Conselheiro, he's Don Pedro Antônio, he's Antônio Mariz, he's Peri, he's Peri-val, he's Persival, he's Antônio Gala-Foice, he's Antônio Galarraz, he's Sinésio Sebastião, son of Don Pedro Sebastião, and it goes on and on."[32] Yet: "That's why I was saying: it's all only one thing, it's the Monarchy of Don Sebastião of Brazil, of the Backlands, of Portugal, of Africa and of the Empire of the Stone of the Kingdom!"[33]

The kingdom is the same, the war is the same—just as the spirit acts upon human history with one purpose and the characters, although different, repeat the same names: Sebastião, João, Pedro, Antônio. The traces of likeness serve to identify, to denounce, and to reveal what is hidden.

According to our initial hypothesis, the strategy of interpretation by harmony, as elaborated by Joachim of Fiore, is manifested as one procedure—and perhaps the main procedure—used in Suassuna's novel to regulate and reduce the understanding of the manifold and diverse types of signifiers throughout the narrative. Yet if this argument seems somehow not yet convincing, we can still explore another route, which focuses on characteristic traces of Joachite thought present in the festivities of the Empire of the Divine Holy Spirit. The next section follows this route.

The Three States and the Utopia of the Divine

Near the end of the book (Pamphlet LXXXIV: "The Envoy of the Divine"), we find two paradigmatic passages in which the task or mission of one of the novel's main characters, who, as the equally narrator himself states, is the "reason and honor" of the entire cavalcade, in our opinion, is given in Joachite terms.[34] In these two passages, the three Joachite states (*status*) are highlighted, with each commanded by a figure of the Trinity—the Father, the Son, and the Holy Spirit—and each figure plays the same role attributed to him by Joachite doctrine.

According to Joachim, the Father, throughout the Old Testament, presents himself as a terrible and cruel God characterized by the use of strength, war, and slavery; the Son, throughout the New Testament and the history of the church, presents himself as a more tender God, who preaches love, redemption, forgiveness, and grace; and the Holy Spirit, crowning this sequence, would come to establish a new and more perfect kingdom of grace and total spiritual freedom. In a famous passage of the *Concordia* (f. 112a), Joachim of Fiore says that the first state is characterized by submission to the law, by slavery, exasperation, fear, by the elders, by the winter and nettles; the second is characterized by grace, filial servitude, faith, the young, by the spring and roses; the third, in turn, is characterized by amplified grace, complete freedom, charity, the children, the summer and lilies.

Similar characteristics, attributed by Joachim to each of the states of the world, can be found in this passage of *A Pedra do Reino*:

> This banner that I bring here with me, and that I've never abandoned since the day when I took my mission with our prince, is the banner of Pentecost, is the banner of the Crown, of the Sun and of the fires of the Divine Holy Spirit. It celebrates the day in which the fire of Pentecost burned forever our brute flesh and our pagan blood, ironing us with the divine seal, a sign to remind us to the end of times that our passage through this brown land of the Backlands, through this immense *segre* that is the World, is a mere banishment, a mere exile. The Father came to raise, to punish and to expel. The Son came

> to redeem and forgive. The Holy Spirit comes to reign and illuminate! The Kingdom of the Father is over, and we are approaching the end of the Kingdom of the Son. The Kingdom of the Holy Spirit is about to begin, and woe to those who are found with a stain of sin on their blood.[35]

A second passage illuminates, behind the questions, the same characterization of the three states of the world. Moreover, it is a friar who answers these questions, explaining that the Third Kingdom is that of the divine Holy Spirit:

> "Mr. Friar, forgive me for asking, but we need to know it in order to be ready!"—cried near us the one-eyed singer Lino Pedra-Verde. "Are you Friar Simão, the holy friar of the Serra do Rodeador and of the Stone of the Kingdom? Is the young man who's come with you our Prince, the Saint-of-the-white-horse, who comes to command the Backlands men to our War of the Kingdom? Is it true that he's come to avenge his Father, to prove being his Son and at the same time to bring the fire of the Holy Spirit to put an end to the injustices and the sufferings of the world?[36]

In this passage, a new element appears that indicates a possible answer to the riddle proposed on the novel's first pages, after the sudden reappearance of the "dangerous" and "mysterious" young-man-on-the-white-horse: that Sinésio Sebastião would be the very envoy of the divine. And he would come to repair all the evil and injustices committed, to reveal himself as Son, and to begin the much-awaited Kingdom of the Spirit. In Suassuna's novel, a strategically constructed ambivalence allows one to trace the equivalence between the history of the main character's personal life (that of Sinésio Sebastião) and the history of the world. The polysemy of the terms and the multiplicity of readings within the narrative, two characteristics that pervade the entire plot, eventually acquire a unity of sense and meaning. Curiously, it is here possible to obtain the same result through two different reading strategies: the literal and the figurative.

Literally, we have the following conclusion of the story: Sinésio Sebastião, who had disappeared on the tragic day when his father—the King of the Fifth Empire of the Stone of the Kingdom, Don Pedro Sebastião Garcia-Barreto—had his throat mysteriously cut, reappears to avenge the Father (his own father), to prove he is his Son (who had disappeared without a trace), and then to succeed him and command the new kingdom, which is the spiritual kingdom.

The figurative (or aesthetic) interpretation is the following: the young-man-on-the-white-horse, like so many other men who had disappeared during the War of the Kingdom (Saint George, Saint Sebastian, Don Sebastião, Antônio Conselheiro, Antônio Villar), returns triumphantly to avenge the Father (likewise the action of the avenging God of the Old Testament, in the first state of the Joachite world), to prove himself the son (when he reappears, disenchants, or resuscitates), putting an end to the second period (referring to the second Joachite state) and eventually beginning a new Kingdom of the Spirit.

Moreover, the two passages just cited are meaningful in situating the cavalcade—marking both the initial and final episodes of the novel—in a chronological moment analogous to the one in which Joachim of Fiore, back in the late twelfth century, thought he was writing his works: the moment when the Kingdom of the Father had reached its end, the Kingdom of the Son was about to be completed, and the Kingdom of the Spirit, after its blossoming, was beginning to produce its first ripe fruits.

NOTES

1. Suassuna, A. *Romance d'A Pedra do Reino e o príncipe do sangue do vai-e-volta*, 6th ed. (Rio de Janeiro: José Olympio Editores, 1995). On Rede Globo's miniseries, see http://pt.wikipedia.org/wiki/A_Pedra_do _Reino.

2. See N. D. Rossatto, *Joaquim de Fiore: Trindade e nova era* (Porto Alegre: EdiPUCRS, 2004), p. 360; *O simbolismo das festas do divino* (Santa Maria: NedMidia/UFSM, 2003); and "L'Abate Gioacchino e la 'Festa del Divino': Una celebrazione luso-brasiliana dell'Età dello Spirito," *Florencia* (Bulletino del Centro Internazionale di Studi Gioachimiti) XVIII–XIX, nos. 18/19 (2005): 173–185. See also O. F. Bauchwitz, "Joaquín de Fiore en el contexto utópico de Oswald de Andrade: La antropofagia como consumación de la historia," *Florencia* (Bulletino del Centro Internazionale di Studi Gioachimiti) XVIII–XIX, nos. 18/19 (2005): 51–57; J. A. Mourão and J. E. Franco, "A influência de Joaquim de Flora em Portugal e na Europa," in *Escritos de Natália Correia sobre a utopia da Idade Feminina do Espírito Santo* (Lisbon: Roma, 2005).

3. Christopher Colombus, *Libro de las profecías* (Madrid: Alianza editorial, 1992); *Book of Prophecie* (Barcelona: Libros Clie, 1991). On the Franciscans, see L. Duch, *La memòria dels sants: El projecte dels franciscans a Mèxic* (Barcelona: Publicacions de l'Abadia de Montserrat, 1992); J. Phelan, *The Millennial Kingdom of the Franciscans in the New World* (Berkeley: University of California Press, 1970). On the Jesuits: A. Milhou, "El mesianismo joaquinita del círculo jesuíta de Francisco de Borja (1548–1550)," in *Storia e figure dell'Apocalisse fra '500 e '600: Atti Del 4 Congresso Internazionale di studi gioachimiti* (San Giovanni in Fiore, September 14–17, 1994) (Rome: Viella, 1996), 203–24. About the same theme in general:

T. Todorov, *La conquista de América: La cuestión del otro* (México: Siglo XXI editores, 1987); M. Bataillon, *Evangelisme et millénaurisme au nouveau monde* (Paris: PUF, 1959); C. Bernand and S. Gruzinski, *Histoire du Nouveau Monde: De la découverte à la conquête, une expérience européenne—1492–1550* (Paris: Librairie Arthème Fayard, 1991).

4. See http://pt.wikipedia.org/wiki/Irmandades_do_Divino_Espirito_Santo and http://pt.wikipedia.org/wiki/Joaquim_de_Fiore.

5. Joachim of Fiore, *Concordia Novi ac Veteris Testamento* (Frankfurt: Minerva, 1964), 135ff; E. Randolph Daniel, ed., *Liber de Concordia Novi ac Veteris Testamenti [Transactions of the American Philosophical Society* 73, no. 8] (Philadelphia: American Philosophical Society, 1983), 336; Joachim of Fiore, *Expositio in Apocalypsim (Liber introductorius in Apocalypsis)* (Frankfurt: Minerva, 1964), 224ff.; Joachim of Fiore, *Psalterium decem chordarum* (Frankfurt: Minerva, 1964), f. 259v–260r. On prophecy in the thought of Joachim of Fiore, see M. Reeves, *The Influence of Prophecy in the Later Middle Ages: A Study in Joachimism* (Notre Dame, IN: University of Notre Dame, 1993), 592; B. McGinn, *The Calabrian Abbot: Joachim of Fiore in the History of Western Thought* (New York: Collier Macmillan Publishers, 1985).

6. J. Lupi, "Origens das festas do Divino Espírito Santo," in *O simbolismo das festas do divino*, ed. N. D. Rossatto (Santa Maria: NedMidia/Ufsm, 2003), 13–32.

7. J. Lupi, "A doutrina de Joaquim de Fiore sobre o Espírito Santo," in *O simbolismo das festas do divino*, ed. N. D. Rossatto (Santa Maria: NedMidia/Ufsm, 2003), 47–58.

8. Vieira's prophetic conception is sketched in three main works: *Esperanças de Portugal* (Hopes of Portugal; 1659), the unfinished *História do Futuro* (1659), and *Clavis Prophetarum* (1663). For more on the theme, see J. Beseelaar, *Antônio Vieira: Profecia e polêmica* (Rio de Janeiro: Eduerj, 2002), 508.

9. About the possible presence of Joachite ideas in the millenarian thought of Antônio Vieira, see M. de Martini and N. D. Rossatto, "Milenarismo na obra profética de Padre Antônio Vieira," *Revista Letras*, no. 43 (2011).

10. See Rossatto, "L'abate Gioacchino e la 'festa del divino'"; VVAA, "O Império do Divino Espírito Santo," p. 2, accessed October 1, 2010, from http://www.emportugal.com/in/icone/CimperioES.htm; VVAA, "O Culto do Império do Espírito Santo," p. 2, accessed October 1, 2010, from http://portugalsecreto.no.sapo.pt/dsebastiao.htm; C. R. Brandão, *O Divino, o Santo e a Senhora* (Rio de Janeiro: Funarte, 1978).

11. See N. D. Rossatto, "Simbólica e mística do Divino: Remanescentes joaquimitas na cultura luso-brasileira," *Sociais e Humanas* 19, no. 1 (2006): 9–20.

12. About Canudos, see *Os sertões*, by Euclides da Cunha, and *La guerra del fin del mundo*, by Mario Vargas Llosa. Also: R. B. Graham, *A Brazilian Mystic, Being the Life and Miracles of Antonio Conselheiro* (New York: Books for Libraries Press, 1971). About the Contestado, see E. Serpa, *A guerra do contestado (1912–1916)* (Florianópolis: Editora da UFSC, 1991); M. Auras, *A guerra do contestado: A organização da irmandade cabocla* (Florianópolis: Editora da UFSC, 2001).

13. J. S. Martins, *Fronteira: A degradação do Outro nos confins do humano*, 2nd ed. (São Paulo: Contexto, 2009), 165.

14. Ibid., p. 177, n. 70.

15. H. Mottu, *La manifestation de l'esprit selon Joachim de Flora: Herméneutique et théologie de l'histoire d'après le "Traité sur les Quatre Évangiles"* (Neuchâtel-Paris: Delachaux et Niestlé, 1977), 11.

16. L. Verardi, *Gioacchino da Fiore: Il Protocollo di Anagni* (Cosenza: Edizioni Orizzonti Meridionali), 1992.

17. See J. Cletison, "Festas do Divino Espírito Santo," NEA (Núcleo de Estudos Açorianos), accessed November 12, 2003, from http://www.nea.ufsc.br/artigos_joi.php.

18. Suassuna, *Romance d'A Pedra do Reino*, p. 35.

19. Ibid., p. 49.

20. The Figure of the World, in Joachim of Fiore, corresponds to Tavola XV of the *Liber Figurarum*, included in M. Bitonti and S. Oliverio, *Gioacchino: Abate di Fiore* (San Giovanni in Fiore: Amministrazione Comunale di San Giovanni in Fiore/Centro Internazionale di Studi Gioachimiti, 1998), 67.

21. Beato de Liébena, *Comentarios al Apocalipsis: Miniaturas del Beato de Liébena*, códice de Fernando I y Doña Sancha (Barcelona: Moleiro Editor, 1995).

22. Suassuna, *Romance d'A Pedra do Reino*, 562.

23. Ibid., 561.

24. M. Reeves and B. Hirsch-Reich, *The Figurae of Joachim of Fiore* (Oxford: Clarendon Press, 1972), 336; Bitonti and Oliverio, *Gioacchino*; L. Tondelli, M. Reeves, and B. Hirsch-Reich, eds., *Liber Figurarum: Il Libro delle Figure dell'Abate Gioacchino da Fiore* (Turin, 1953); C. D. West and S. Zimdars-Swarts, *Joachim of Fiore: A Study in Spiritual Perception and History* (Bloomington: Indiana University Press, 1983).

25. Suassuna, *Romance d'A Pedra do Reino*, 709.

26. Ibid., 269, 434.

27. Ibid., 503, 512–13.

28. Ibid., p. 698–702.

29. In the original text: "E é aí que se vê, mesmo, o motivo do medo deles: é que São Sebastião é o mesmo São Jorge, montado no cavalo branco matando o Dragão; e é o mesmo Dom Sebastião, que liberta a Onça castanha e manda ela matar o Porco branco que vem do estrangeiro! E é o mesmo Dom Pedro Sebastião, pai de Dom Sinésio Sebastião e que foi degolado! Todos esses são uma pessoa só" (Suassuna, *Romance d'A Pedra do Reino*, 598–99).

30. In the original text: "É claro, Doutor, que quem deu o cavalo branco ao Rei era o mesmo São Jorge, que apareceu no Pajeú! É o São Sebastião que apareceu na Pedra do Reino, que é o mesmo Dom Sebastião que apareceu naquela Tróia, naquela África que foi o Império de Canudos" (Suassuna, *Romance d'A Pedra do Reino*, 704).

31. In the original text: "Um dos Reis da Pedra do Reino chamava-se João Antônio, e terminou indo para o Crato, no Sertão do Ceará. E se esse tal Dom Antônio, que deu o cavalo a Dom Sebastião, era Prior do Crato, vá ver que era ele quem estava na Batalha da África—o nosso Rei da Pedra do Reinoera ele quem estava na batalha da no Sert, João Antônio, Prior do Crato! E é isso mesmo, porque todos são uma pessoa só—Dom Sebastião Barbosa, São Sebastião, Dom Antônio Galarraz, Dom João Quaderna, Dom Antônio Conselheiro, Dom Pedro I—todo esse pessoal santo e guerreiro . . ." (Suassuna, *Romance d'A Pedra do Reino*, 704).

32. In the original text: "Cada vez que ele (o homem do cavalo-branco) aparece, adota um nome diferente, de acordo com as necessidades e perigos da Guerra do Reino! É Dom Sebastião, é Dom Pedro, é Dom Pedro Sebastião, é Dom Antônio Conselheiro, é Dom Pedro Antônio, é Antônio Mariz, é Peri, é Peri-val, é Persival, é Antônio Gala-Foice, é Antônio Galarraz, é Sinésio Sebastião, filho de Dom Pedro Sebastião, e por aí vai" (Suassuna, *Romance d'A Pedra do Reino*, 704–5).

33. In the original text: "É por isso que eu estava dizendo: tudo isso é uma coisa só, é a Monarquia de Dom Sebastião, do Brasil, do Sertão, de Portugal, da África e do Império da Pedra do Reino!" (Suassuna, *Romance d'A Pedra do Reino*, 703).

34. Suassuna, *Romance d'A Pedra do Reino*, 45.

35. Ibid., 725.

36. In the original text: "Seu Frade, me desculpe eu perguntar, mas a gente precisa saber, pra se garantir!"—gritou, perto de nós, o Cantador caolho, Lino Pedra-Verde—"O Senhor é Frei Simão, o frade santo da Serra do Rodeador e da Pedra do Reino? O Rapaz que veio com o senhor é o nosso Prinspe, o Santo-do-cavalo-branco, que vem comandar os Sertanejos para a nossa Guerra do Reino? É verdade que ele veio para vingar o Pai, provar que é o Filho e, ao mesmo tempo, trazer o fogo do Espírito Santo para acabar com as injustiças e os sofrimentos do mundo" (Suassuna, *Romance d'A Pedra do Reino*, 726).

WORKS CITED

Auras, M. *A guerra do contestado: A organização da irmandade cabocla*. Florianópolis: Editora da UFSC, 2001.

Bataillon, M. *Evangelisme et millénaurisme au nouveau monde*. Paris: PUF, 1959.

Bauchwitz, O. F. "Joaquín de Fiore en el contexto utópico de Oswald de Andrade: La antropofagia como consumación de la historia." *Florencia* (Bulletino del Centro Internazionale di Studi Gioachimiti) XVIII–XIX, nos. 18/19 (2005): 51–57.

Beato de Liébena. *Comentarios al Apocalipsis: Miniaturas del Beato de Liébena*, códice de Fernando I. Sancha y Doña Sancha. Barcelona: Moleiro Editor, 1995.

Bernand, C., and S. Gruzinski. *Histoire du Nouveau Monde: De la découverte à la conquête, une expérience européenne—1492–1550*. Paris: Librairie Arthème Fayard, 1991.

Beseelaar, J. *Antônio Vieira: Profecia e polêmica*. Rio de Janeiro: Eduerj, 2002. 508.

Bitonti, M., and S. Oliverio. *Gioacchino: Abate di Fiore*. San Giovanni in Fiore: Amministrazione Comunale di San Giovanni in Fiore/Centro Internazionale di Studi Gioachimiti, 1998. 79.

Brandão, C. R. *O Divino, o Santo e a Senhora*. Rio de Janeiro: Funarte, 1978.

Cletison, J. "Festas do Divino Espírito Santo." In NEA (Núcleo de Estudos Açorianos). Accessed December 11, 2003, from http://www.nea.ufsc.br/artigos_joi.php.

Colombus, Christopher. *Book of Prophecie*. Original manuscript with English translation. Barcelona: Libros Clie, 1991.

———. *Libro de las profecías*. Madrid: Alianza editorial, 1992.

Cunha, E. *Os sertões: A campanha de Canudos*. São Paulo: Círculo do Livro, 1983.

Duch, L. *La memòria dels sants: El projecte dels franciscans a Mèxic*. Barcelona: Publicacions de l'Abadia de Montserrat, 1992.

Graham, R. B. *A Brazilian Mystic, Being the Life and Miracles of Antonio Conselheiro*. New York: Books for Libraries Press, 1971.

Joachim of Fiore. *Concordia Novi ac Veteris Testamento*, 135ff. Frankfurt: Minerva, 1964 [Venice, 1519].

———. *Expositio in Apocalypsim (Liber introductorius in Apocalypsis)*, 224ff. Frankfurt: Minerva, 1964.

———. *Psalterium decem chordarum*, f. 259v–260r. Frankfurt: Minerva, 1964 [Venice, 1527].

Llosa, M. V. *La guerra del fin del mundo*. Barcelona: Editorial Seix Barral, 1997.

Martins, J. S. *Fronteira: A degradação do Outro nos confins do humano*. 2nd ed. São Paulo: Contexto, 2009.

Mottu, H. *La manifestation de l'esprit selon Joachim de Flora: Hermenéutique et théologie de l'histoire d'apres le "Traité sur les Quatre Évangiles."* Neuchâtel-Paris: Delachaux et Niestlé, 1977.

Mourão, J. A., and J. E. Franco. *A influência de Joaquim de Flora em Portugal e na Europa: Escritos de Natália Correia sobre a utopia da Idade Feminina do Espírito Santo*. Lisbon: Roma, 2005.

Phelan, J. *The Millennial Kingdom of the Franciscans in the New World*. Berkeley: University of California Press, 1970.

Reeves, M., and B. Hirsch-Reich. *The Figurae of Joachim of Fiore*. Oxford: Clarendon Press, 1972. 336.

Rossatto, N. D., ed. *O simbolismo das festas do divino*. Santa Maria: NedMidia/UFSM, 2003.

———. *Joaquim de Fiore: Trindade e nova era*. Porto Alegre: EdiPUCRS, 2004. 360.

———. "L'Abate Gioacchino e la 'festa del divino': Una celebrazione luso-brasiliana dell'Età dello Spirito." *Florencia* (Bulletino del Centro Internazionale di Studi Gioachimiti) XVIII–XIX, nos. 18/19 (2005): 173–85.

———. "Simbólica e mística do Divino: Remanescentes joaquimitas na cultura luso-brasileira." *Sociais e Humanas* 19, no. 1 (2006): 9–20.

Serpa, E. *A guerra do contestado (1912–1916)*. Florianópolis: Editora da UFSC, 1991.

Suassuna, A. *Romance d'A Pedra do Reino e o príncipe do sangue do vai-e-volta*. 6th ed. Rio de Janeiro: José Olympio, 1995.

Todorov, T. *La conquista de América: La cuestión del otro*. México: Siglo XXI editores, 1987.

Tondelli, L., M. Reeves, and B. Hirsch-Reich, eds. *Liber Figurarum: Il Libro delle Figure dell'Abate Gioacchino da Fiore*. 2 vols. Turin, 1953.

Verardi, L. *Gioacchino da Fiore: Il Protocollo di Anagni*. Cosenza: Edizioni Orizzonti Meridionali, 1992.

Vieira, Antônio. *Defesa ante o tribunal do Santo Ofício*. 2 vols. (introduction and notes by Hernâni Cidade), Vol. I: XL–342, Vol. II: XXII–396. Bahia: Universidade da Bahia, 1957.

———. *Clavis prophetarum [Chave dos profetas]*. Book III. Edição crítica Arnaldo do Espírito Santo, 789. Lisbon: Biblioteca Nacional, 2000.

VVAA. "O Culto do Império do Espírito Santo," p. 2. Accessed October 1, 2004, from http://portugalsecreto.no.sapo.pt/dsebastiao.htm.

———. "O Império do Divino Espírito Santo," p. 2. Accessed October 1, 2004, from http://www.emportugal.com/in/icone/CimperioES.htm.

———. *Storia e figure dell'Apocalisse fra '500 e '600: Atti del 4 Congresso Internazionale di studi gioachimiti*. San Giovanni in Fiore, September 14–17, 1994. Rome: Viella, 1996.

West, C. D., and S. Zimdars-Swarts. *Joachim of Fiore: A Study in Spiritual Perception and History*. Bloomington: Indiana University Press, 1983.

NOELI DUTRA ROSSATTO is a professor in the Graduate Program on Philosophy (MA and PhD), Department of Philosophy, Federal University of Santa Maria, Rio Grande do Sul, Brazil. She may be reached at rossatto.dutra@gmail.com.

MARCUS DE MARTINI is a professor in the Undergraduate Course on Languages (Portuguese Language and Literature), Department of Vernacular Language and Literature, Federal University of Santa Maria, Rio Grande do Sul, Brazil. He may be reached at marcusdemartini@gmail.com.

PAULO MOREIRA

National Identity in Brazil and Mexico in the Twentieth Century

ABSTRACT: In the first decades of the twentieth century, Latin American intellectuals and artists articulated new forms of national identity that responded to the peculiar modernization of the region. These new articulations offered possibilities but also imposed limits that reached a crisis in 1968 in Brazil and in Mexico, when the process of modernization in the two countries reached a point of inflection. In the contrasting images of the Homem Cordial as the symbol of the Brazilian insistence on smooth transitions and of the revolution as the awakening of Mexico from the long slumber of the formalistic liberalism of the nineteenth century lie two faces of this national identity, and this paper examines their potentials and their weaknesses.

KEYWORDS: Latin America, national identity, modernization, Alfonso Reyes, Ribeiro Couto, Sérgio Buarque de Holanda.

Most people recognize the great importance, at least on a symbolic level, of the generation of writers, painters, architects, and philosophers who participated in the Ateneo de la Juventud,[1] a society for study and lectures founded after a famous series of conferences in 1907 and 1908 and active until 1914, after which its most prominent members continued to participate in the cultural, artistic, and political life of Mexico.[2] Their questioning of positivist tenets in the Escuela Nacional Preparatoria against the *científicos* (a group instituted as a government faction) and their defense of lay education against the interference of conservative Catholics gained symbolic momentum as actions preceding the revolution that ended Porfirio Díaz's rule, which lasted from 1884 to 1911. The Ateneo de la Juventud thus came to symbolize (to a great extent by its members' own account) the new country that emerged after the Mexican Revolution, despite the actual ambiguity of the group's relationship with both the old regime and the new.[3]

The two most influential members of the Ateneo, José Vasconcelos and Alfonso Reyes, also left their marks on the urban fabric of Rio de Janeiro—and it is reasonable to say that Brazil left a mark on their intellectual life as well. Vasconcelos visited Brazil in 1922 for the international celebration marking Brazil's centenary as an independent state. As the head of the largest international delegation, Vasconcelos brought with him as a gift an imposing statue of the Aztec emperor Cuauhtémoc, a version of which stands in Mexico City's Paseo de la Reforma to this day. Ironically, this statue was a relic from Porfirio Díaz's longtime relationship with the U.S. firm Tiffany & Co. and an example of *indigenista* art with which the anti-American and ardent Hispanist Vasconcelos was not at all comfortable.[4] The second Cuauhtémoc still cuts an imposing figure in a square of the same name in Aterro do Flamengo, surrounded by a cactus garden donated by none other than Alfonso Reyes, when he was ambassador in Rio de Janeiro in the 1930s. In "Las estatuas y el pueblo," Alfonso Reyes approvingly cites the Brazilian poet Murilo Mendes to note that *Cariocas* (inhabitants of Rio de Janeiro) had by then adopted Cuauhtémoc as theirs, turning the emperor into "un inmenso amuleto, una 'mascota,' una imagen propiciatoria de la Buena suerte" (an enormous amulet, a "mascot," a proptitous image of good luck) (64).

Besides attending the centennial festivities in the capital, Vasconcelos visited Salvador, São Paulo, Campinas, Santos, Belo Horizonte, Ouro Preto, Barbacena, and Juiz de Fora, and insisted on traveling from Rio de Janeiro to Uruguay by train instead of ship to "ver el país, no las olas, que son iguales en su multiplicidad inumerable" (see the country, not the waves, with their identical, innumerable multiplicity) (*La raza cósmica*, 1925, 131–32). Vasconcelos's enthusiasm for Brazil's achievements and cultural vibrancy resembles at times what Brazilians humorously call *ufanismo*,[5] but the account of this trip to Brazil is of no small importance in the works of the great *oaxaqueño*. The trip (and its continuation down to Uruguay and Argentina) makes up the bulk of Vasconcelos's still influential *La raza cósmica—Misión de la raza iberoamericana*, whose prologue prophesies the coming of the "fifth race" (a mingling of the existing white, black, yellow, and red) destined to found a "New Rome" in Latin America.[6]

Almost a decade after Vasconcelos's trip, Alfonso Reyes arrived in Rio de Janeiro as the Mexican ambassador. In contrast with Vasconcelos's brief stay, Reyes lived in Rio until 1936 and participated intensely in the city's intellectual life. The diplomat cultivated the friendship of all kinds of intellectuals, from

Alceu Amoroso Lima and Gilberto Freyre to Carlos Lacerda and Graça Aranha; Cândido Portinari illustrated for him, and Cecília Meireles counted on Reyes for material on the Mexican education policies during the debates around the Escola Nova. Reyes was so integrated into the city's cultural life that he was the only foreigner at the celebration of Manuel Bandeira's fiftieth birthday,[7] and one of Bandeira's best-known poems, "Rondó dos Cavalinhos,"[8] describes Reyes's farewell banquet at the Jockey Club: "Alfonso Reyes partindo, / E tanta gente ficando . . ." (Alfonso Reyes leaving, / And so many people staying . . .) (*Libertinagem*, 85).

While in Rio de Janeiro, Reyes was also quite prolific: he wrote thirteen of the fourteen issues of his *Monterrey—Correo literario*, a one-man literary journal;[9] some of his best short stories; an exquisite book of poems entirely dedicated to Rio de Janeiro (*Romances de Río de Enero*); a collection of short essays, *Historia natural das Laranjeiras* (illustrated by Reyes himself); and several pieces for newspapers and magazines, such as Augusto Frederico Schmidt's *Literatura*, that were later incorporated into his *Obras completas*.[10] And whereas Vasconcelos handed the Cuauhtémoc statue to the city, Reyes left his mark through a more modest, personal gift to his beloved Jardim Botânico: a small statue of Xochipilli, the Aztec spring god of flowers.[11]

Beyond the many interesting anecdotes and their monumental traces in Rio de Janeiro,[12] there remains the challenge of reading with contemporary eyes what these Mexican intellectuals wrote about or in Brazil and what these texts reveal about the particular gaze of a foreigner who is also a fellow Latin American. I want to focus on two short essays written by Reyes: "México en una nuez," a well-known text written in Brazil in 1930, and "Brasil en una castaña," a less known piece published twelve years later. The titles point to an obvious relationship between the two essays, which first appeared together in Reyes's *Obras completas* in 1959. But "México en una nuez" and "Brasil en una castaña" also share something less obvious. These two essays were conceived as bridges between different nationalities within Latin America: Reyes read "México en una nuez" in the Teatro Rivadavia in Buenos Aires during a festival for the Amigos de la República Española in 1937,[13] and "Brasil en una castaña" was first published in *El Nacional*, the Mexican government's quasiofficial newspaper, in 1942.[14]

"México en una nuez" and "Brasil en una castaña" are part of what Reyes elsewhere called the creation of a "Gramática comparada entre las naciones" ("Palabras sobre la nación argentina," 28), a project with two articulated aims:

"hemos comenzado apenas a compararnos unos con otros y . . . de semejante comparación ha de nacer un conocimiento más exacto del proprio ser nacional" (we have just started to compare ourselves, one with the other, and . . . from a similar comparison will be born a more precise knowledge of our own national being) (28). To propose that people get to know each other in order to better know themselves was Reyes's way of defending cultural cosmopolitanism as a form of nationalism. Comparative texts with the national character in view, "México en una nuez" and "Brasil en una castaña" are thus also an interesting part of a greater corpus of texts written by Latin American intellectuals mainly in the first half of the twentieth century, with their defining trait a consistent exploration of the nation as a theme.

In *El ensayo mexicano moderno*, José Luis Martínez defines modern Mexican essayists by their focus on "su historia, su cultura, sus problemas económicos y sociales, sus creaciones literarias y artísticas, su pasado y su presente" (their history, their culture, their economic and social problems, their literary and artistic creations, their past and their present) (Martínez 2001, 17), which is a common trait of Brazilian essayists in the period as well. These texts are intellectual exercises in national reinvention through self-examination that helped forge renewed identities for these Latin American countries as they grew into more modern, industrialized nations. This redefinition of national identity generally tries to distance itself from the ethnocentric pessimism of the previous generation, for whom "todo lo que valía la pena venía de fuera y a todo lo autóctono, fuera nativo o criollo, se le tenía por atrasado" (all that was worthwhile came from abroad and all the autochthonous, be it native or *criollo*, was supposed to be backward) (Brading 9), but it otherwise varies greatly in terms of style, approach, and ideology.

Several writers, many somehow connected to the *modernistas* of 1922, published essays on Brazil in the first half of the twentieth century. Among these are some who, as with their Mexican counterparts, are still influential because, even though their approaches or ideas might have been partially contested or at least contextualized, much of the current national imaginary and identity are still indebted to their books. Gilberto Freyre's *Casa-Grande e Senzala* (1933), Sérgio Buarque de Holanda's *Raízes do Brasil* (1936), and Caio Prado Jr.'s *Formação do Brasil Contemporâneo* (1942) are, in this sense, classics but also hallmarks of national historiography with solid foundations in scholarly research. In México the same could be said about books such as Reyes's *Visión de Anáhuac* (1920), Vasconcelos's preface to *La raza cósmica* (1925), Samuel Ramos's *El perfil del hombre y de la cultura en México* (1934), and Octavio Paz's *El laberinto de la soledad* (1949).

Alfonso Reyes's exquisite style always couples verbal ingenuity with uncompromising clarity of expression. A relaxed, conversational tone infuses Reyes's erudition and formal inventiveness with unpretentious readability. This constant effort toward clarity has been described as Reyes's ideal of social commitment: a writer's unfailing disposition for dialogue with the reader as a foundation for literary democracy, a sort of "antiautoritarismo en la forma" (Monsiváis 49). Another important aspect of the modern humanist Reyes's epistemology is that, while drawing from different fields of knowledge (history, geography, philosophy, anthropology, and so on), his approach is, in his own words, ultimately literary: "Cada uno mira el mundo desde su ventana. La mía es la literatura" (Each of us has our own window onto the world. Mine is literature) (IX, 29). Accordingly, Reyes's arguments almost invariably center on images at once didactic and aesthetic,[15] from which the main ideas spring by parallel analogy as the images are at once interpreted and evoked. As Reyes himself explains:

> La síntesis histórica es el mayor desafío a la técnica literaria. La palabra única sustituye al párrafo digresivo; el matiz de certidumbre . . . establece la probidad científica; el hallazgo artístico comunica por la intuición lo que el entendimiento solo abarcaría con largos rodeos. (Historical synthesis is the greatest challenge to literary technique. One word alone substitutes for a digressive paragraph; the tinges of certitude . . . establish scientific probity; the artistic solution communicates by intuition what knowledge could only encompass through long circumlocutions.) (*México*, 184)[16]

Since Reyes was a self-proclaimed classicist dedicated to a modern reinterpretation of classical culture, these images are often derived from the Greeks or Romans.[17] This reliance on evocative/illuminating images is especially prominent in short pieces such as "México en una nuez" and "Brasil en una castaña," which, as their names indicate, try to encapsulate in a few pages the essential features of national character.

Another of Reyes's important traits as an essayist is his determination not to take sides in the major ideological debates of his time. This has been interpreted as a sign of Reyes's omission or simply a general lack of interest in politics. In a recent article, "Un hombre de letras," Mario Vargas Llosa writes with evident impatience about Reyes, given his status as a public intellectual who seemed always to be in tune with the powers that be in Mexico, a man very much unlike Vargas Llosa himself, known for his combative style and vocal defense of his liberal beliefs. It should be said that in this alignment with the government, the founder of El Colegio de México is far from being an exception in Mexico or in Latin America. Furthermore, Reyes did get engaged, albeit perhaps against his will, in an argument with nationalists such as Héctor Pérez Martínez, who questioned Reyes's "evidente desvinculación de México" in the 1930s. Nevertheless, like others involved in this polemic, Reyes does not question nationalism as an ideology but prefers instead to claim that his cosmopolitanism is the best way to serve México as a nation—an argument that resurfaces, as we have seen, in his justification of inter-American studies.[18]

The fact is that Alfonso Reyes was a classic liberal whose emphasis was never placed on the explicitly political. Reyes has been described as the last *modernista*,[19] and his beliefs include an idealist notion of true knowledge, which, free from flattering insincerity or rigid dogma as well as from strict subjection to political ends, could dismantle all stereotypes and demagogical, melodramatic mystification. In practice this idealist view of knowledge as inherently neutral led Reyes to a sort of intellectual equanimity, attempting what sometimes became a strained synthesis between two opposing lines of thought—for example, between cosmopolitanism and nationalism or between political engagement and the supremacy of the aesthetic.

The opening of "México en una nuez" exemplifies Reyes's reliance on the illuminating image: the encounter of American peoples and the Spaniards that marks the birth of Mexico is described as "el choque del jarro contra el caldero. El jarro podía ser muy fino y muy hermoso, pero era el más quebradizo" (the clash of the jug against the cauldron. The jug could be very fine and very beautiful, but it was also more brittle) (42). Ever the classicist and the diplomat, Reyes evokes the *Iliad* to interpret the Conquest simultaneously as a tragedy (for the indigenous population) and an epic (for Spain and the church). The American peoples, endowed with an astonishing artistic sensibility, are doomed to defeat by their military frailty; the Spaniards, with an endless capacity for intrigue and deceit, are able to accomplish the extraordinary end of conquering populations and territories several times larger than theirs. This tragic/epic simultaneity enables Reyes to refrain from openly embracing either of the two opposing views of the conquest. Reyes tries to side neither with the Hispanistas, who defended the Spanish colonial heritage as central to modern Mexico, nor with the Nativistas, who defended the centrality of indigenous cultures in the establishment of a free, independent culture. Reyes repeats in "México en una nuez" a key maneuver from his most famous essay, *Visión de Anáhuac*, when he evokes the shared experience of living in the high planes of Anáhuac, "base bruta de la historia" (crude basis of history), as that which unites indigenous and Spaniard descendants in present-day Mexico, affirming that "no soy de los que sueñan en perpetuaciones absurdas de la tradición indígena, y ni siquiera fío demasiado en perpetuaciones de la española" (I am not one of those who dream of absurd perpetuations of indigenous traditions and do not expect too much of the perpetuation of the Spanish ones) (*Visión de Anáhuac*, 101). Instead, Reyes subtly defends the need to establish meaningful contemporary interpretations of national history that transcend such stark oppositions in an effort to build a national identity that does not deny either of its major strains.

Another evocative image, this time a humorous one, opens "Brasil en una castaña": Reyes accounts for the magnitude of the country's natural landscape as the result of the work of a "demiurgo o agente mediador encargado de gobernar la obra," a young artist who "usaba demasiado materiales y tenía la fuerza de la inexperiencia" (187). The effect centered on the image derived from the classics (this time from Hesiod) is again dramatic, but neither tragic nor epic. The underlying assumption in this case is the centrality of nature for the construction of an idealistic view of Brazil. This assumption becomes clearer as Reyes claims that when such creative exuberance was applied to the inhabitants of this country of superlatives, it originated "el diplomático nato, y el mejor negociador que ha conocido la historia humana" (188), enabling Brazilians to "desahacer, sin cortarlo, el Nudo Gordiano." Without explicitly quoting *La raza cósmica*, Reyes implies that Brazilians are indeed some kind of "cosmic race," albeit less grandiose and certainly less bellicose than Vasconcelos's messianic "new Romans."

A similar contrast between Mexico and Brazil appears when Reyes writes about the indigenous populations in the two countries. Whereas the pre-Columbian Aztecs are fierce oppressors of the other proud peoples of the central valley, the Brazilian Indians live in a perfect symbiosis with the luxuriant environment, inspiring Rousseau's "buenos salvajes," their poetry translated by Montaigne and then Goethe.[20] Reyes implies that in Brazil the colonization shifts the land and its inhabitants from the realm of geography to that of history: the Portuguese disrupt this symbiosis between Indians and their environment and, by accelerating changes in the ecology, turn Brazil into subject matter for historians.

Contrasts between geography and history appear in both "México en una nuez" and "Brasil en una castaña" and center explicitly on the idea that "la historia es mucho más veloz que la geografía" (51) and, implicitly, on the traditional view that culture is inherently Western and that the American peoples belong to the realm of the natural. But even after the arrival of the Portuguese and independence, history in Brazil still moves with the "robustez y lentitud de las erosiones geológicas" (188), in a stately *natural* rhythm that contrasts sharply with the "vaivenes coléricos y algo improvisados con que se suceden las etapas en las demás naciones americanas" (188). For Reyes, the explanation for this comparatively much greater instability in Spanish Latin America is that the liberal republics implanted after independence were *artificial*, that is, not natural regimes, which demanded political maturity from nations yet in their first infancy. For Reyes the gigantic dimensions of Brazil, its primary characteristic as established dramatically in the opening of "Brasil en una castaña," *naturally* demand slow, smooth historical transitions from its people. For Reyes the establishment of a monarchy after independence exemplifies one of the smooth transitions that supposedly have given Portuguese America time for political maturity before the arrival of the republic.

Again a vivid image clarifies Reyes's interpretation of Brazilian historical changes: "la historia es la piedra que cae en el lago dormido" (189). The contrast with Reyes's Mexico is even clearer. In Mexico the cauldron and the fragile jar collide; in Brazil the stone plunges into the sleeping lake: two striking images describe two types of encounters of Europeans and American peoples in the New World. The first is an encounter between man-made artifacts, whereas the second involves natural elements. Both evoke the collision between something hard and something soft and inexorable outcomes, but the indigenous element in Mexico resists and therefore breaks whereas its Brazilian counterpart accepts and thus incorporates the arriving Europeans. In Brazil "esta intrusión [of the stone into the water, of the Portuguese into the continent] no es necesariamente violenta" (189): the water ultimately engulfs the stone and the scenery reacquires a stately calmness.

As Reyes moves into the colonial period, geography and history seem to continue to guide the parallels between Mexico and Brazil: the history of Brazil is understood primarily as the history of man's struggle against a bountiful but indomitable nature, whereas in Mexico colonization takes place between "cruel realities" ("la repartición de la tierra") and "bloody euphemisms" ("la encomienda de almas") (44). Whereas Brazilian history is a succession of economic cycles related to the exploitation of natural resources (the Pau-Brasil tree, sugarcane, gold, coffee, rubber, cotton), Mexican history is politics as a great tragedy of blood, from the conflicts among the crown, the colonizers, the church, and indigenous people during colonial times to the bloody wars fought by Caudillos, Liberals, and Conservatives to the long slumber of the Porfiriato peace until the painful reawakening of the revolution. Commenting on the vicissitudes of Mexican history, Reyes solemnly declares that "a la majestad de la Historia no siempre conviene el que los grandes conflictos encuentren soluciones fáciles" (History's majesty does not always accommodate easy solutions for great conflicts) (45) and that this history of violent conflict gives Mexico its identity: "la cara del nuevo pueblo se va dibujando a cuchilladas" (the face of the new people is carved by knife strokes) (49).

An eloquent defense of the Mexican Revolution closes "México en una nuez"—an oratorical piece directed at an Argentinian public suspicious of the radical changes and the instability of the first years of the revolution. The revolution has put an end to years of self-denial in which Mexico's Hispanic and indigenous heritages and cultures were a source of embarrassment to the fantasy of a peaceful francophone, liberal republic under Porfirio Díaz's iron fist. The revolution is thus a moment of precious self-discovery, a chance to realize the country's true potential and recover the treasures of the past, Spanish and indigenous alike. Reyes's last words in "México en una nuez" are a proud and reassuring declaration in defense of the revolution, in a context in which the so-called excesses of the revolution, especially in terms of land reform and laicization, were seen with great suspicion by other governments in Latin America:

> Algunos nos han compadecido con cierta conmiseración. Ha llegado la hora de compadecerlos a nuestro turno. ¡Ay de los que no ha osado descubrirse a sí mismos, porque aún ignoran los dolores de este alumbramiento! Pero sepan—dice la Escritura—que sólo se han de salvar los que están dispuestos a arriesgarlo todo." (Some have pitied us with certain commiseration. The time has come for us to pity them. Woe to those who have yet to dare to dis-

> cover themselves, for they still ignore the pains of this enlightenment! But know this—the Scripture says—that only those willing to risk it all will save themselves.) (56)

Oratorical eloquence also closes "Brazil en una castaña," but in this case Reyes produces an enthusiastic panegyric to a nation of dazzling beauty and never-ending generosity and happiness:

> Y de todo ello resulta una hermosa y grande nación que nunca perdió la sonrisa ni la generosidad en medio del sufrimiento, ejemplar a un tiempo en el coraje y en la prudencia, orgullo de la raza humana, promesa de felicidad en los días aciagos que vivimos, fantástico espectáculo de humanidad y naturaleza, cuya contemplación obliga a repetir con Aquiles Tacio: "¡Ojos míos, estamos vencidos!" (And of all that results a beautiful and great nation that has never lost its smile nor its generosity amid suffering, exemplary at once of courage and prudence, pride of the human race, promise of happiness in the sour days in which we live, fantastic spectacle of humanity and nature, whose contemplation obliges one to repeat after Aquiles Tacio: "We are beaten, my eyes!") (195)

Achilles Tatius is known as the author of the Greek "novel" *Leucippe and Clitophon* of AD 2 In this passage Clitophon expresses his wonder at the sight of Alexandria, a remarkable spectacle of Hellenistic civilization in both human and natural terms.[21]

In sum, there are two European nuts in American soil: the walnut (Mexico) is dry, wrinkled, hard, and bitter; the sweet chestnut (Brazil) is moist, smooth, soft, and mild. In between the two essays, in a poem written in 1932 called "El ruido y el eco," a third nut—or, actually, a pair—appears in Reyes's imagination, the coconut:

> Si aquí el coco de Alagoas
> labrado en encaje, allá
> la nuez de San Juan de Ulúa,
> calada con el puñal.

In one small stanza Reyes makes masterly use of a succinct and many-layered symbol, takes advantage of the multiple meanings of *labrar* ("to carve" but also "to embroider") and *calar* ("to pierce" but also "to hemstitch"). Here we have a direct contrast between Brazil and México around two different forms of craft with material from the same source, the coconut. From Brazil comes the delicate embroidery made with coconut fiber from the northeastern state of Alagoas—traditionally the domestic work of women. From Mexico come the elaborate carvings on the coconut shell to make cups or coin banks—work that demands great physical strength due to the hardness of the shell and that was associated with the inmates in the notoriously brutal "Mexican Alcatraz" of San Juan de Ulúa, a fort with a long, painful history, built by the Spaniards in 1528 in Veracruz.[22] For Reyes Brazil and Mexico are exemplars of the Latin American capacity to articulate aesthetically European and non-European cultures, but Brazil would always be the country of the "en encaje," the gentle face of a tropical, lush Latin America, contrasted with Mexico, the country "con el puñal," the somber face of a troubled, bloody history.

One could explain Reyes's enthusiasm for Brazil by looking into his biography. When he arrived in Rio de Janeiro, Reyes had already been living abroad for seventeen years. In 1913 his father, Bernardo Reyes—one of the most prominent generals of the Porfiriato—was gunned down in front of the Palacio Nacional as he took part in a failed attempt to overthrow the revolutionary government. Soon afterward another general of the Porfiriato, Victoriano Huerta, succeeded in a counterrevolutionary coup d'état. But after Reyes refused an invitation to be secretary for the new president, the son of the eminent Gen. Bernardo Reyes was advised not to stay in the country. Alfonso Reyes thus left Mexico, later entering diplomatic service, to escape the country's turmoil. But those were not to be tranquil years: Reyes left Paris during World War I, experienced financial hardship in Spain, and then encountered a belligerent mind-set in Argentina's intellectual circles and more political instability with Hipólito Yrigoyen's second term as president.

Reyes arrived in Brazil a mere six months before the 1930 revolution, but the Mexican ambassador was subsequently deeply impressed by Getúlio Vargas's capacity for building broad coalitions out of left- and right-wing *tenentes*, the military, dissenting oligarchs, conservative Catholics, unions placed under the wing of the state bureaucracy, and so on. Vargas's deft maneuvers from left to right, seducing former enemies and ostracizing old allies with a great sense of timing, were followed closely by the ambassador and contrasted sharply in his mind with years of violent instability of a revolution that, in Reyes's words, "llevaba diez años de buscarse a sí propia" (55).

However, beyond Reyes's personal traumas and his personal admiration for Vargas and the apparently affable Brazilian intellectuals and politicians, we should not underestimate how much "Brasil en una castaña" reflects views that had wider acceptance in the day's Brazilian intellectual circles. Unlike José Vasconcelos, who, after a brief visit, fantasized about the Brazil of Epitácio Pessoa as a benevolent dynamo on its way to challenge Anglo-Saxon supremacy in the continent, Reyes cultivated relationships with important Brazilian intellectuals, was an avid reader and a thorough researcher, and had great curiosity toward all things Brazilian. A very eloquent demonstration of Reyes's deep knowledge of Brazilian affairs can be found in the six-hundred-plus pages of the second volume of *Misión Diplomática*, a recent compilation of diplomatic briefs from 1930 to 1936.

In fact, Reyes's *Monterrey—Correo Literario* contains the first public appearance of a much-discussed term in Brazil to this day. The *Homem Cordial* makes this first public appearance in a letter from the modernist Rui Ribeiro Couto entitled "El Hombre Cordial, producto americano" and published in the eighth issue of Reyes's journal. At the center of Ribeiro Couto's argument is the idealization of a gentle colonization, an adventure in a welcoming, fertile land, an adventure "alimentada pelas redes nupciais de índias bravias e pela sensualidade dócil de negras fáceis": He continues: "O egoísmo europeu, batido de perseguições religiosas e de catástrofes econômicas, tocado pela intolerância e pela fome, atravessou os mares e fundou ali, no leito das mulheres primitivas e em toda a vastidão generosa daquela terra, a Família dos Homens Cordiais, esses que se distinguem do resto da humanidade por duas características: o espírito hospitaleiro e a tendência à credulidade. Numa palavra, o Homem Cordial" (3).

Ribeiro Couto claims the Homem Cordial as the symbolic middle ground in the battles between what he calls the primitivism of *indianismo* and the classicism of *hispanismo* in Latin America, a synthesis not unlike the one favored by Reyes himself in "México en una nuez." But it is important to note that at the core of what is framed as a magnanimous synthesis between Western and non-Western aspects of Latin American culture lies an idealization of colonization as a romance (a presence in the imagination of the Brazilian elites beginning with José de Alencar's historical novels) with markedly patriarchal roles assigned to the colonizer (male) and his indigenous/slave counterpart (female), who functions as a double for the fertile native land.[23] Furthermore, it should be noted that whereas Reyes assigns this narrative specifically to Brazil, for Ribeiro Couto this "Civilização Cordial" was the greatest contribution of *Latin*

America to the civilized world, then enveloped in the turmoil that would result in World War II. After all, this contribution is presented as the result of a process that turned European selfishness and the skepticism of the colonizer into Latin American hospitality and the credulity of the Homem Cordial.

In accordance with Ribeiro Couto but restricted to Brazil, Alfonso Reyes uses the term *cordialidade* in "Brasil en una castaña" as a benign trace of Brazilian identity. But the concept has had myriad uses in Brazil and is known nowadays primarily as a prominent term in Sérgio Buarque de Holanda's 1936 classic *Raízes do Brasil*. Buarque de Holanda, who dutifully points to Ribeiro Couto's letter to Reyes as the source for the "expressão feliz" (146), offers a much less enthusiastic view of the colonization and, consequently, of the Homem Cordial. The negative aspects of the concept might not be so evident at first, and the author strives to be more explicit in a second edition of *Raízes do Brasil* in 1947: "Se eliminam aqui, deliberadamente, os juízos éticos e as intenções apologéticas."[24] A third edition in 1956 includes an essay by one of the main intellectual forces behind the dictatorship of the Estado Novo, the right-wing modernist Cassiano Ricardo,[25] a source of some of the "juízos éticos e as intenções apologéticas" to which Buarque de Holanda had referred in the book's second edition. Cassiano Ricardo exemplifies the discomfort of the right with Buarque de Holanda's use of *cordialidade* with such dissonant views of the history and character of Brazil: "Sérgio alterou, descaracterizou nosso homem cordial" (293).[26] Buarque de Holanda's curt reply restates his different view of the matter and proclaims: "Creio que nunca chegaríamos a entendimento perfeito acerca de alguns aspectos tratados e vejo que será inútil esmiuçar todos os pontos de sua réplica" (311).

Here we have progressives and conservatives battling for a definition of *cordialidade*.[27] The status of *Raízes do Brasil* as an indisputable classic and the removal of Cassiano Ricardo's letter in its following editions seem to attest to the victory of the progressives in this matter.[28] Nevertheless, conservatives continued to use the term *cordialidade* to define Brazil's national character—drawing on the original appearance of the term in *Monterrey* in order to complain against "foreign" ideologies that "offended" Brazilians' inherent desire for a peaceful social order. Ricardo's letter became an extended essay, "O homem cordial" (Ricardo 1959, 7–46), and the centerpiece of a 1959 collection of articles. Telling evidence of Alfonso Reyes's influence in seeing Brazil as a benign culture of conciliation was that Reyes—together with Sérgio Buarque de Holanda—gets cited in an influential newspaper column in support of a concurring argument about the country's "social and political traditions" at an important historical crossroads for the country:

> Essa cordialidade, que Alfonso Reyes atribuía a toda a América Latina e Sérgio Buarque de Holanda considera tipicamente brasileira, não me parece sinal de mau caráter. Ou de falta de caráter. É a marca de um caráter eminentemente humano, lírico, compreensível, racional, que faz da composição e não da oposição a lei de nossa psicologia nativa e da nossa conseqüente história política. Temos tido também as nossas lutas cruentas e guerras civis que duraram mais de decênio, como a dos Farrapos, campanhas sangrentas como a de Canudos, repressões violentas como as coloniais, para mostrar que o sangue da nossa gente também corre. Mas é a exceção que confirma a regra. Se alguma coisa devemos cultivas em nosso caráter nacional, e preservar em nossa história, como típica de nosso Humanismo brasileiro, é precisamente essa tendência inata às soluções pacíficas das nossas mais graves crises políticas. Mesmo com os tanques nas ruas . . . É a marca da nossa gente, da nossa História da nossa civilização. Cultivamo-la com carinho. E o 30 de março a confirmou uma vez mais. (222)[29]

The newspaper was the *Jornal do Brasil* at its apex,[30] the author was Alceu Amoroso Lima a.k.a. Tristão de Athayde, "o grande crítico do modernismo" (Barbosa 1964, 9), and the text was written a few days after President João Goulart was overthrown. The military coup d'état, referred to in the previous passage as "o 30 de Março" (March 30), is, for Amoroso Lima, a confirmation "com os tanques nas ruas" (with tanks on the streets) of Brazil's inherent tendency to seek peaceful conciliatory solutions.

The conservative credentials of Alceu Amoroso Lima were then indisputable.[31] However, by 1964 he was amid a transition from the rabid anticommunist conservatism of the 1930s[32] to becoming one of the mainstream denouncers of the authoritarianism and brutality of the military regime that would remain in power for twenty years. This gradual change did not mean any loss of identity as a Catholic intellectual: the fundamental point of inflection in Amoroso Lima's transition was not 1964 but rather the changes Pope John XXIII brought to Catholicism in 1962 with the Second Vatican Council. The civil opposition to the dictatorship prized Amoroso Lima's support precisely because of his impeccable conservative credentials, which placed him above suspicion and practically immune to the accusation of spreading communist propaganda. In 1964, however, Amoroso Lima seemed to express agreement with Cassiano Ricardo, who claimed that "toda a revolução brasileira termina em acordo, e a pena mais rigorosa para os nossos crimes políticos nunca passou do exílio" (Ricardo 1959, 41).[33]

A few years earlier, in 1960, Amoroso Lima wrote an affectionate portrait of Alfonso Reyes, "Homem de Proa," recalling their friendship in Rio de Janeiro since their first meeting amid Vargas's ascent to power. Reyes captivated the young Catholic leader with diplomatic tact and gentleness. The Mexican ambassador had offered asylum to figures of the First Republic and showed a vivid interest in Amoroso Lima's recent conversion to Catholicism.[34] For Amoroso Lima, Reyes was Latin America's greatest humanist, who "sabia analisar, agudamente, o espírito latino-americano quando por exemplo afirmava que éramos a expressão típica do *homo cordialis*" (147). In the early 1930s the Mexican diplomat portrayed Amoroso Lima as "el maestro definidor de las derechas juveniles" (*Mission Diplomática*, 122). The compliments to Amoroso Lima's intelligence and articulateness were tempered, however, by the knowledge that the right-wing youth in Brazil "tienden invariablemente a una estrecha doctrina de nacionalismo católico y autoritario": "De trato insinuante y algo sinuoso, tiene el valor de quien se siente apoyado por las clases pudientes, por la Iglesia y por cierta sorda inercia nacional."

As the twentieth century moved along, a growing number of Brazilian and Mexican intellectuals and artists felt uneasy with the limitations imposed not only by the tenets of positivism and naturalism but also (and perhaps most decisively) by classical liberalism in its particular Latin American mold. The epistemological, aesthetic, and political challenges to this status quo by Mexican and Brazilian intellectuals and artists gained decisive symbolic leverage with the acute political crises that occurred in the two countries.

But these decisive crises were set apart by more than ten years, and they differed in their trajectory: in Mexico the crisis happened at full speed with the fall of Porfirio Díaz in 1911 and only resolved to a certain stability in the 1930s. In Brazil the crisis flared up during the election campaign of Arthur Bernardes in, of all years, 1922, but the cultural and political establishments managed somehow to contain the confrontation, which slowly built to the end of the so-called First Republic and the turbulent 1930s. The Porfiriato and the First Republic were identified at least symbolically with positivism's cultural hegemony,[35] and these regimes' failings would spark changes in the ideas and careers of intellectuals and artists who, in the following decades, would play a prominent role in Mexican and Brazilian culture.

The twelve-year gap between the two "centennial generations"—1910 in Mexico and 1922 in Brazil—explains, to a certain extent, the more visible role of the avant-gardes on the Brazilian scene.[36] The *ateneístas* Alfonso Reyes and José Vasconcelos—men of Manuel Bandeira's generation—played in Mexican letters the galvanizing role of younger *modernistas* such as Mário de Andrade, Lucio Costa, and Gustavo Capanema in Brazil. Vasconcelos founded the Universidad Nacional Autónoma de México (UNAM)—the university's motto, "por mi raza hablará el espíritu," is his—and Reyes founded in 1940 and presided over El Colegio de México, a research institution sponsored by the federal government, Banco de México, UNAM, and the Fondo de Cultura Económica.[37] These are arguably still the two main academic institutions in modern Mexico.

It should be no surprise, then, that Mexican historians claim the refutation of late nineteenth-century aesthetics in Mexican poetry occurred with Enrique González Martínez's "Tuércele el cuello al cisne"—a fairly conventional sonnet —whereas the same refutation in Brazil is identified with the scandals of the Semana de Arte Moderna. Were Brazilians ironically compensating for "slow, gradual, and cautious" political change with fiery radical literary rhetoric? Was Mexico's legendary classicism, its attachment to the introspective "épica en surdina," a form of self-preservation during years of violent revolutionary turmoil, thus the relative unimportance attached to its avant-garde?

Instead of viewing this pair as mutually exclusive exceptionalisms, I believe we should take with a grain of salt these historical accounts and their emphases either on continuities or ruptures. We should think in broader terms, differentiating between Modernismo, in Portuguese, with a capital M (a specific set of avant-garde movements from the 1920s), and modernism, in English, with a lowercase m (something that includes but reaches beyond all the avant-gardes). The literary and cultural histories of Brazil and Mexico in the first half of the twentieth century can be seen, then, as two slightly diverging paths against the spread and development of modernism in Latin America.

The uneasy feeling about positivism and naturalism and about Brazilian liberalism predated 1922, and writers such as Lima Barreto and Monteiro Lobato should not dwell in the limbo called "pré-Modernismo," nor should writers such as Graciliano Ramos and Guimarães Rosa, who felt a deep aversion to the aesthetics of the Modernismo of the 1920s, be thought of as "second and third generation Modernistas." In Mexico the "Generación del Centenario" did not represent such a radical rupture with prerevolutionary positivism or *modernismo* (with the term used here in its Hispanic meaning), and likewise the following generations in Mexican literary circles did not simply accept the guidance and continue the work of the *ateneístas*. Somewhere in between the excessive emphasis on the continuities between generations in México and the myth of 1922 as a complete rupture with an utterly obsolete past lies a more accurate view of the period, one that sees the respective histories of early twentieth-century Mexico and Brazil in their variety and complexity. Beyond the undeniable differences and specificities, Mexico and Brazil also have a lot in common.

For that matter, I do not want to give the impression that Alfonso Reyes could simply be placed in the long line of conservative thinkers of Brazil or Latin America. This is not just because Reyes was of the old Latin American school but also because he was mostly uninvolved with politics and never expressed faith in authoritarian solutions such as those repeatedly proposed by Alceu Amoroso Lima and Cassiano Ricardo starting in the 1930s. Reyes's views of Brazil, like Stefan Zweig's more famous impressions recorded in his *Brasil: País do Futuro*, are overly optimistic but not completely unrealistic. "México en una nuez" and "Brasil en una castaña," remarkable exercises in Latin American comparativism, are stylistic gems in which Reyes captures two different aspects of the region. One Latin America is acutely aware of, though not necessarily pessimistic about, the continent's violent history and difficult relationship with its European models. The other Latin America is proud and confident, perhaps too much so at times, in the future of a new, exciting culture, imagined as a felicitous synthesis of several racial or cultural strains in a fertile, tropical melting pot.

In Brazil, the process started with the coup d'état in April 1964 and culminated with the AI-5 decrees, which essentially annulled Brazilians' constitutional rights in December 1968, doing away with any illusions about the possibility of peacefully resolving the contradictions exacerbated by Latin America's modernization, rapid industrialization, urbanization, and the Cold War. In Mexico the October 1968 massacre of civilians in Tlatelolco marked the end of illusions about the perpetual continuation of the Mexican revolution embodied by the Partido Revolucionario Institucional (PRI) as a progressive and constructive force guiding the modernization of Mexico with its nationalist rhetoric. In Brazil the years that followed, "Os Anos de Chumbo," would see the creation of a powerful, repressive modern apparatus that included systematic torture and murder and bore no trace whatsoever of the *cordialidade* that Amoroso Lima hoped the military regime would embody. In Mexico the nationalist and progressive official rhetoric contrasted more and more with the encroachment of U.S. capitalism and the repressive paramilitary apparatus of the Halcones, and the title of a famous essay, "Atento aviso: El que haya encontrado la Revolución mexicana, favor de devolverla" (Aguilar Camin 1984, 5), captures the spirit of the time. In *La jaula de la melancolía*, Roger Bartra signals Tlatelolco (and, we could add, AI-5 in Brazil) as the end of a era, "por la obvia imposibilidad para explicar la circunstancia trágica de 1968 por medio del mito de 'lo mexicano'" (Bartra, 21). There and then, both the myth of the gentle, natural-born diplomat in "Brasil en una castaña" and that of the redeeming revolution that finally brought a country to confront and recognize itself in "Mexico en una nuez" suddenly looked ancient and insufficient.[38]

NOTES

1. The group was renamed the more nationalistic Ateneo de México in 1912. That influential generation has also been called "la generación del centenario" because of the festivities of the centennial of Mexican independence in 1910.

2. In addition to José Vasconcelos (1882–1959) and Alfonso Reyes (1889–1959), it is worth mentioning Pedro Henríquez Ureña (1884–1946), Antonio Caso (1883–1946), Julio Torri (1889–1970), Martín Luis Guzmán (1887–1977), Enrique González Martínez (1871–1952), Jésus T. Acevedo (1882–1918), Manuel M. Ponce (1882–1948), and Diego Rivera (1886–1957).

3. Justo Sierra, Porfirio Díaz's minister of education, was a strong influence on some of the *ateneístas* and supported their efforts to curb the influence of positivists and fight attempts to undermine laical education by Catholic groups. The mere fact that Don Porfírio himself was invited to one of their activities should not be underestimated as a sign of the group's insider status in the Porfiriato. In this sense it is interesting to contrast Carlos Monsiváis's prologue (32–42) and Alfonso Reyes's own account of that time in "Pasado inmediato (fragmento)" (133–74), both found in the anthology *México—Alfonso Reyes*. In "Notas sobre la cultura mexicana en el siglo XX," Monsiváis moves further to question the actual relevance, novelty, and depth of the famed conferences in which Antonio Caso refuted positivism (*Historia general de México*, 968–76).

4. For a very interesting account of this trip and a study of its particular significance for Vasconcelos, see Mauricio Tenorio's "A Tropical Cuauhtemoc—Celebrating the Cosmic Race at the Guanabara Bay."

5. The noun *ufanismo* is a common ironic reference derived from the title of Afonso Celso's *Por que me ufano de meu país*, a nationalistic primary school textbook written in 1902, in which the author enumerates countless reasons for patriotic pride.

6. Proof of the extraordinary endurance of the terminology created by Vasconcelos can be seen in unlikely places such as the work of Darcy Ribeiro, a left-wing nationalist and an anthropologist famous for his passionate defense of indigenous cultures. In Ribeiro's *O povo brasileiro*, a late addition to the tradition of essays about national identity in Latin America intended to be his intellectual testament, and an instant best seller in Brazil in 1995, Vasconcelos's term *New Rome* appears prominently in the last chapter, "O destino nacional" (441–49), again related to the mingling of the races and the glorious future of the Brazilian nation.

7. The book *Homenagem a Manuel Bandeira* contains Reyes's "Acto de presencia," which also appears in *Genio y figura de Alfonso Reyes* (203). Fred Ellison's article "Alfonso Reyes y Manuel Bandeira: Una amistad mexico-brasileña" offers a thorough account of the friendship between the two intellectuals.

8. Bandeira also refers indirectly to Reyes in "Rondó do Palace Hotel" and briefly cites the Mexican several times in his *crônicas*, particularly in "Tempo de reis," in which Reyes is featured as a patron in a small popular restaurant in Rio de Janeiro (*Poesia e prosa*, 377–78).

9. *Monterrey—Correo literario de Alfonso Reyes* lasted from 1930 to 1937. Considered by José Emilio Pacheco as a sort of precursor to the modern-day blog (Pacheco, 23), the literary journal was, in spite of its modest scope, one of the most important initiatives in the '30s in terms of inter-American dialogue.

10. *História Natural das Laranjeiras* was first published in book form in 1955 in the ninth volume of Reyes's *Obras completas*. Most of Reyes's writing done in or about Brazil is concentrated in the ninth and tenth volumes of his *Obras completas*.

11. "Ofrenda al Jardin Botánico de Río Janeiro" (*Obras completas*, vol. IX, 89–92) refers to the speech given during the ceremony inaugurating the statue in 1935. The speech is featured on the first page of the thirteenth issue of *Monterrey—Correo Literario de Alfonso Reyes* together with photographs of the Cuauhtémoc in Flamengo and the cactus garden and the Xochipilli in the Jardim Botânico. The speech is dedicated to Paulo Campos Porto, director of the Jardim Botânico from 1931 to 1938, with whom Reyes cooperated on the cactus garden around the Cuauhtémoc in Flamengo. Reyes compliments the Jardim Botânico for its remarkable collection of Mexican cacti and reveals that he himself delivered *peyotl* seeds from México to Campos Porto.

12. Fred P. Ellison's *Alfonso Reyes e o Brasil* is a thorough account of Reyes's years in Rio de Janeiro.

13. A sign of the essay's prominent position in Reyes's oeuvre is that in 1996, when

the Fondo de Cultura Económica published Reyes's volume for the collection "Cultura para todos" (low-cost paperback editions of Mexican classics), the book was called *México en una nuez y otras nueces*.

14. Initially called *El nacional revolucionario*, the newspaper was created in 1929 at the national convention of the PRN (the newly founded revolutionary party that would become the PRM in 1938 and the PRI in 1945) and would move away from the revolutionary rhetoric of Lázaro Cárdenas to become the government's mouthpiece in the 1940s.

15. Luis Leal once aptly described Reyes's prose as "poesía y saber unificados a través de un acercamiento basado en la reminiscencia y la evocación" (poetry and knowledge unified through an approach based on reminiscence and evocation) (Leal, 15).

16. The essay "Justo Sierra y la historia patria" (175–98), from which this passage comes, is particularly illustrative, since in it Reyes lays out what are for him the essential qualities of a great historic essay.

17. The *ateneístas*—the group's name is particularly meaningful—were fundamentally classicists who wished to rescue ancient Greek and Roman culture from the oblivion to which it had been banished by positivist materialism and the stale rhetoric of academicism. At the core of Vasconcelos's ambitious literacy plans for Mexican education was the creation of school libraries with a collection of carefully translated classics (e.g., Homer, Aeschylus, Euripides, and Plato, as well as Dante, Goethe, and Cervantes), published in editions of twenty to fifty thousand volumes.

18. In his account of the 1932 argument with the nationalists, Guillermo Sheridan confesses without much subtlety that "A mí también me irrita la ambigüedad de Reyes, enfermo de diplomacia, y que solo en su correspondencia (ni siquiera en su diario) externase su verdadera opinion sobre 'las ruindades del nacionalismo' y sobre la forma en que se había lacerado con esas acusaciones" (I see Reyes's ambiguity as irritating as well. It is infected by diplomacy and it is only in his private letters that he expressed his true opinion about 'the evils of nationalism' and about how he had gotten hurt with those accusations) (Sheridan, 52). The discrepancies found in Reyes's opinions are not contradictions but instead reflect natural differences between public and private realms. Anyway, it is difficult to define precisely which of the two supposedly conflicting opinions is the "true" one. The truth of the matter is that Sheridan, in his determination to combat nationalism, wishes to define too sharp a contrast between the two fields as they played out in the 1930s. By comparison, in "A vuelta de correo" (vol. VIII, 427–49), for example, Reyes prefaces his reply to Héctor Pérez Martínez with language that is much less marked by clearly opposed divisions.

19. Julio Ortega affirms that "Alfonso Reyes debe haber sido el último modernista: entre Rubén Darío (que era capaz de sumar Góngora a Verlaine) y Jorge Luis Borges (que era capaz de añadirle compadritos a Shakespeare)" (*Teoría literaria*, 12–13).

20. In 1933 Reyes published in *El libro y el pueblo* his translations of fragments of pre-

colonial indigenous poetry that had previously been translated into French and Portuguese. See "Poesía Indígena Brasileña," in Alfonso Reyes, *Obras completas*, vol. IX, 86–88.

21. In Spanish: "Miraba esto, iba a ver lo otro, corría a contemplar lo del más allá y me atraía lo que aún me quedaba por ver. Y así recorriendo todas las calles, cautivo de un anhelo insaciado ante tanto espectáculo, exclamé extenuado: '¡Ojos míos, estamos vencidos!'" In English: "There were sights I saw, sights I aimed to see, sight I achcd to see, sights I could not bear to miss . . . my gaze was overpowered by what I could see before me, but dragged away by what I anticipated. As I was guiding my own tour around all these streets, lovesick with the sight of it, I said to myself wearily: 'We are beaten, my eyes!'" (77).

22. The fort on the island of San Juan Úlua was ironically one of the last bastions of colonial Mexico; surrendered by the Spaniards only in 1825, it functioned as a prison from the late eighteenth until the twentieth century, with famous inmates such as Fray Servando Teresa de Mier and Benito Juárez (*San Juan de Ulúa—Biografía de un presidio*, 112–26). The exquisitely carved coin banks made in San Juan Ulúa are now much sought-after antiques. See Sandra Kraisrideja's "Carved Coconuts Highlight Mexico's History," *North County Times*, August 3, 2005.

23. In *As raízes e o labirinto da América Latina*, Silviano Santiago points back to Pero Vaz de Caminha's letter to the king of Portugal, which announced the "discovery" of Brazil, as the foundational text holding the first linguistic sign of such imaginary in relation to the colonization (84, 89–94).

24. Perhaps, in his attempt to negate the apologetic reading of the *cordialidade*, Sérgio Buarque de Holanda might have exaggerated its negative aspects. Pedro Meira Monteiro rightly observes that, for Buarque de Holanda, at least in *Raízes do Brasil*, "os valores liberais . . . se colocavam como uma *opção* individual, que parecia *excluir* os valores cordiais. Se nos mantivermos no plano da reflexão do historiador, dificilmente vislumbraremos, no próprio ensaio, uma saída clara para o impasse" (*A queda do aventureiro*, 291).

25. Cassiano Ricardo was one of the founders of the nationalistic Verdeamarelo, together with Menotti del Picchia and Plínio Salgado. Without adhering to Integralismo, the Brazilian version of fascism, Ricardo became an intellectual leader of nationalist right-wing *modernistas* and one of the most powerful figures in Getúlio Vargas's dictatorial Estado Novo (1937–1945). As with other conservative or authoritarian figures of Brazilian Modernismo, Ricardo was either neglected or else mentioned briefly and with embarrassment until Luiza Moreira's *Meninos, poetas e heróis*, a pioneering reading of Ricardo's main works.

26. In this lengthy text, Cassiano Ricardo complains that in the second edition of *Raízes do Brasil* "pretendendo explicar a palavra, Sérgio alterou, descaracterizou nosso *homem cordial*" (293) and, furthermore, Cassiano Ricardo contests the adequacy of the term *cordialidade*—he prefers the openly apologetic *bondade*, "primeiro fundamento da nossa democracia social" (294).

27. Another important point of view on the discussion of the Homem Cordial

comes from the *modernista* Oswald de Andrade, in a short piece called "Um aspecto antropofágico da cultura brasileira: O homem cordial," presented at the first Congresso Brasileiro de Filosofia in 1950. In this text, Oswald, returning to the *antropofagia* of the 1920s after a long period of communist militancy, claims to agree with Sérgio Buarque de Holanda's definition (he includes a long quote from *Raízes do Brasil*) but offers a completely different genealogy to the Homem Cordial, closer to that of Ribeiro Couto. For Oswald, the Homem Cordial is a remnant of the culture of Brazil's precolonial indigenous matriarchal society. This *matriarcado* was, furthermore, ready for a comeback of sorts (with Oswald seeing traces of it in the thought of Kierkegaard, Mallarmé, Karl Jaspers, and Sartre) as humanity faces fear without any help from heaven.

28. Cassiano Ricardo's "Variações sobre o homem cordial" and "Carta a Cassiano Ricardo" were originally published in 1948, in the second and third issues of the magazine *Colégio—Revista de cultura e arte*, edited by Roland Corbisier (1914–2005), former *integralista* and founder in 1955 of the government-sponsored research institution ISEB (Instituto Superior de Estudos Brasileiros). The model for this institution, which was co-conceptualized by Hélio Jaguaribe and Gilberto Amado, was the Collège de France and Reyes's Colegio de México (its original name was to be Colégio do Brasil). After the 1964 coup d'état, ISEB was closed down, its library incorporated into the Escola Superior de Guerra, and its members investigated by the military.

29. I thank my colleague Alexandre Nodari for pointing to this quote in a different context.

30. For a brief assessment of *Jornal do Brasil*'s positions during the military dictatorship, see Beatriz Kushnir's *Cães de Guarda: Jornalistas e censores do AI-5 à constituição de 1988*.

31. Converted to Catholicism in the late 1920s by his mentor Jackson de Figueiredo, the modernist Alceu Amoroso Lima became the great intellectual leader of the conservative Catholic layman movement in the 1930s, with remarkable influence in Getúlio Vargas's Conselho Nacional de Educação, where he battled in the name of the church and private interests against the reformers of the Escola Nova. For an account of the debates in the council and the roles played by Amoroso Lima and the other members, see Sergio Miceli, "O Conselho Nacional de Educação: Esboço de Análise de um Aparelho de Estado (1931–7)," in *Intelectuais à Brasileira* (2001), 293–341.

32. Anticommunism was an essential part of the Catholic right wing. In 1935, for example, in a chapter not very subtly called "666" in his book *Pela Ação Católica*, Alceu Amoroso Lima warns that "do outro lado do Vístula, espreitam os novos bárbaros, velam os que levantam estátuas a Judas, velam os que ergueram sobre o trono soviético aquele mesmo Animal do Apocalipse" (49).

33. Among other things in his essay, Cassiano claims that "o problema das minorias raciais e culturais é quase inexistente entre nós" (39) and that "não temos problemas de desocupados, da falta de terra, da violenta diferença de classes, do ódio de raças e

religiões, da excessiva diferença de cultura ou riqueza" (40). I believe these statements stand alone without commentary.

34. It is a sign of Alfonso Reyes's diplomatic acumen that he cultivated at the same time the friendship of Alceu Amoroso Lima and Graça Aranha. As implied earlier, Reyes also quietly supplied Cecília Meireles with material about Mexican education policies as she battled on the other side of the political spectrum for the reformers of the Escola Nova (Soares 258–79).

35. The most visible traces of positivist influence are the political power of the *científicos* in Mexico and the motto "Ordem e Progresso" still displayed on the Brazilian flag. In one of his last books, Sérgio Buarque de Holanda would question the prominent role of positivism in the ending of the monarchy and the establishment of the republic. Nevertheless, the perceived influence of the tenets of positivism went well beyond those who professed to follow strictly Auguste Comte's doctrines. Positivism's ideological hegemony extended its reach, even in diluted or distorted forms, to practically all the elites in Latin America and was taken into account by those who wished to challenge them.

36. Nevertheless, the relative importance of the avant-gardes in Brazilian culture and their trajectory since the 1920s has been a topic for discussion. As the relationship between the Ateneo and both the Porfiriato and the revolution have been distorted to make the *ateneístas* seem in tune with the new regime, the role of the *modernistas* and their cultural clout have been exaggerated by post hoc accounts that try, for example, to enhance the connection between the Modernismo of the '20s and later developments in Brazilian culture such as *concretismo* and *tropicalismo*. This has distorted our views of the culture in the period, especially with the providential erasure of the many influential right-wing *modernistas* such as Tristão de Atayde, Cassiano Ricardo, Plínio Salgado, and Menotti del Picchia. For a brief exposition of the theme, see Randal Johnson's "Rereading Brazilian Modernism."

37. Vasconcelos was a very important presence for the *muralistas* and writers such as the poet Carlos Pellicer, whereas Reyes also helped and guided several young poets, from Villaurrutia and other *contemporáneos* in the 1920s to the young Octavio Paz, in a role not unlike Mário de Andrade's in Brazil.

38. A paradigmatic example of this insufficiency is Octavio Paz's "postdata," adding to his *Labyrinth of Solitude* an anachronistic attempt to build a parallel between the brutal repression and the student massacre planned and executed by the administration of Gustavo Díaz Ordaz and pre-Columbian sacrifices. See Bartra (160–61).

WORKS CITED

Aguilar Camin, Hector. *Saldos de la revolución*. Mexico: Ediciones Oceano, 1984.

Andrade, Oswald de. "Um aspecto antropofágico da cultura brasileira: O homem cordial." *A utopia antropofágica*. São Paulo: Editora Globo, 1990. 157–59.

Bandeira, Manuel. *Homenagem a Manuel Bandeira*. Rio de Janeiro: Officinas Typographicas do "Jornal do Commercio," 1936.

———. "Tempo de reis." *Poesia e prosa*. 2 vols. Rio de Janeiro: Aguilar, 1958. 377–78.

———. "Rondó do Palace Hotel." In *Libertinagem—Estrela da manhã*, edited by Giulia Lanciani. Madrid et al.: ALLCA XX, 1998. 85.

———. "Rondó dos Cavalinhos." In *Libertinagem—Estrela da manhã*, edited by Giulia Lanciani. Madrid et al.: ALLCA XX, 1998. 83.

Bartra, Roger. *La jaula de la melancolía—Identidad y metamorfosis del mexicano*. Barcelona et al.: Grijalbo, 1987.

Brading, David A. "Prólogo—Alfonso Reyes y América." *América*. México: FCE, 2005. 7–27.

Buarque de Holanda, Sérgio. *Raízes do Brasil*. São Paulo: Companhia das Letras, 1999.

Ellison, Fred P. "Alfonso Reyes y Manuel Bandeira: Una amistad mexico-brasileña." *Hispania* 70, no. 3 (September 1987): 487–93.

———. *Alfonso Reyes e o Brasil*. Rio de Janeiro: Topbooks, 2002.

Freyre, Gilberto. *Casa Grande & Senzala*. Rio de Janeiro: Record, 1992.

Johnson, Randal. "Rereading Brazilian Modernism." Texas Papers on Latin América, no. 89–04. Austin: Institute of Latin American Studies, University of Texas at Austin, 1989. http://lanic.utexas.edu/project/etext/llilas/tpla/8904.pdf.

Kraisrideja, Sandra. "Carved Coconuts Highlight Mexico's History." *North County Times*, August 3, 2005.

Kushnir, Beatriz. *Cães de Guarda: jornalistas e censores do AI-5 à constituição de 1988*. São Paulo: Boitempo, 2004.

Leal, Luis. "Presentación." In *Visión de Anáhuac*, by Alfonso Reyes. México: UNAM, 2004.

Lima, Alceu Amoroso. *Cultura Inter-Americana*. Rio de Janeiro: Agir, 1962.

———. "30 de março." *Revolução, reação ou reforma?* Rio de Janeiro: Tempo Brasileiro, 1964. 221–22.

———. "Homem de proa." *Companheiros de viagem*. Rio de Janeiro: José Olympio, 1971. 145–49.

Martínez, José Luis. *El ensayo mexicano moderno I*. Mexico: Fondo de Cultura Económica, 2001.

Micelli, Sérgio. "O Conselho Nacional de Educação: Esboço de Análise de um Aparelho de Estado (1931–7)." In *Intelectuais à Brasileira*. São Paulo: Companhia das Letras, 2001. 293–341.

Monsiváis, Carlos. "Notas sobre la cultura mexicana en el siglo XX." *História general de México*. México: El Colégio de México, 2000.

———. "Prólogo." *México—Alfonso Reyes*. México: FCE, 2005. 32–42. Monteiro, Pedro Meira. *A queda do aventureiro: Aventura, cordialidade e os novos tempos em Raízes do Brasil*. Campinas: Editora da UNICAMP, 1999.

Moreira, Luiza. *Meninos, poetas e heróis: Aspectos de Cassiano Ricardo do modernismo ao Estado Novo*. São Paulo: EDUSP, 2001.

Nodari, Alexandre. "45 anos do Golpe: Terrorismo e cordialidade." *Consenso, só no paredão*, May 19, 2009. http://www.culturaebarbarie.org/blog/2009/05/45-anos-do-golpe-terrorismo-e.html.

Ortega, Julio. "Prólogo." *Teoría literaria—Alfonso Reyes*. México: FCE, 2007. 7–13.

Pacheco, José Emilio. "Monterrey de Alfonso Reyes." *Edición facsimilar de los quince fascículos de "Monterrey—Correo Literário" de Alfonso Reyes*. Monterrey: Fondo Editorial de Nuevo León, 2008. 23–31.

Paz, Octavio. *El laberinto de la soledad*. México: FCE, 1959.

Prado, Paulo. *Retrato do Brasil—Ensaio sobre a tristeza brasileira*. Rio de Janeiro: José Olympio, 1962.

Prado Jr., Caio. *Formação do Brasil Contemporâneo*. São Paulo: Livraria Martins Editora, 1942.

Ramos, Samuel. *Perfil del hombre y la cultura de México*. México: UNAM, 1963.

Reyes, Alfonso. "A vuela de correo." *Obras completas*. Vol. VIII. México: Fondo de Cultura Económica, 1958.

———. "Brasil en una castaña." *Obras completas*. Vol. IX. México: Fondo de Cultura Económica, 1959.

———. "México en una nuez." *Obras completas*. Vol. IX. México: Fondo de Cultura Económica, 1959.

———. "Poesía Indígena Brasileña." *Obras completas*. Vol. IX, 86–88. México: Fondo de Cultura Económica, 1959.

———. "Romances del Río de Enero." *Obras completas*. Vol. X. México: Fondo de Cultura Económica, 1960.

———. "Visión de Anahuác." In *Prosa y Poesía*, edited by James Willis Robb. Madrid: Cátedra, 1975. 69–127.

———. *Misión Diplomática—Tomo II*. México: Fondo de Cultura Económica, 2001.

———. "Justo Sierra y la historia patria." *México—Alfonso Reyes*. México: FCE, 2005. 175–98.

———. *Edición facsimilar de los quince fascículos de "Monterrey—Correo Literário" de Alfonso Reyes*. Monterrey: Fondo Editorial de Nuevo León, 2008.

Reyes, Alicia. *Genio y figura de Alfonso Reyes*. México: Fondo de Cultura Económica, 1997.

Ribeiro, Darcy. *O povo brasileiro*. São Paulo: Companhia das Letras, 2006.

Ribeiro Couto, Rui. "El Hombre Cordial, producto americano." *Monterrey*, no. 8 (March 1932): 3.

Ricardo, Cassiano. *O homem cordial e outros pequenos estudos brasileiros*. Rio de Janeiro: Ministério da Cultura/Instituto Nacional do Livro, 1959.

Santiago, Silviano. *As raízes e o labirinto da América Latina*. Rio de Janeiro: Rocco, 2006.

Santiago Cruz, Francisco. *San Juan de Ulúa—Biografía de un presidio*. Mexico: Editorial Jus, 1966.

Sheridan, Guillermo. *México en 1932: La polémica nacionalista*. México: FCE, 1999.

Soares, Gabriela Pellegrino. *Semear Horizontes: Uma história da formação de leitores na Argentina e no Brasil, 1915–1954*. Belo Horizonte: UFMG, 2007.

Tatius, Achilles. *Leucipe and Clitophon*, translated by Tim Whitmarsh. London: Oxford University Press, 2003.

Tenorio, Mauricio. "A Tropical Cuauhtemoc—Celebrating the Cosmic Race at the Guanabara Bay." *Anales del Instituto de Investigaciones Estéticas* XVI, no. 65 (1994): 93–137.

Vargas Llosa, Mario. "Un hombre de letras." *El País*, Sunday, February 20, 2005.

Vasconcelos, José. *La raza cósmica—Misión de la raza iberoamericana—Notas de viajes a la América del Sur*. Paris: Agencia Mundial de Librería, 1925.

Zweig, Stefan. *Brasil: País do futuro*. Porto Alegre: LP&M, 2006.

PAULO MOREIRA is an assistant professor at Yale University, and he has a PhD in comparative literature. His main areas of interest are American, Brazilian, and Mexican twentieth-century literature, cinema, and modernism. He has a forthcoming book about Faulkner, Guimarães Rosa, and Rulfo from Editora UFMG and received the Morse Fellowship to write a book about Mexican and Brazilian artists and intellectuals. His second book, *Literary Relations between Mexico and Brazil: Deep Undercurrents*, is forthcoming with Palgrave Macmillan. He may be reached at paulo.moreira@yale.edu.

SHEILA KHAN
Translated by Carmen Ramos-Villar

Narrativizing the Other-Empire in Silence
On Portuguese Postimperiality/Postcoloniality

ABSTRACT: This papers aims, within the theoretical framework presented by Boaventura de Sousa Santos and Paula Meneses—named *epistemologias do sul* (Southern epistemologies) and based on the working tool that the same sociologists called *sociologia das ausências* (sociology of absences)—to offer a complementary analysis proposed as the *sociologia pós-colonial das ausências* (postcolonial sociology of absences). This approach is inspired by the creation of an interventive methodology that aims to reflect, on the one hand, the state of Portuguese research in postcolonial studies and its sensibility toward realities thought to be marginal and, on the other, to identify the lines of dialogue and cooperation between such studies and the people who inhabit the space and time of this Portuguese postimperiality/postcoloniality.

KEYWORDS: identity, Southern epistemologies, postimperiality/postcoloniality.

> We have in ourselves a great excess of mythified memory, adding up to our centuries-old memory as Europeans. And above all we have this excess or overload of dream which, as with Baudelaire's albatross, prevents us from consenting or adhering to the demands of reality.
> —Eduardo Lourenço

I.

Much has been written about the loss of the Portuguese African colonies, and what came out of it was not enough to rescue from silence and forgetfulness the lives and identities that the Portuguese empire forged and imagined on the other side of itself (Khan 52–53). Eduardo Lourenço, in his brilliant autopsy of the Portuguese identity, mirrored in his *O Labirinto da Saudade*, interprets this founding moment of postcoloniality in the following terms: "Strange was our 'empire,' and stranger still the people who, having suddenly seemingly lost *their soul's soul*, appear to be mostly shocked with the invasion-flood of the living stones of that imperiality, randomly stacked up at the Portela airport. *What we had been as Portuguese from the metropolis*, what we were as real or potential owners of distant lands, was severed, and remained severed almost until the end of one of the world's most unusual colonizing adventures" (Lourenço, 43–45).

Despite Lourenço's brilliance here, I would point out that what in the past remained *severed* is still reflected in the impossibility of dialogue or encounter between the imperial center in Portugal and the lived experience on the other side of the imperial divide. In line with this reality, I have seen in much recent fiction, autobiography, and journalism[1] evidence of this abyssal postimperiality and postcoloniality, as reflected in two nonintersecting strains: on the one hand, the celebration of a multicultural Portugal, picturing itself as a modern and European nation because of the presence of diverse peoples in the Portuguese territory; and, on the other, the walls of silence and forgetfulness that have been built between that discourse and that celebration and the individuals who participated in colonialism, who remain absent and peripheral in this great Portuguese postcolonial narrative. As for the profusion of published works on the return to Portugal proper of many Portuguese and the colonial Others,[2] we learn from these works the following the lesson: the Other, once the subject of the discourse defined and formed according to the colonizer's cultural and civilizational parameters (Mignolo 2011), is today, as I write, entirely marginalized. There is widespread ignorance of the Other's historical, cultural, subjective, and mnemonic trajectory. Indeed, this Other remains not only subdued by the sense of cultural and social inferiority with which he or she was tagged but also left out of a Portugal that claims to be postcolonial and multicultural. Like two sides of a bridge that cannot be crossed, today's "multicultural" European nation and its forgotten Other—and the corresponding sense of historical awareness—seem to be ununitable. I will not invoke here the various analyses of a few works that I mention on the first note: namely, the work undertaken by Margarida Calafate Ribeiro (2004, 2012) and Ana Margarida Fonseca (2010) clearly focuses on this fracture in public memory post–April 25, 1974. My task pushes me toward a more sociological framework, where a critical approach to considering the two sides of Portuguese postimperiality and postcoloniality are still missing. As I point out in another work:

> If contributions, namely literary ones, show us with some degree of propriety and clairvoyance the impact of that overseas experience upon the lives and

social perceptions that the Portuguese built about themselves, the opposite is not as evident, tangible, or visible. We refer to those who, having participated in the social and political colonial and colonizing architecture, are nowadays the heirs of that steady presence of the Portuguese in Africa and about whom so little is known—or, in other words, there is very little curiosity to know how [their lives] are like, today, the lives of the ex-colonized. (Khan 49)

We now turn to observations drawn from a research endeavor titled *Portugal Híbrido, Portugal Europeu? Gentes do "Sul" mesmo aqui ao lado* (Hybrid Portugal, European Portugal? People from the "South" Right around the Corner) (Khan 2011).[3] It is one brief question that remains unanswered in the forgetful fog of postimperiality and postcoloniality (Ribeiro 1998). It is important to stress here that the simultaneous use of the terms *postcoloniality* and *postimperiality* converge in a sole analytical criterion, structured upon the idea that the colonies represented, both rhetorically and ideologically, the mirror image of the imperial center, which thought of itself as the source of civilization and progress. Thus, several "Portugals" were recreated on various continents: South America, with Brazil; Asia, with India and East Timor; and Africa, with Angola, Cape Verde, Guinea Bissau, São Tome and Principe, and Mozambique. To enter the field of Portuguese postimperiality/postcoloniality, we must read both sides of the mnemonic and historical experience of the changes pre- and post-April 25, including the social and cultural awareness by those who were first subjected to, and then forgotten by (i.e., the human wreckage of), a Portuguese nation that now imagines itself to be European and multicultural. The narration of the past and the work of building the historical awareness of the present cannot simply mirror a country's triumphs—it has a "memory duty" as well (Levi 2010). It has to constitute a gesture of historical humility toward everyone who helped build the Portuguese imagery upon the faith of an "empire as imagination of the center" (Ribeiro 3).

II.

To think about the abyssal sides of this Portuguese postimperiality/postcoloniality would imply recognizing that the "South" as a metaphor on which to base a hegemonic occidental posture, as well as its colonial and imperial adventure of the worlds of Others, was not obliterated with the effective and political denial of the unfit occupation by the colonizer, that same colonizer who, while abandoning the colonized territories in the territorial sense, did not do so either ideologically or culturally: the virus of the coloniality and the rhetoric of Western superiority have thus been transformed into a division into global North and global South. In the Portuguese sense, for which an interior global South exists right around the corner, the lack of memory, dialogue, recognition, or historical and social participation is especially pronounced. As noted by the sociologist Boaventura de Sousa Santos:

> Western modern thought is an abyssal thought. I argue that this is as true today as it was during the colonial period. Modern thought continues to operate with abyssal lines which divide the human and the subhuman world, in such a way that the principles of humanity are not jeopardized by inhuman practices. The colonies represent a model of radical social exclusion which subsists nowadays in Western modern thought and practices, in the same way it did in the colonial cycle. Today, as before, both the creation and the denial on the other side of the line are a part of hegemonic principles and practices. (Santos 23–31)

Coloniality and power, as ably put forth by the Peruvian sociologist Aníbal Quijano (2000), are not just a long permanence of hegemonic thought cultivated in the past; on the contrary, that very epistemological posture is multiplied by the colonization of being, knowledge, and thought (Lander 2000; Walsh et al. 2002; Schiwy and Ennis 2002; Maldonaldo-Torres 2008). Alongside this statement, Walter Mignolo (2007) uses the concept of *colonial difference* as an analytical and interpretive tool, so as to better contextualize the colonial and postcolonial sides at issue. In Santos's opinion, the colonial difference is not so much embodied in epistemological, ontological, and gnoseological hegemony but rather in the denial of history, of time, of the Other's space, and, as a consequence, in the absence of a cognitively accurate vision of the Other (Santos 2007, 2008) as a source from which spring other, pluri-diversified versions of reading, organizing, and interpreting the human world. The acting, living, and ethical horizons are thus polarized according to this rhetoric of labeling the Other as human "damage," with no time or place to which the assets of modern and Western thought would be, on the one hand, a way of salvation and, on the other hand, and insidiously, an instrument of racism, exploitation, and subjective, identitarian, and cultural degradation. The colonial difference, as a construction and a reflex of the power and being of coloniality, and of the rhetoric of Western epistemological hegemony itself, cannot be separated from this trap that imprisons every one of those who are not understood by the Western vocabulary and not recognized in the space and time of their criteria of modernity, civilizational maturity, and progress. As a consequence of this duplicity, the abyssal thought (Santos 2007) is also a thought whose human reality is felt and internalized unevenly, as we can see from this very enlightening description by Walter Mignolo: "A lake looks different when you are sailing on it than when you are looking at it from the top of the mountains which surround it. Different perspectives on modernity are not only a question of the eyes, then, but also of *consciousness* and of physical location and power differential—those who look from the peak of the mountain see the horizon and the lake, while those inhabiting the lake see the water, the fish and the waves surrounded by mountains, but not the horizon" (Mignolo 466).

As a result of this epistemological and cultural extremism, the "universe on this side of the line," a herald of progress and of technical, economic, and historical development, neither sees nor assumes the existence of the other side, since "the division is so strong that 'the other side of the line' disappears as a reality, it becomes nonexistent, it is actually produced as nonexistent. This means it doesn't exist in any relevant or comprehensible form" (Santos 3–4). What the coloniality of power and being, hand in hand with the rhetoric of modernity, has once presented to us as an abyssal world remains—in the Portuguese case of postimperiality/postcoloniality—a reality frozen in time, surviving every effort for emancipation and liberation of Others and holding captive their political and historical autonomy. In Portugal, the historical difference has become consubstantiated as a postcolonial difference, in the sense that the present matrix still thinks and interprets the world of Others as "nonexistent," or produced as invisible, absent, and marginal, aside from the new architecture of Portuguese postcolonial imagery. The theoretical efforts to overcome this cognitive and human handicap are many, and they assume various conceptual and methodological formulations (Smith 1999; Chakrabarty 2000; Connell 2007; Burawoy 2008; Mignolo 2009; Santos and Meneses 2010),[4] but they all converge in the same intent: to eliminate from the human world the arrogance of Western thought, and to bet on the diversity of other knowledges, other experiences, other wisdoms wrongly set as peripheral in the grand frame of world thought. In order to serve its scope, this reflection will be based, on the one hand, on the theoretical systematization set forth by Santos and Meneses in *Epistemologias do sul*, or Southern epistemologies, and, on the other, on the *postcolonial sociology of absences* (Khan 2011b), which uses as an inspirational, epistemological model the methodological efforts from the *sociology of absences (sociologia das ausências)* (Santos 2002, 2008), which have been used as a guideline for the analysis of reality on the various working and research projects of the Portuguese sociologist Boaventura de Sousa Santos.

The Southern epistemologies as a theoretical system and a lever for change, when compared to the Western and hegemonic thought paradigm, try to rescue the "South" and to translate it beyond an elementary and fixed conception, in which the South is the context of incomprehensible human knowledges and realities, with a meek possibility of dialogue with the modern logical and scientific practices of reflection and action of the Western world. As a first gesture of rupture, the Southern epistemologies are based upon the work of challenging and questioning the validity of this universal arrogance of a thought that sees itself as the center, as the only parameter for analysis and understanding toward the human grammars that it accepts as existing, while validating, at the same time, knowledges and expertises that, as alternatives to this monolithic knowledge, coexist with and are recognized by this theoretical frame as valid knowledge that contributes epistemologically to a better understanding of the global world. If "on the field of knowledge, the abyssal thought consists of conceding modern science the monopoly of the universal distinction between true and false," and, thus, "on the other side of the line, there is real knowledge; there are beliefs, opinions, magic, idolatry, intuitive and subjective understandings" (Santos 5), then the Southern epistemologies bring with them tools that try to break down, to weaken, and to contradict this postulate, while remaining alert and sensitive to the infinite and manifold copresence of other cultural, historical, and social experiences, based on the willingness to create an epistemological equity among knowledges that are different in space and time. From that point of view, the sociology of absences, as a tool for observation, recognition, and valorization of these other knowledges, is a part of a process of identification and utilization of these other knowledges, with the aim to "[transform] impossible objects into possible ones and, from there, to transform absences into presences. This is done by focusing on the fragments of social experience that were not socialized by the metonymic totality" (Santos 246). Complementary to this methodological praxis, the postcolonial sociology of absences that I have derived (Khan 2011b) aims to transform silences and absences, socially produced as nonexistent, into social presences by bestowing upon them, thus, visibility, recognition, and validity toward an interpretation that is more transparent, concrete, and interventive regarding what is today the postimperiality/postcoloniality of Portuguese expression, based on the social, human, and ontological contributions of these people from the "South," this South right around the corner. I will try, therefore, using this new methodological vocabulary and syntax, to strengthen my argument: The global South is not just a remote and unattainable reality, or at least it does not elude our ability to look, think, and act. Quite the opposite, it becomes, to all those who consider this judgment legitimate, rightful and reliable, a field of infinite possibilities that has consisted hitherto of voices that are absent and socially mute, since they are surrounded by a social and historical blindness and inertia. The postcolonial sociology of absences is inspired by the creation of an interventive methodology that aims to reflect, on the one hand, the state of Portuguese research in the field of postcolonial studies as well as its sensibility toward realities thought to be marginal and, on the other hand, to identify the lines of dialogue and cooperation between these studies and the people who inhabit the space and time of this Portuguese postimperiality/postcoloniality.

III.

How to narrativize the Other-empire in silence? The way I see it, we face a disturbing aporia in applying this question to Portuguese postimperiality and postcoloniality. This is because if, on the colonial past, according to Nelson Maldonaldo-Torres, there is "the idea that people cannot survive without the theoretical or cultural conquests of Europe" (Maldonaldo-Torres 77), this very obstacle and cognitive limitation are heirs to an epistemological imperialism and colonialism that label the Other as marginal and invisible within a logic of Western and abyssal thought (Santos, 2007). Therefore, in the case at stake, we have an Other-empire or, to be more accurate, an Other-post-empire whose prefixes are still rooted in practices of social exclusion, social blindness, and a meek historical awareness. This is the global South that is no longer a geographically distant South, since the presence on Portuguese territory of these Other-people brought along our very own interior South, which goes against walls of silence, abyssal ignorance (Lourenço 2001), and a meek historical humility on the part of those who once built and fed the imagery of a nation as an imperial center.

Over two years, 2007–2008, I directed a documentary aimed at bringing to light the reflection, be it academic, subjective, or interpretive, of postimperial and postcolonial Portugal. In order to do so, I filmed interviews of immigrants from Mozambique, all of whom had Portuguese nationality (Khan 2009), and also researchers, thinkers, and writers, so as to understand today's sense of our own social South. The witnesses, the voices, the subjective and analytical records that will be presented and analyzed in this essay are a result of my postdoctoral project (Khan 2011b).

One of the questions raised by this social sample, and according to the theoretical and methodological framing just explained, involved a possible relationship between what I defined as *research or interpretation postcolonialism* and *everyday postcolonialism*. For the reader who is less familiar with these terms, what I call *research or interpretation postcolonialism* is the scientific knowledge produced by universities and research centers, including the literary contributors who undoubtedly have engendered not only Portuguese-speaking postcolonial studies but also postcolonial studies in general. Meanwhile *everyday postcolonialism* should be understood as daily practices, life routines, the ways in which individuals incorporate memories and identity narratives into their way of being, and the ways in which these cultural and identitarian assets are represented in people's strategies of interaction with Portuguese society. Thus, the programmatic and methodological use of a *postcolonial sociology of absences* has become a tool that is both effective and critical toward the Other-post-empire and postcolonial in silence (Cruzeiro 2004). Therefore we can say, as the researcher of Portuguese postcolonial studies Margarida Calafate Ribeiro has noted so opportunely, that bringing the past to the place of the present is a necessary step, since those who shared and still share a given life experience, be it colonial or postcolonial, apart from that subjective and interpretative evocation, assume an active role as builders and narrators of this postimperiality/postcoloniality: "[From] a work of remembering the past that was [which] imposes [itself] whatever its position is, until they realize the true dimension of their own experience—because only by narrating do they realize fully the personal and collective dimension of their own experience—[from] a work of search[ing] for the amplitude of truth and the nature of the power that supported it so as to build a possible representation and, thus, [is] deniable or questionable" (Calafate 138).

These dimensions, both the personal and the collective, given that the postcoloniality of power and knowledge can be denied and questioned and that it boasts of its multicultural aspect, are clearly inscribed in the way in which many

Mozambicans I interviewed enunciate and narrativize the state of play of postcolonial Portugal. Florinda Pott, a Mozambican with Portuguese citizenship who is retired from public service, when invited to reflect on this postcoloniality, states that little is known on the life experience of those who, in the times of Mozambique's political independence, chose to carry on with their life projects in the ancient imperial metropolis. She said as follows: "I think there is little, we have very little information on that. I have no information whether there is anything, any institution that does this kind of work, I don't know. I was never approached by anyone until now, by you; nobody every questioned me. Nothing. I know nothing. If there is, if there is something, I know nothing about it; I have no knowledge of an institution that ever cared to know how do people from Mozambique live here in Portugal" (Khan 74).

Adriano Malalane, a Mozambican and a lawyer who once practiced at the cultural center known as the Casa da Moçambique, assumes, in his interview, a rather critical position toward Mozambicans' confrontation with Portuguese society, given the evident social blindness of the host: "Portuguese society doesn't seem to me to be interested in knowing the Mozambican as such. As an autonomous entity, as a separate group, I don't think there is such a sensibility" (Khan 72). Actually, in his opinion, the very small size of this Mozambican community could be promoting its invisibility; however, according to his understanding of the everyday reality, this criterion cannot justify the notorious divide between the scholarly and interpretational world of research/reflection postcolonialism and everyday postcolonialism. The lines that mark this divide can be identified, on the one hand, with the rapid evolution of the daily reality and, on the other, with the way in which Portuguese society positions itself toward that everyday reality, including the logic of assimilation and absorption of the Other applied to postcolonial immigrants:

> It could be a source of inspiration for the scholars, the daily life, the things that go on. But I don't think so. The Portuguese society has not taken [a] position; it hasn't, so to speak, it has not built the foundations on how to look at those realities. Because, for a certain period, the people who came from the ex-colonies were supposed to integrate and to lose their identity, until they were considered, in a way that is less than accurate, Portuguese. It didn't make sense, in those first years, to consider that there were Mozambican, Guineans . . . they were Portuguese from the colonies. Little by little,

> Portuguese society began to gain consciousness that not everybody was Portuguese. And the scholars, those, it wasn't until much later, I think, that they looked at this reality as a possible study subject. And it is notorious, from the papers I have read, interviews, conferences, that they don't have a very deep knowledge of the daily life of those communities and their relationship with the Portuguese society. (Khan 72–73)

Eugénio Lisboa, an essayist and literary critic, takes a very strong position in his interview concerning the way in which the human experiences of Portuguese colonization are clearly underestimated and undervalued within a rhetoric of modern and *europeistical* "Portugality." In his opinion, "The Portuguese, since they began thinking of joining Europe, they became blond. But they became blond both physically and spiritually, as if, all of a sudden, they became Europeans who had nothing to do with Africa" (52). Within this argument, the additional contents of his answer strengthen his position: "I think there is a great lack of attention toward everything that came from overseas. I mean, people here[,] I have the impression that they see the overseas [areas] with the eyes of that period of fourteen years of war" (52).

This lack of attention that Eugénio Lisboa talks about is, in the opinion of Inocência Mata, a scholar who specializes in African literatures in the Portuguese language, explained by Portuguese society's inability to see the Other, with its vision distorted by a coloniality of memory and being (see Maldonado-Torres 2008) that remains very much present in Portuguese society. If Portugal "decolonized" its African territories and, over that historical continuity, has lost its image as an imperial and colonial power, this does not imply a deep and complete decolonization of the minds, of the core of Portuguese identity, and this core is always itinerant, in an inconstant and oscillatory production of a dignified image of a center. Hence, understanding the blurring of the social, cultural, and historical languages of the Other is also an exercise of deconstruction of Portuguese society, as well as of the state of its abyssal postcoloniality. Still, according to this scholar and to her reading of this postcoloniality, it is a priority to understand the following:

> The Portuguese people have never learned how to deal with the Other, and that learning [is] thirty years old, let's not forget that the Portuguese colonialism was an assimilatory one. It is a way of colonialism in which the Other could only be integrated in the Portuguese society if he were like the ones

> in the Metropolis. And, even being like them, it depended on where he was born, because there was the underdog white man, so imagine the black man. It is necessary as well, when we analyze these matters, we need to bear in mind some realities. The truth is that the Portuguese never learned to deal with the difference, and this learning is thirty years old. From this point of view, he is a good student . . . above all, for someone who is in Portugal for twenty years, like myself, it is possible to see how the relationships changed, there was a change in the relationships—truth be told, for us it is always very little. *The independence of the colonies took place thirty years ago . . . and it didn't happen in a democratic situation* [my emphasis]. (53–54)

The learning that Inocência Mata refers to in her reflection is due, in the opinion of the other interviewees, to a clear attempt at homogenizing the human differences in the Portuguese social fabric. In that sense, underlying this homogenization is not only an effort to formalize the abyssal lines but also a need to ghettoize these human margins into a place where the Other becomes both invisible and culturally distant. In addition, there is a localization that is socially deprived of civilian tools, without which these peripheries become anodyne, passive, and thus incapable of reaching a space of confrontation that is critical and prominent in Portuguese society because, as explained by Manuela Ribeiro Sanches, a specialist in postcolonial studies, "the Other is always someone who we know where he is, we even know where he lives, we think they all live in ghettos" (Khan 54). As a consequence, the abyssal walls that have been built are not only places of invisibility but, more important, the universe of production and formation of acritical social margins. In the opinion of Ana Mafalda Leite, a researcher of African literatures in the Portuguese language: "What I think, and I may be wrong, I cannot make radical statements, but I think that, generally speaking, even though Portugal has a very strong capacity of absorbing the Other, it has a great inability to see him as different. This capacity of absorption is, at the same time, an ability to make the Other invisible. I can't explain this theoretically, why this happens; or, on the other hand, what I think that seems to be happening lately is that there is a worry about the Other in the sense of understanding his difference, more than recognizing his difference and his importance" (54–55).

In the Portuguese context, the overcoming of these abyssal lines remains inalterable if we compare it with its rhetoric of modernity and coloniality along its colonial past. To some of those who took part in this study, overcoming that epistemological limitation might include recognizing that the sense of continuity and historicity of this very context is inescapably intertwined with the Other's inherited life experience. However, that reality seems to be, for some interviewees, always postponed, always in retrograde motion, always delayed, when read in the light of a proposal of postcolonization that would involve breaking the link with old and retrograde ways of being and thinking that once served an empire "as imagination of the center." The denial of the existence of a culturally polysemous and polyphonic reality is then the defense of a monoculture of a knowledge and a way of being that "sits" on and asphyxiates other knowledges, other wisdoms, and other voices, perceived as blank pages of a history of which they are undoubtedly a part. Another property of this postimperiality/postcoloniality "on this side of the line" in Portugal brings us to an idea that the journalist Jorge Araújo defines as territorial limbo or, put differently, "nobody's land." The following excerpt from this journalist's interview is a good illustration of his thought:

> I think it is something that doesn't draw enough attention, and which is of the utmost importance, it concerns this generation born of Mozambicans, Cape Verdians, who were born in Portugal, and who live in nobody's land. This is what worries me. These kids were born in Portugal, and the Portuguese don't see them, so to speak, unless they win the triple jump, they don't see them as Portuguese; but they are no longer Mozambican, no longer Cape Verdian. The case of Cape Verde, that I know best, people that have an almost mythical idea that Cape Verde is but coconut trees, which isn't true, but [people] who are here, in the Cova da Moura neighborhood, and whom the Portuguese think are not Portuguese. *And they live in a nobody's land, a place where anything goes, and I think the academy doesn't pay much attention to this* [my emphasis]. (56)

Another question I set out as a challenge to think critically about this side of the line was (a) Do you think the Mozambicans have visibility in Portuguese society? About this question the answers are mostly unanimous concerning a total invisibility of the Mozambican in the space and time of the present moment of Portuguese postcolonialism. Once again, the discussion covered the inability of the Portuguese to engage in critical self-analysis, on the one hand, and, on the other, their inability to view knowledge as horizontal—that is, to view not the Mozambican, the Angolan, the Cape Verdian as polyphonic and subjective but rather as part of a monolithic Other. Sónia Polanah, a librarian who was born in Mozambique, reflects on this matter, associating the lukewarmness with a vision of a Portuguese society that is socially uncommitted and uncaring toward its Others:

> They don't even realize that they, themselves, have that mixture. But they think, I suppose they think they are a bit pure. I tell you this because sometimes it happens that someone comes along with kinky hair and I say—"Wow, you must have black blood." "Oh no I don't." "Like hell you don't!" I mean, I think they don't actually realize, but then again they don't care to know. I think we have, we were brought up to understand our generations, we were taught that our grandmother is black, who she lived with, what came from there. . . . Here, I think they're pretty proud of being the white ones. Here, in the university, I never realized any of that, quite honestly. Of course, there are a whole lot of meetings of African literatures, and it's all very nice, very pretty indeed, but I've never seen the preoccupation of wanting to understand who he actually is, the African, or the Mozambican, or the Angolan, or the Indian, or the Chinese. I've never seen that, to be quite frank. I've honestly never seen that, what I do see is that it is very nice to talk about multiculturalism, and all that stuff, it's all very nice . . . (Khan 57)

Margarida Paredes, a writer, also points out this detachment toward the Others, in this case Mozambicans living in Portugal, by recalling a vision that tends to choke out other cultural dynamics and idiosyncrasies. In this writer's opinion, making visible this or that one cannot occur, because the Other, or the Others, is almost always labeled under one single designation and automatically "swallowed" by that "dead sea" with no other cosmology and no chance of a concrete identification as Mozambican. Of course, as pointed out by the Mozambique-born lawyer Adriano Malalane, this analysis must necessarily encompass the numeric element, since the number of Mozambicans who live in Portugal is not very expressive, in the sense that, statistically, they are always counted as Portuguese, because they adopted Portuguese citizenship (e.g., Khan 2009). However, in Margarida Paredes's opinion, this lack of visibility has to do with the following:

> I wouldn't isolate the Mozambican, I would say Africans, generally speaking. I think the Africans, who represent Portugal in sports events, have plenty [of] visibility, but not as African people. It goes like this, they are depicted as

> Portuguese, and I have the impression that this visibility depends on the fact that they are victors; as soon as they are losers, they become African and are no longer Portuguese. This is how I see it. About the African communities, generally speaking, they are always very ill treated. . . . The immigrant African communities, when there are, for instance, crimes involving African people, there is always the need to say that the person is of African origin, so they identify the race, and I think they are not well treated. (Khan, 58–59)

In her essay "Estranhos em permanência: A negociação portuguesa na pós-colonialidade," of undeniable importance for critical thought regarding Portuguese postcoloniality, Inocência Mata writes as follows:

> It is undeniable that Africans brought to the Portuguese "civilization" new values, new habits and cultural traditions. . . . However, in that process of enrichment of the Portuguese culture the people who bring along the cultural signs of that celebrated contribution are not always valued and understood, and they have been often omitted in the "great account of the Portuguese nation." Thirty years after the colonial empire has been politically dismantled, the nation's speech . . . continues to textualize the Africans who live here, as well as their descendants, as the Others!" (Mata 289; see also Fonseca 2010)

Even if ours continues to be a country of immigrants, we have no literature or cultural tradition of trying to understand who they are, what they feel, and how they live, these people who inhabit, from that abyssal cartography of postcolonial Portugal (see Fonseca 2010), the other side of the line. Even if my following remark may contradict what I just said, I think that, in these last few years, the only novel that testifies to this internal abyssal cartography of Portuguese postimperiality/postcoloniality is António Lobo Antunes's *O Meu Nome é Legião* (My Name Is Legion) (2007), in which the author, beginning with the allegorical description of a supposed neighborhood—which could be any of the peripheral neighborhoods in greater Lisbon—also enacts a metonymic construction of all those who are not on this side of the line but who inhabit it as invisible and absent social actors. In that sense, this novel draws our attention to the question of whether there is a continuous, decent, and lucid dialogue between research/reflection postcolonialism and everyday postcolonialism (for an example of the everyday version, see Antunes 2007). The positions on this question call for attention because, if in some testimonials we see an auspicious and optimistic vision, others converge in a space in which there are still insecurities and a few expectations regarding the future of the relationship between these two postcolonial worlds. In the opinion of Margarida Calafate Ribeiro, that relationship exists and establishes itself through metaphorical language, since "the social does not speak scientifically" (Khan 69). Clearly against this opinion, the essayist Eugénio Lisboa states that "*there is often in the scholarly speeches a great dose of alienation. It is another world. There is a great deficit of attention toward everything that came from overseas* [emphasis added]" (69). This deficit emerges from a certain Portuguese tendency of not knowing how to face and accept the Other as their neighbor and, in a way, as part of a historical, social, and cultural parcel. In many ways, as Eduardo Lourenço (2001) puts it, we forget the past and, indeed, we actually wanted to set loose our African past. Immediately, within that huge imagination of ourselves as center, we, in turn, direct ourselves toward another center of self-representation and identification, which has now concentrated itself on the European continent. To the researcher Manuela Ribeiro Sanches, who specializes in postcolonial studies, this is a complicated matter, because it will not be possible to beat around the idea of a "divorce of sorts" between everyday postcolonialism and that of research. In a similar sense, we might say that this divorce is contemporized, slowly, through the acknowledgment that a growing number of studies are dedicated, so to speak, to the everyday life on the other side of the line. However, in Sanches's opinion:

> Well, that is a complicated question. On the one hand, I think that very little has been made, but there are very meritorious things that, fortunately, are appearing [and] these questions are beginning to be discussed in a perspective that is different from the one that was in use immediately after April 25. I would say that it is a perspective that is still, let's put it this way, very anticolonial. Therefore it is a reaction, a militancy, that is fully legitimate and justified after all the experience of the colonial war, of the independence of the colonies. Nowadays, I think there are two things, people's inability, that I think is general, and I am not talking just about scholars, to speak openly about these issues. On the other hand, it is blatant that there are everyday experiences that testify [to] that reality. Now, to what extent does the academic theory encompass or bear in mind these experiences, I think in some cases it does. I would say, for example, namely, the field of anthropology, or even sociology. Now, obviously there is always some kind of divorce. (Khan 70)

Rosa Cabecinhas, a researcher, concurs by showing a common dichotomization in language describing Portuguese society, as revealed by her studies with respect to Africans as Others. From this linguistic tendency stems a poor and precarious production of theoretical and methodological proposals. These proposals tend to prioritize the knowledge of the life experiences and identitary dynamics of these people who continue, in her opinion, to be set aside in a place of forgetfulness and invisibility and whom postcolonial studies ends up mirroring with a near absence of careful and zealous incorporation of those life experiences into reflections and work projects: "I don't think so, they are little reflected. I think that sometimes there is that divorce between the academic community and the researchers and, let us say, common sense, I mean people in their daily lives, in their everyday lives. And, often, the researchers involve themselves in reflections and don't consult or question the Others enough to bear in mind these elements of reflection, which can be somewhat dissonant regarding the paradigms that are established" (Khan 71).

To some of the Mozambican immigrants who were interviewed, the search for a new identity by Portuguese society during postcolonization has demonstrated an unequivocal lack of interest in recognizing in these Other African, these Other-post-empires, human centers that irradiate knowledge, expertise, and practices that in many ways reflect the cultural crossing that started with the project of Portuguese colonization overseas. However, paradoxical as it may seem, these cultural crossings are held and kept on the margins in the way Portuguese society convokes new narrative dimensions—on the one hand, as a multicultural and European country and, on the other, as a nation that still depends on this grand imagery with which it instrumentally celebrates its link to Africa, supposedly through lusophony—in short, with its old and labile lusotropicalism.

IV.

If Portugal once turned its back on Europe so as to be able to imagine itself as an imperial center, with the loss of its empire and its colonies, Portugal has needed to remodel its own image before itself and before other European countries and, thus, by turning toward Europe, it has placed in a less dignified and visible place its colonial memory. Yet it has turned that memory less into a source of a critical self-knowledge than into an impulse to celebrate and, thus, hide its historical weaknesses. Suffering from a hesitant and fragile self-expression, Portugal sometimes stands by revitalizing its lusotropicalist rhetoric, and other times by picturing itself as European just as well. This identitarian reshuffle is not, as it is easy to understand, isolated from the postcolonial context of the present. On the contrary, this imagery compulsion stands, as the writer Lídia Jorge points out, beside "a long tradition of that need [of the Portuguese] to hide from themselves" (Khan 42). A foundational question of the documentary therefore asked: (b) Do you think that Portugal and, somehow, Portuguese society in general are aware that their history was made from the crossing with other cultures, other people? In your opinion, is Portugal aware of its cultural hybridism?

This question raised a clear problem associated with the identitarian fluctuation from which Portugal suffered and suffers still, given the need to make up for the loss of its imagery concerning its last imperial project in Africa. Consequently, it became urgent and imperious, with Portugal inevitably adjusting its "position" in the space of the European postimperial puzzle, and recreating a new cultural, geopolitical, existential, and global disposition. Going back to its peripheral position, it begins a new journey and a new process that is no longer territorial, but rather symbolic and ontological so as to, once again, imagine itself as the center of a project called Europe. In the opinion of high school teacher and poet Delmar Gonçalves, a Portuguese citizen born in Mozambique: "I think they don't realize, some pretend they don't. Because there are many people who know and prefer, simply, to ignore, to play ignorant and, above all, among the decision makers, those with political power, people who work at the universities, they prefer to set that matter aside, because they think it will prevent many things. . . . Portugal is a country that aspires, actually, to be a European country, a modern and modernist one, and it's aware of its own limitations, mostly on the economic level" (Khan 43).

However, that Africa, even if marginalized and silenced, is a reality from which Portugal cannot escape, be it culturally or epidermically. To deny or to forget the contaminations of other peoples, other knowledges, enormously perplexes both Helder Macedo, a professor and writer, and Maria João Seixas, a journalist. For these two individuals, Portugal weaves a total and blunt ahistoricity when it "hides" the Others from itself, and by "hiding" from itself its own trajectory and the wellspring of culture that underlies it. They echo the thought formulated by Maria Manuel Cruzeiro, who, in her 2004 essay "As mulheres e a Guerra Colonial: Um silêncio demasiado Ruidoso" (Women and the Colonial War: A Silence That Is Too Noisy), explicitly highlights the following structural formulation of Portuguese society: "We pretend that everything is OK. We are exquisite managers of silence, even when we speak. Particularly when we speak. On this, said Adolfo Casais Monteiro: 'the Portuguese are not the least bit inclined toward their self-knowledge. They like very much to talk about themselves, but that's very far from actually knowing oneself'" (Cruzeiro 31). It could be said that there are many blank pages in the self-representations that Portuguese society builds, and also that there are plenty of other stories, other presences, other narratives that certainly complete and complement these noisy silences of the postcoloniality "from this side of the line"; let's hear, then, these precious noises in the words of Macedo and Seixas:

> What is strange, as well, another thing the Portuguese forget, and shouldn't forget, in general, is that the Portuguese, the Portuguese are mestizos, we are, we, Portuguese, are mestizos from everything there is out there, including Africans. You know as well as I do that—statistics are precarious—in the 16th century it is estimated that 10 to 12 percent of the population of Lisbon was black. In Évora, it went up to, it is thought to have reached around 18 percent. Well, these people weren't eaten [interviewee laughs], the Portuguese weren't cannibals, I mean, they were integrated: the Moors were integrated, the Jews were integrated. We are a mixed race, there is no such thing as the Portuguese race, there is a mixture." (Khan 44–45, filmed interview with Helder Macedo)
>
> . . . I think the Portuguese are, in the best case scenario, prudish toward their own History and, in the worst case scenario, indifferent to it. And, in that sense, the answer to your question is, mostly, no. I think that hour has not arrived yet, if it ever will. No, I don't think so. But what I do think is that the Portuguese lack the curiosity concerning their own History. It's very common, not about the negritude, or African people, or those from India, but it is very common to say that we all have Jewish blood; we are all Jewish. It's frequent, it's common, everyday. But it doesn't cross anybody's mind to say we all have African blood. And it obviously doesn't happen in the same scale. *But, just the other day, I was listening to Helder Macedo, and he always says that, back in the 15th and 16th century, 10 percent of Lisbon's population was black. Ten percent is a lot, and it leaves a trace. Lisbon was a wonderfully libertine town, very open to miscegenation.* And, therefore, many of us have black blood, from that time. However, when we say "we all have Jewish blood in our veins," most people don't know the History of the Jewish people in Portugal, and what the Jews in

> Portugal, what the Jews had to go through, to suffer, either those who left or, mostly, those who stayed. And by saying this we are minimizing the recognition of the Jewish people in Portugal. I mean, when people say "but there is no antisemitism in Portugal," there isn't. But it isn't consciously that there is no antisemitism. We don't give a damn, and we should [my emphasis]. (45, filmed interview with Maria João Seixas)

Strangeness, prudishness, lack of knowledge about its own historicity, and the various identitarian formulations all add to the critical debate the awkwardnesses of this postcoloniality, as well as the historical absences that constitute it. Recalling Lídia Jorge's remarks, the prudishness of a self-knowledge that is clear, multifold, and critical brings us, generally speaking, toward other structural and structuring weaknesses of the Portuguese as a whole. According to Jorge: "I think the Portuguese have a complex about themselves, that is, I think the Portuguese know they occupy one small space, so to speak, of the world's territory and, at the same time, they are aware that they did something that they can't quite define. And one thing that characterizes us is a sort of fear of looking ourselves in the mirror, I think we are ill put before ourselves, we don't know very well who we are and we are afraid of knowing who we are. Mostly, I think we don't like *to theorize about ourselves* [my emphasis]" (46).

This impossibility or inability to theorize, to rationalize, the Portuguese identity is clearly consonant with the remarks of Manuela Ribeiro Sanches, in whose view this prudishness stems from an awareness, meek as it may be, of subalternity, which is anchored to the fixation and the concretization of the stages of Portugal's imagination of itself as a center, even if a minor center, when compared to the other European centers. According to Sanches, this subalternity locatable in the speech of the Portuguese identity is the explicit result of a continuous effort, of a search, and, simultaneously, of a denial between being hybrid and being European, between being a mestizo culture and attempting to disguise the idea, as Lídia Jorge writes, that we "do not transport a superior culture, and, if we can put it this way, a cultivated culture, and this is bad for us. I mean, it is bad because we didn't elevate ourselves, and we didn't elevate the others, and by not doing so, with that fear, I mean, a kind of prudishness . . . I think we lost, precisely, that notion of perspective that makes one say 'I am a mixture' or 'I am not a mixture.' . . . But what the Portuguese do mostly is not wanting to be aware, not wanting to rationalize who they are. . . ." (Khan 47).

Along the same lines, Sanches expresses her thought based on two vectors of Portuguese identification:

> There is a very curious moment going on here, a certain ambivalence, which is, on the one hand, [that] we [are] wanting to be hybrid but in certain contexts we don't, we want to become European. But what is it to become European? To become European is, many times, as well, also to abandon what we think is the delay, the living in another time, stop being primitive, become whiter. Of course here the whiteness I refer to is, let us say, metaphorical. And so it is very complicated, because, often, we think, "How can Portugality be defined?" It cannot be defined as mestizo. It can be defined as an heir of the discoveries, as the people who gave the world new worlds, hence, the Portuguese expansion, a word that keeps being used in a more generous mission, that is milder, theoretically, than other colonial stories. I think it is a complicated issue in Portugal. (47)

A reading that diverges from this twofold notion of Portuguese identity appears in the interview with the anthropologist João Pina Cabral, for whom Portugal can no longer be characterized though rhetoric that celebrates the past that is an heir of the discoveries and, in turn, the belief and imagery of a country that "gave new worlds to the world." Quite the contrary, he says, there is no space or cultural platform that allows a retrospective vision of the current Portuguese time, because "Portugal has reconstructed its identity, from the end of the eighties, as a European nation and, therefore, with a geostrategic position that is not compatible with the colonization efforts" (Khan 48). However, these colonization efforts continuously return within the postcolonial narrative, in the sense that, without that glorified past, there cannot be, according to the lawyer Adriano Malalane, the possibility for Portuguese identity to refine and retouch the image of itself before a Europe in which Portuguese society is still in a semiperipheral position, as well as a contrasting one. These contrasts issue from matters of economic, social, and cultural development and impel Portugal to inevitably reclaim and evoke its link, be it historical, cultural, or linguistic, with the colonized African territories—with the corresponding logic involving affections, continuities, and hybrid human experiences:

> There are moments in which Portugal turns toward Brazil, and it being a product of Portugal, the link is very strong. Then there are times in which

> Portugal forgets Brazil, and wants to turn toward other European countries, and then again it feels it isn't Europe, Portugal never assumes itself as a European country, for example, it never does. *It is interesting that Portugal, in my opinion, only assumes itself as a European country in its relationship with Africa, or with Brazil, in its relationship with the other European countries, Portugal is always out of Europe, it looks like a foreign body inside Europe. So I think Portugal hasn't found its identity yet* [my emphasis]. (Khan 49)

Rosa Cabecinhas, meanwhile, stresses an inclination to create nostalgic scenarios and to praise them according to an exponential rhetoric focusing on the contributions the Portuguese left to the people, on the gestures, on the common language, on the former colonial possessions:

> I think Portugal continues to have the structural problem of being, simultaneously, a center and a periphery. We continue to see ourselves as the center of a great empire, and I think that is still very much present. Even this nostalgia for Africa that we see in people nowadays, the Portuguese jet set stating it is going back there to cure a kind of homesickness, that kind of idealism from the time in which we were there . . . But people talk about Africa with a lot of nostalgia, a lot of idealism, and I ask myself—why is that? Is it the fascination of Africa or is it the fascination of our Africa, "our," in quotations. But, on the other hand, we have another reality as well, as a member of the European Union. And as a member of the European Union, we look at the statistics and we can't but feel depressed, right? And I think that is what explains that which many talk about regarding that manic-depressive character of the Portuguese mentality: we are either euphoric or depressive. It depends on whom we compare ourselves to: if we look at our ex-empire we even feel a little comforted because "we left and it became a whole lot worse than it was, so it means that, after all, we were doing something over there"; I see this speech over and over again. When we look at our European colleagues, we become depressed, we see the statistical data . . . *And, of course, we are always doing this back-and-forth motion, according to the group to whom we compare [ourselves]: this or that one* [my emphasis]. (49–50)

Prudishness, apprehension, fear of theorizing and rationalizing who we are, identity swings around a symbolic construction of a center—all these characteristics, assumed as historical deficiencies of the Portuguese society's self-gnosis, constitute a perfect menu for understanding what is postcoloniality "on the other side of the line." In fact, if postcoloniality "on this side of the line" offers us a heterogeneous and manifold portrait regarding what concerns the various precarious dynamics of the Portuguese identity, the other side of the line, on the contrary, can be reduced, for many interviewees, to a space that is homogeneous, silenced, and formed according to a criterion of an abyssal epistemological line, in which the Other ceases to have specific cultural and social characteristics, where the postcolonial differences remain heirs of the coloniality of power, of being and of knowing (and here I recall Walter Mignolo's 2000 and 2007 reflections on *colonial differences*), and where there is no visibility or dialogue on other side of the line, but just the need to strategically absorb the Other as a way of building invisible social walls that, however, are dialogically and historically insurmountable. This side of the line is not only the other face of postimperiality/postcoloniality but also of a postimperiality/postcoloniality that idly creates itself, as the journalist Seixas remarks, an introverted and restrictive window in its vision of the copresence of other human landscapes, other cosmologies, other narratives that are, in fact, a part of the Portuguese postcolonial tissue (Khan 2006). In that sense, according to Seixas, we are speaking about a look that is not outward but rather inward: from a "window [which] didn't open, but not outward, it would be open inward and it hasn't yet. Because we need to know how to look inward so that we can, afterward, be completely and fully in the outside. I think we don't know how to look at ourselves. And we can't, without understanding our own core, get to the core of others" (Khan 51). To many individuals with whom I talked and reflected on the social and cultural landscape of the postcolonial/postimperial Portuguese context, the search for a new identity narrative after decolonization and the influx of immigration from the former colonies has been accompanied, undoubtedly, by a lack of interest in recognizing, on the one hand, these African Others and, on the other—and I repeat—of accepting them as subjects of the Portuguese African experience and as sources of other knowledges, theorizations, and historical and cultural explanations that legitimately merit a space to be heard in the interest of a just historicity of Portuguese society, from both a synchronic and a diachronic point of view.

Finally, and as a conclusion, this paper has tried to be a polyphonic narrative to which I invited not only people from the "South" but also thinkers and researchers of Portuguese postimperiality/postcoloniality. After all, the South of this journey of mine is still just around the corner, but this project concerns a South that I tried to listen to, and to learn from, with new ways of looking at the landscape of this everyday life that belongs to all those who are a part of Portuguese history and who are not unwritten pages but rather human pages to be read and imprinted on our minds and ways of living. The answer to the central question of my postdoctoral manuscript—if I may restate it, "People from the 'South' Right around the Corner"—lies, I think, in the encounter and recognition of other narratives and other knowledges that will indeed complete the puzzle of Portuguese historicity, because, as the postcolonial studies scholar Manuela Ribeiro Sanches puts it:

> It is not just the work of mourning. It is, as well, to know that the memories are not only our own, they are the memories of all the others that we still don't know how to listen to. Because the question, as it is usually said in postcolonial studies, is not only knowing if the subordinate can speak, the question is also whether we are willing to listen. I also think that sometimes we are so worried about our own mourning, with our own stories, with our war, which is normal, that sometimes we forget a little about the other stories that are still to be told. I mean, I don't really know what postcolonial Portugal is, but it has to be this constant questioning. . . . (Khan, 126)

NOTES

1. In this list of publications on the return, the following titles can be pointed out: António Lobo Antunes's novel *As Naus* (2002), which in my opinion inaugurates this narrative urgency of breaking public forgetfulness regarding the painful return process, accompanied more recently by Margarida Paredes, *O Tibete de África* (2006); Júlio Magalhães, *Os retornados* (2008); António Trabulo, *Os Retornados—O Adeus a África* (2009); Manuel Acácio, *Balada do Ultramar* (2009); Leonel Cosme, *O Chão das Raízes* (2009); Isabela Figueiredo, *Caderno de Memórias Coloniais* (2009); Aida Gomes, *Os Pretos de Pousaflores* (2011), and, finally, Dulce Maria Cardoso, *O Retorno* (2011).

2. It is important to refer to the three novels that allow us to enter the space of the colonial-Other in the postcolonial/postimperial period: Lídia Jorge, *O Vento Assobiando nas Gruas* (2002); Joaquim Arena, *A Verdade de Chindo Luz* (2006); and Raquel Ochoa, *A Casa-Comboio* (2010).

3. This book was a result of my postdoctoral project, originally titled *African Mozambican Immigrants in the Former "Motherland": The Portrait of a Postcolonial Portugal*. This manuscript of the book, finished in 2011, has been submitted to the Almedina publishing house under CES/Almedina.

4. This epistemological effort to "decolonize Europe" is not an isolated attempt, since other recent reflections have attempted to concretize this critical examination of the hegemony of Occidental thought (see Hountondji 2002; Encarnación 2010; Bhambra 2010; Cassano 2010; Mignolo 2011). In the wider frame of present research, other proposals have been put forth concerning an operational plurality of designations, such as "epistemologias do Sul" (Santos and Meneses 2010), "epistemic disobedience" (Mignolo 2009), "Southern theory" (Connell 2007), "subaltern global sociology" (Burawoy 2008), "provincializing Europe" (Chakrabarty 2000), and "decolonizing methodologies" (Smith 1999).

WORKS CITED

Antunes, António Lobo. *O Meu Nome é Legião*. Lisbon: Publicações Dom Quixote, 2007.

Bhambra, Gurminder K. "Sociology after Postcolonialism: Provincialized Cosmopolitanisms and Connected Sociologies." In *Decolonizing European Sociology: Transdisciplinary Approaches*, edited by E. Gutiérrez Rodríguez, M. Boatca, and S. Costa (UK: Ashgate, 2010), 33–47.

Burawoy, M. "Rejoinder: For a Subaltern Global Sociology." *Current Sociology* 56, 3 (2008): 435–44.

Cassano, F. "South of Every North." In *Decolonizing European Sociology: Transdisciplinary Approaches*, edited by E. Gutiérrez Rodríguez, M. Boatca, and S. Costa (UK: Ashgate, 2010), 213–24.

Chakrabarty, D. *Provincializing Europe: Postcolonial Thought and Historical Difference*. Princeton, NJ: Princeton University Press, 2000.

Connell, Raewyn. *Southern Theory*. UK: Polity Press, 2007.

Cruzeiro, Maria Manuela. "As Mulheres e a Guerra Colonial: Um silêncio demasiado ruidoso" *Revista Crítica de Ciências Sociais* 68 (April 2004): 31–41.

Fonseca, Ana Margarida. "O meu nome é solidão: Representações da pós-colonialidade na ficção de Lobo Antunes." *VI Congresso Nacional Associação Portuguesa de Literatura Comparada / X Colóquio de Outono Comemorativo das Vanguardas*, pp. 1–17 (Universidade do Minho, 2009/2010), accessed July 18, 2010, from http://ceh.ilch.uminho.pt/Pub_Ana_Fonseca.pdf.

Hountondji, Paulin J. *The Struggle for Meaning: Reflections on Philosophy, Culture and Democracy in Africa* (Athens: Ohio University Press, 2002).

———. "Knowledge Appropriation in a post-Colonial Context." In *Indigenous Knowledge and the Integration of Knowledge Systems*, edited by Catherine A. Odora Hoppers (South Africa: New Africa Books, 2002), 23–38.

Khan, Sheila. "Identidades sem chão: Imigrantes Afro-Moçambicanos: Narrativas de Vida e Identidade, e Percepções de um Portugal pós-colonial." *Luso-Brazilian Review* 43, no. 2 (2006): 1–26.

———. *Imigrantes Africanos Moçambicanos: Narrativa de Imigração e de Identidade e Estratégias de Aculturação em Portugal e na Inglaterra*. Lisbon: Editora Colibri, 2009.

———. "O 'Sul' mesmo aqui ao lado: Cartografias Identitárias Abissais do Pós-Colonialismo Português." In *Intersecções Identitárias*, edited by Ana Maria Brandão and Emília Rodrigues Araújo. Famalicão: Ediçóes Húmus, 2011a. 49–64.

———. *Portugal híbrido, Portugal europeu? Gentes do "Sul" mesmo aqui ao lado*. Manuscrito submetido a Coimbra: CES/Editora Almedina, 2011b.

Lander, Edgardo, ed. *La colonialidad del saber: Eurocentrismo y ciencias socials: Perspectivas latino-americanas*. Buenos Aires: CLACSO, 2000.

Levi, Primo. *O dever de memória*. Lisbon: Editora Cotovia, 2010.

Lourenço, Eduardo. *O Labirinto da Saudade*. Lisbon: Gradiva, 2001.

Maldonaldo-Torres, Nelson. "A topologia do ser e a geopolítica do conhecimento: Modernidade, império e colonialidade." *Revista Crítica de Ciências Sociais* 80 (March 2008): 71–114.

Mata, Inocência. "Estranhos em permanência: A negociação portuguesa na pós-colonialidade." *Portugal não é um país pequeno*, edited by Manuela Ribeiro Sanches. Lisbon: Edições Cotovia, 2006. 285–315.

Mignolo, Walter. *Local Histories/Global Designs: Coloniality, Subaltern Knowledges, and Border Thinking*. Princeton, NJ: Princeton University Press, 2000.

———. "Delinking." *Cultural Studies* 21, no. 2 (2007): 449–514.

———. "Epistemic Disobedience, Independent Thought and Decolonial Freedom." *Theory, Culture & Society* 26, nos. 7–8 (2009): 159–81.

———. *The Darker Side of Western Modernity: Global Futures, Decolonial Options*. Durham, NC: Duke University Press, 2011.

Quijano, Aníbal. "Modernidad, colonialidad y América Latina." *Neplanta—Views from South* 3 (2000): 533–80.

Ribeiro, Margarida Calafate. "Percursos Africanos: A Guerra Colonial na Literatura Pós–25 de Abril." *Portuguese Literary and Cultural Studies* 1 (Fall 1998): 125–52.

———. *Uma História de Regressos: Império, guerra colonial e pós-colonialismo*. Porto: Edições Afrontamento, 2004.

———. "O fim da história de regressos e o retorno a África: Leituras da Literatura contemporânea portuguesa." In *Itinerâncias: Percursos e Representações da Pós-Colonialidade*, edited by Elena Brugioni, Joana Passos, Andreia Sarabando, and Marie-Manuelle Silva. Famalicão: Editora Húmus, 2012. 89–99.

Santos, Boaventura de Sousa. "Para uma sociologia das ausências e uma sociologia das emergências." *Revista Crítica de Ciências Sociais* 63 (October 2002): 237–80.

———. "Para além do pensamento abissal: Das linhas globais a uma ecologia dos saberes." *Revista Crítica de Ciências Sociais* 78 (October 2007): 3–46.

———. "A filosofia à venda, a douta ignorância e aaposta de Pascal." *Revista Crítica de Ciências Sociais* 80 (March 2008): 11–43.

Santos, Boaventura de Sousa, and Maria Paula Meneses, eds. *Epistemologias do Sul.* Coimbra: Edições Almedina, 2010.

Schiwy, Freya, and Michael Ennis, eds. "Knowledge and the Known: Andean Perspectives on Capitalism and Epistemology." Special Dossier, *Neplanta—Views from South* 3, no. 1 (2002): 1–98.

Smith, Linda Tuhiwai. *Decolonizing Methodologies: Research and Indigenous Peoples.* London: Zed Books, 1999.

Walsh, Catherine, Freya Schiwy, and Santiago Cástro Gómez, eds. *Indisciplinar las ciencias sociales: Geopolíticas del conocimiento y colonialidad del poder: Perspectivas desde lo Andino.* Quito: Universidad Andina Simón Bolívar y Abya-Yala, 2002.

SHEILA KHAN is a researcher at the Centro de Investigação em Ciências Sociais (CICS), University of Minho. She received her PhD from the University of Warwick, Centre for Research in Ethnic Relations, did her master's degree at ISCTE, Lisbon, and finished her first degree in sociology at the University of Minho. Her research interests focus on postcolonialism (Mozambique and Portugal), African Mozambican immigrants in Portugal, the history and literature of Mozambique, life and identity narratives, memory, documentary, the epistemologies of the South, and decolonizing methodologies. She is the author of *Imigrantes Africanos Moçambicanos: Narrativa de Imigração e de Identidade e Estratégias de Aculturação em Portugal e na Inglaterra* (2009, Edições Colibri). She has also published articles and chapters in refereed journals and books dealing with her topics of specialty. She may be reached at sheilakhan31@gmail.com.

Reviews

JOÃO CABRAL DO NASCIMENTO.

Além-Mar: Poemeto épico que fez Joam Cabral do Nascimento para narrar a história tormentosa das caravelas que aportaram à Ilha do senhor Infante na madrugada do século XV.

> Living with the other, with the foreigner, confronts us with the possibility or not of *being an other*. It is not simply—humanistically—a matter of our being able to accept the other, but of *being in his place*, and this means to imagine and make oneself other for oneself. . . . Split identity, kaleidoscope of identities: can we be a saga for ourselves without being considered mad or fake?
> —Julia Kristeva, *Stranger to Ourselves*, pp. 13–14

> We also view cultural memorization as an activity occurring in the present, in which the past is continuously modified and redescribed even as it continues to shape the future.
> —Mieke Bal, *Acts of Memory*, p. vii

On May 15, 1917, under the title "Perpetuando uma data: A descoberta da Madeira" (Perpetuating a Date: The Discovery of Madeira), the *Diário da Madeira*, a local newspaper, published an article promoting the recent commemorative proposal put forward by João Augusto Pina to the Funchal District General Board (Junta Geral). The initiative was aimed at celebrating the 1420 arrival of the explorer Gonçalves Zarco to Madeira within a context in which the figure was already frequently referenced artistically on the island. From the perspective of João Pina, the historical event thus demanded a notable act of commemoration that should serve "as a lesson to all" that Madeira simply could not remain "in a disgraceful state of forgetfulness regarding this memorable date" (Anonymous 1917, 1). At the national level, this voyage "represent[ed] . . . the audacious beginning of *our* [the Portuguese] maritime golden era" (Anonymous 1917, 1), and at the archipelago level it provided *the* founding moment of Madeira as a community and hence deserved to be present within the "spirit of all Madeirans in a very particular fashion" (Anonymous 1917, 1).

In truth, the project proposed by João Pina incorporated a clear literary challenge to the island's intellectual community in calling for the production of "a literary work, of a historical character, but with a popular aspect and primarily designed for the less learned classes . . . in order to turn this work into an abundant repository of information and news that may be of particular interest to all" (Anonymous 1917, 1). On Madeira in May 1917, literature was thus understood as an effective and necessary *place of memory*; a cultural and artistic phenomenon that might significantly contribute toward the reconstruction of the symbolical-identity of the nation, with *nation* here understood in generic terms as a community endowed with a shared consciousness of identity. This is a symbolical-identity (re)construction that, as Maria José Canelo (2001) so appropriately points out, coexists with (and sometimes even preexists) the political-administrative and institutional (re)construction of the same nation.

In referring here to *places of memory*, we clearly draw upon the concept put forward by Pierre Nora (1989), who defines *lieux de mémoire* as places crystallizing the collective memory of the nation. According to this French historian, the process of creating these *lieux de mémoire* seeks very precisely to ensure the (re)connection of a community's present with a past that should not or cannot be forgotten on pain of jeopardizing the sociocultural and even political cohesion and survival of the group in question in the present and into the future. This is a danger that, also according to Nora (1989, 7), has grown more acute in modern societies (above all, those especially exposed to processes of modernization and globalization) and where history and its archives have been substituted for the traditional organic memory of the past.

Indeed, as Paul Ricoeur so well notes (Ricoeur 2006, 10), the creation of *lieux de memoire* does not annul the awareness of the inevitable dangers of cultural amnesia, whether such is determined by the pact of vertiginous modern life and the fluidity of its values or by the conflicts and traumas of a diverse nature that were, in truth, experienced by the European, Portuguese, and Madeiran societies in the 1910s: namely, World War I; internal political conflicts aggravated during the first Portuguese republic; and social and economic-financial crises. And we should certainly not overlook how, in Madeira, the precariousness inherent in international warfare and internal political conflict would bring about the decline of the Port of Funchal, thus worsening the prevalent conditions of poverty, hunger, and disease. This furthermore condemned the island to the anguish of isolation and abandonment, a situation punctuated by the December 1916 and 1917 German torpedo attacks on Funchal.

These last events, irrespective of the Atlantic isolation and the physical distance between the archipelago and the mainland, where these conflicts were open and ongoing, illustrate how the *local* reality of Madeira, far from actually corresponding to some image of an *Atlantic Eden cut off from the rest of the world* (an image put forward as an *ufanismo* in romantic eighteenth- and nineteenth-century travel literature and especially among English-language writers and in tourism marketing campaigns, particularly those run by British companies with economic interests in the island), was never actually cut off from the cross-border social, political, economic, and cultural trends taking place on a more global scale.

However, we note that Mieke Bal (1999), who reconceptualizes the *lieux de mémoire* as *acts of memory*, highlights that these "acts of memory are performed by individuals in a cultural framework that encourages these acts" either because the subjects engaged in them (for whatever personal or collective reason) feel that these acts of memory "were much needed" (Bal, 1999, xiii) or because "each act of memory [really is] a projection of desire, of political agency, and of erasure" (xiv–xv).

Within this conceptual and contextual framework, we seek to interpret as a place of memory *Além-Mar*, an epic short poem written in 1916 and published in February 1917 by Cabral do Nascimento, a Madeiran intellectual of Luso-British and Jewish origins.

We would here highlight the apparent oddity behind the fact that João Pina, in presenting his commemorative project to the Funchal Council, made no reference to the poem by Nascimento, published a few months earlier and subject to widespread comment in the Madeiran press. We would consider that the explanation for this silence includes the differentiated approaches held by the two thinkers regarding Madeiran identity and its respective relationships, whether with the Portuguese nation-state or with other communities.

The heroic commemorations planned by João Pina verged on positions adopted by other Madeiran intellectuals who (monarchists or republicans) understood Madeira as a *glorious feat* of the Portuguese and as the *Lusitanian daughter* of Zarco. They correspondingly strove to erase from the local collective memory any contribution from other cultures and peoples to the societal formation and cultural identity of the archipelago. Indeed, they took up a line of identity thinking very close to the ethnically homogenizing exclusive nationalism identified by Sérgio Campos Matos as a dominant trend in the discourse on the nation and much promoted in Portugal throughout the period of the first Portuguese republic (Matos, 2002).

This perspective opened up clear distance with the ancestral Madeiran cultural imaginary that could not break with the strong British presence and influence in Madeira from the eighteenth century onward. We refer here to the story of the British pair—Ana d'Arfet and Roberto Machim—whom legend labeled as the first inhabitants on the island. This imaginary was deeply rooted in the island's cultural memory, circulated through both popular culture and literature.[1]

An interesting contrast with the identity discourse driven by exclusivist nationalism is the story "Portugal and Britain: What Does the Alliance Represent?" published in the *Diário da Madeira* in the immediate aftermath of the German declaration of war on Portugal.[2] This article (among other significant texts in the press) clearly states the need felt in Madeira to highlight the British commitment to defending Portuguese territory whenever it was threatened by any enemy, including during the Napoleonic campaigns when British troops twice occupied the archipelago. Furthermore, in 1916, British involvement was forecast as a likely future outcome given the manifest incapacity and lack of interest of the Portuguese republic in meeting the demands, needs, or intentions of the island communities. Here we should remember that throughout the 1910s and 1920s, Madeira was labeled the "Portuguese Ireland."

Therefore, it should similarly be of little surprise that, running counter to the heroicizing and essentializing tendencies of exclusivist nationalism that dominated the Portuguese and Madeiran identity discourse of the period, the Luso-British Cabral do Nascimento chose to poetically rewrite the history of the settling of the island.

In fact, *Além-Mar* restores the figure of Zarco and the "tormented history of the Caravels who dropped anchor off 'Ilha do Senhor Infante' in the early years of the 15th century" (Nascimento 1917, cover). Nevertheless, the work takes on a tone of *countermemory*, stripping both its lead figure and his history of the heroic air that others attribute to them. Additionally, in dialogue with the aforementioned literary and popular tradition, Cabral do Nascimento granted the British Roberto Machim and Ana d'Arfet the status of the first inhabitants of Madeira and attributed his Zarco with the mission of seeking out a "divine" and "dreamed after" island where it would be possible to engage in *dialogue with and learn* the history of these first and non-Portuguese inhabitants (Nascimento 1917, 8).

This is precisely the point where Nascimento deconstructs the heroics of Zarco, rewriting the narrative of his voyage of discovery. The island initially dreamed of and sought after by Zarco corresponds to an updated version of Paradise; an island haven for those fleeing the despair and desolation left behind on the "promontory said to be Sagres" (Nascimento 1917, 5), this symbolic place readable as a synecdoche for continental Portugal or contemporary Europe itself. Nevertheless, at the end of the poem, the island spotted by Nascimento's antihero corresponds instead to (and only to) an island of "sad anguish" (1917, 10), the island of the dead where Portuguese arrivals only briefly encounter the shadows of these British *others*; an island where, in fact, it is no longer viable to reestablish any homogeneous identity unit that is anything but stable or not disturbing.

We thus find that it was against this homogenizing, glorifying, and heroic discourse on identity produced by both the Portuguese state and the dominant sectors of Madeiran intellectuals that Cabral do Nascimento questioned the idea of the modern nation, established in the wake of the expansionist movement out over the Atlantic, as well as reflecting on the identity profiles possible within these modern nations exposed to instability, fluidity, heterogeneity, and conflicts of value that, above all, derived from human mobility between nations and cultures.

More than conceiving of Madeiran cultural identity as a *pure sample* of a supposed homogenous "Portugalidade," installed on the island, ab initio, with the arrival of Zarco, Nascimento understood the construction of the Madeiran nation, both in *Além-mar* and other later texts, as a tensional and transnational process, generating a heterogeneous and fragmentary identity profile, undergoing constant reelaboration.

Madeira, to Nascimento, while remaining Portuguese, simply could not ignore the problematic but unquestionably *inclusive differentiation* (as put forth by Ulrich Beck 2007) in relation to Portugal. This representation of the island would certainly not have struck him as odd, either in terms of his family genealogy or his island and mainland experience. Nascimento was a Portuguese citizen from Madeira with nonexclusively Portuguese lineage and, whether in Lisbon or in Funchal, perceived himself as different/differentiated in relation to the *others* with whom he partially identified and shared a certain sense of identity.

Nevertheless, in the case of this Madeiran intellectual, the nostalgia of the absolute (which, I would argue, underlies this way of conceiving the nation and, to a great extent, would seem to derive from a modern crisis experienced by a fragmentary *self* that finds itself prevented from any single and absolute center) never took on the "restorative" character that Svetlana Boym attributes to a certain nostalgic experience (Boym 2001, 41). Far from any idyllic Atlantic Paradise, or even an island on which all cultures somehow harmoniously coexist, Madeira is represented deceptively in the work of Nascimento as an illusory island: an apparent Paradise where, in truth, only death and despair are encountered as well as the fragmentary ruin of that perfect whole dreamed. In this representation of an unnamed island (identifiable as Madeira but also, due to the anonymity that it is presented with, with the contemporary world of the poet), Portugal and Great Britain appropriately take on this profile of the disconnected fragments of Madeiran identity, that of the *other-selves*, paradoxically strange and familiar within the cultural identity that Nascimento reconstructs *in* and *of* Madeira.

NOTES

1. See Frutuoso 1998; Tomás 1635; Melo 1975; Medina e Vasconcelos 1806; Gouveia 1907.

2. March 9, 1916—the date of the German declaration of war on Portugal; March 28, 1916—the publication date of "Portugal and Britain: What Does the Alliance Represent?"

WORKS CITED

Bal, Mieke. "Introduction." In *Acts of Memory: Cultural Recall in the Present*, edited by Mieke Bal, Jonathan Crewe, and Leo Spitzer. Hanover, NH: University Press of New England, 1999. vii–xv.

Beck, Ulrich. *The Cosmopolitan Vision*. Cambridge, UK: Polity Press, 2006 [2004].

Boym, Svetlana. *The Future of Nostalgia*. New York: Basic Books, 2001.

Canelo, Maria José. "Nações em revista(s)." In *Entre ser e estar: Raízes, percursos e discursos da identidade*, edited by Maria Irena Ramalho and António Sousa Ribeiro. Porto: Ed. Afrontamento, 2001. 437–72.

Fernandes, Maurício. "Inaugura-se uma estátua." *Atlântico: Revista de temas culturais* 3 (Fall 1985): 225–28.

Frutuoso, Gaspar. Section XVI of *Saudades da terra*. 1998. Accessed August 15, 2008, from http://www.azoreangenealogy.com.

Gouveia, João. *Atlante: Tragédia d'alma*. Lisbon: Typographia Francisco Luiz Gonçalves, 1907 [1903].

Kristeva, Julia. *Stranger to Ourselves*, translated by Leon S. Roudiez. New York: Columbia University Press, 1991.

Matos, Sérgio Campos. "História e identidade nacional: A formação de Portugal na historiografia contemporânea." *Lusotopie*. Paris: Karthala, 2002. 123–29.

Medina e Vasconcelos, Francisco de Paula. *Zargueida: Descobrimento da Madeira*. Lisbon: Officina Simão Taddeo Fernandes, 1806.

Melo, Dom Francisco Manuel de. *Epanáfora Amorosa: Descobrimento da ilha da Madeira: Ano 1420: A lenda e a história acerca do par amoroso*. Braga: J. Castro, 1975 [1654].

Nascimento, João Cabral do. *Além-Mar: Poemeto épico que fez Joam Cabral do Nascimento para narrar a história tormentosa das caravelas que aportaram à Ilha do senhor Infante na madrugada do século XV*. Lisbon: Livraria Brazileira, 1917.

Nora, Pierre. "Between Memory and History: *Les lieux de mémoire*." *Representations* 26 (Spring 1989): 7–25.

Pita, Gabriel de Jesus. "Decadência e queda da Primeira República analisada na imprensa madeirense da época (1924–1926)." *Atlântico: Revista de temas culturais* 3 (Fall 1985): 194–208.

Ricoeur, Paul. "Memory—Forgetting—History." *Meaning and Representation in History*, edited by Jörn Rüsen. New York: Berghahn Books, 2006. 9–19.

Tomás, Manuel. *Insulana*. Amberes: Caza de Ioam Mevrsio Impressor, 1635.

Veríssimo, Nelson. "Em 1917, a Madeira reclama autonomia." *Atlântico: Revista de temas culturais* 3 (Fall 1985): 229–32.

———. "O alargamento da autonomia dos distritos insulares, o debate na Madeira (1922–1923)." *Actas do II colóquio internacional de História da Madeira*. Coimbra: CNCDP, 1990. 493–515.

ANA SALGUEIRO RODRIGUES is a PhD candidate at Estudos de Cultura (Faculdade de Ciências Humanas—Universidade Católica Portuguesa). She may be reached at asalgueirorodrigues@sapo.pt.

CHATARINA EDFELDT.

Uma história na História: Representações da autoria feminina na História da Literatura Portuguesa do século XX.

Our only duty to history is to rewrite it.
—Oscar Wilde

The quotation I have chosen to start this review certainly applies to a text written by Chatarina Edfeldt, a Portuguese, Brazilian, and African literature professor with a gender, postcolonial, and queer perspective at Stockholm University. As is indicated by the title, *Uma história na História*, her aim is to analyze "o motivo pelo qual as escritoras e respectiva expressão literária têm tido tantas dificuldades em conseguir reconhecimento e consagração nas obras da História da Literatura Portuguesa" (Edfeldt 2006, 19).[1] This shows the necessity of rewriting traditional literary history in order to include the important—although practically invisible—contribution of women in Portuguese literature.

With a well-structured text, she has justified her research claiming the emergence of studies on the exclusion and marginalization of feminine authorship since the 1970s. In this way, she identifies a gap whereby the national literary canon contributes to the invisibility of feminine authorship. According to Edfeldt, this comes from "accumulated errors" and "vicious language and methodology" that need to be reviewed in the contemporary context, and it has increasing interest for questions related to the politics of identity and democracy. The scientific perspective, in this case literary historiography, must question prejudices related to women in the national literary discourse. In other words, Edfeldt has showed the necessity of narrating and recognizing the important role played by women writers, despite the sexual biases built in to our society. She makes this argument on both political and scientific grounds, understanding that history, while perhaps seeming neutral, is subject to dominant rules and ideologies.

The specific problem in literary histories, as Edfeldt points out, comes from the traditional way in which this knowledge is constructed. Generally, the new literary histories rely on what has already been written about literature, reproducing antiquated points of view. The necessity of including women writers is related to the practical importance of literary histories, which are a principal tool in teaching. If syllabi of schools and universities only include canonized works and writers, women writers must be welcomed into this canon. The memory of these works, and these narratives, cannot be lost to future generations. This, in turn, explains the necessity of rewriting literary historiography.

A main focus of Edfeldt's work, in my understanding, is on forces that have contributed to the negligence, marginalization, and exclusion of women writers in literary discourse. That is, she covers not only the importance of including women writers in the national canon, but she has also exposed the strategies used in official discourse that neutralize the feminine contribution. For the corpus, she has selected works that construct a historical narrative of twentieth-century Portuguese literature: "o corpus do presente estudo é constituído por obras que têm como objectivo historiar e construir o discurso da História da Literatura Portuguesa durante o século XX. Assim, incluem obras dos gêneros: história literária narrativa e enciclopédia (dicionários) sobre a literatura e/ou os autores portugueses. Além disso, incluíram-se algumas obras-síntese mais resumidas, de carácter narrativo, por ser um gênero histórico-literário de fácil acesso aos estudantes"[2] (Edfeldt 2006, 32).

Edfeldt has analyzed the structure and organization in these narratives alongside images they reproduce about literature written by women, with particular attention to rhetorical and strategic elements used in the dominant discourse. From this perspective, the study takes a qualitative and historical perspective on important notions such as *women writers* and *women*.

In the first chapter, in addition to the introductory explanation and justification, the author presents her main hypotheses as follows: "Uma constante preocupação com a identidade de gênero do(a) autor(a) se torna decisiva na categorização e organização das histórias literárias. A identidade de gênero da escritora está marcado no discurso historiográfico com tal intensidade que é responsável pela marginalização da sua escrita no mesmo discurso. . . . Numa segunda hipótese, sugere-se que na organização tradicional das histórias literárias a autoria masculina está relacionada directamente com as *correntes literárias*, ao passo que a autoria feminina dificilmente faz parte destas 'narrativas'"[3] (Edfeldt 2006, 29).

Another hypothesis, related to the second one, is that women writers appear as "isolated islands" in literary histories because they are not portrayed as integral and contributing to literary knowledge. In part because they are not considered participants in official discourse on literature, they are banished from the dominant narrative.

The fourth hypothesis contends that this marginalization is related to political and traditional forces, and not to women's artistic ability. In other words, there are qualified women writers who are absent from literary history because of prejudice and political biases propagated without attention and reflection.

Edfeldt has organized her book in an easy and usefully instructive way. Each of the seven chapters has its own delimited objective and explanation, divided into sections in which she develops her main ideas. Identifying and examining her arguments poses no difficulty, as with her analyses about the corpus, discussed earlier. This organization helps the reader understand her point of view as well as illustrating the author's brilliant efforts to reveal how women have been excluded from literary discourse in the past.

To summarize, the first chapter shows her hypotheses, corpus, and central ideas. In the second chapter, she presents the theoretical and methodological framework behind her research—incorporating the theories and concepts of gender studies, critical discourse analysis, and discourse theory, as subjected to a social constructionist scientific perspective. She has used the deconstruction method, interpreting literary historiography as an institutional discourse. Understanding reality as a social construction, she invokes the following important concepts (and their thinkers): Stuart Hall on representation; Foucault on discourse; contingency and questions of power; subject and subject position; antagonism, objectivity, and hegemony; the category *gender* and the image of women as constructed in the literary field; and so on.

Chapers 3 to 7 correspond to the various strategies used in the dominant historical-literary discourse to marginalize the expression of the Other. Thus, the third chapter analyzes the discursive place given to feminine authorship. Notable here is how women were treated as separate from the main historical-literary discourse. In a sparkling evaluation of the corpus, the author shows how different structures used to write literary history deal with the feminine question in different ways. In this process, she compares the narrative and encyclopedic ways of writing historical-literary discourse. The main question of this chapter is why the texts produced by women were analyzed as separate from the official and hegemonic literary histories.

The fourth chapter considers representations of literature written by women before the 1950s. Before this decade, Edfeldt writes, explaining her periodization, the absence of contextualization for women's writing creates a glaring omission. The objective of this chapter is to show that this negligence occurred for political reasons. Women were related to the traditional, private sphere, which was seen as incompatible with the mainstream concepts related to literature.

In the fifth chapter, the author approaches the constructed incompatibility between feminine authorship and literary schools. The focus is on factors in the dominant culture that have restricted women's participation in the institutional literary discourse, investigating the relation between feminine authorship and the evolution of larger forces in the historical-literary discourse.

The sixth chapter emphasizes that literature written by women is not honored with a well-organized genealogy in the historical-literary discourse. According to the author, the associated problem is that knowledge constructed about literature generally is based in the genealogies of literary schools and periods. If feminine authorship does not appear in such categories, women are, in effect, not acknowledged as authors of literature at all. Indeed, this omission comes from the tradition of setting feminine authorship outside the official narrative.

The seventh and last chapter, related to the previous chapter's emphasis on politics, feminism, and feminine authorship, analyzes the ways in which the discourse deals with and represents the terms *feminine*, *emancipated*, and *feminist*. It likewise analyzes how these characterizations interact in the historical-literary discourse, presenting examples of how literature written by women has been understood throughout history.

The book also includes an appendix, which lists women writers banished from the official literary-historical discourse. These details are interesting, even if not central to the research, and they prove the existence of these forgotten women writers.

Uma história na História is an interesting book for helping us understand the need to recast literary history. It shows how we must focus on our constructed memory of the literary past, despite all the critiques applied to history. There are voices who need to be listened to and represented as historical agents. As Edfeldt affirms, it is easier to reproduce traditional approaches to and definitions of literary-historical discourse than to rethink the presuppositions that structure this knowledge. Even as some authors, such as David Perkins, have affirmed the end of literary history, Edfeldt has shown how this knowledge is useful.

Other important issues covered in the book are related to the production of historical knowledge. It seems a paradox that "cuanto más urgentes los reclamos de representación histórica, más se ponen en duda los instrumentos y los recursos para llevar a cabo dicha historización"[4] (Tozzi 2009, 169). However, to understand history and literary history as a discourse that presents or represents reality requires questioning this knowledge in two interrelated ways: epistemic and political. The emergence of different voices in literary history can be seen as a means to question the epistemological presuppotions of traditional literary-historical discourse. And both aspects are implied in the necessity of rewriting literary history.

Reading Edfeldt's book prompts questions in the reader. She has contended that the marginalization of feminine authorship comes from the traditional way of writing literary history. In this sense, it seems important to rethink this traditional approach. That is, it is necessary to rethink not just the position of women in literary history but also the way related knowledge is produced. As she affirms, it is easier to create an appendix to insert the contemporaneous issues in the writing of literary history. However, given the political and epistemic issues raised in the book, it is practically impossible to continue writing literary history as it has been written up until now. All history is the history of the present and responds to the questions important to a determined context.

Another question, regarding the author's discussion of "feminine authorship," is the necessity of caution in order not to homogenize women into an essential core. Thinking about feminine identity implies a preoccupation with the fluidity and flexibility of this identity. And historical changes paired with this fluidity and flexibility, we must remember, have made possible the emergence of feminine voices. Literary historians must therefore keep in mind that they construct their object of knowledge by viewing the literary past through their own lenses of theory and methodology. And, in this sense, it is necessary to think about the concept of women who pass through such constructed literary history.

Even with these questions, Chatarina Edfeldt has produced a relevant analysis on the history of Portuguese literature. Her preoccupation with primary sources, examined with special attention, helps us understand the strategies of dominant discourse that have marginalized feminine authorship. This work may thus help guide future scholars away from making the same (sometimes vicious) mistakes that, in the past, have been reproduced without consideration.

Other histories with other voices are necessary. Writing such books is our only duty to (literary) history.

NOTES

1. [T]he reason women writers and their respective literary expression have struggled so much to achieve recognition and praise in works of Portuguese literary history [my translation].

2. The corpus of the present study is constituted by works that have as their objective to create a history and construct a discourse of Portuguese literary history during the twentieth century. This includes works of the following genres: narrative literary history and encyclopedias (dictionaries) about literature and/or the Portuguese authors. Therefore, it includes some synthetic works resembling summaries, of a narrative character, to make the literary-historical genre easier for students to access [my translation].

3. A constant preoccupation with the identity of the author's genre becomes decisive in the categorization and organization of literary histories. The genre identity of the woman writer is marked in the historiographic discourse with such intensity that it is responsible for the marginalization of its writing in the same discourse. . . . A second hypothesis suggests that in the traditional organization of literary histories masculine authorship is related directly to the literary school, whereas feminine authorship hardly takes part in these "narratives" [my translation].

4. [T]he more urgent the claims of historical representation, the more they put in doubt the tools and resources to carry out such historicization [my translation].

WORKS CITED

Edfeldt, Chatarina. *Uma história na História: Representações da autoria feminina na História da Literatura Portuguesa do século XX*. Montijo: Câmara Municipal Montijo, 2006.

Tozzi, Verónica. *La historia según la nueva filosofía de la historia*. Buenos Aires: Prometeu libros, 2009.

ALINE DE ALMEIDA MOURA holds a master's degree in literature, culture, and contemporaneity from the Pontifical Catholic University of Rio de Janeiro. She holds graduate degrees in history from the Universidade Federal Fluminense (2011) and in literature from the State University of Rio de Janeiro (2010). In her scholarship, she analyzes the conceptual foundations of literary studies, considering their various historical forms. She also studies the historical dimensions of literature, regarding their textual and institutional aspects, focusing on literary history. Her latest publications are "Novos realismos na contemporaneidade: A escrita de história" (2011) and "O real em Mia Couto" (2010). She may be reached at alineamoura@yahoo.com.br.

A. M. PIRES CABRAL.
Artes Marginais; Antes que o Rio Seque; Arado.

In creating his poetic work, António Manuel Pires Cabral soon directed his thematic and geographical compass toward the northeast of Portugal. Born in Trás-os-Montes (Macedo de Cavaleiros) in 1941, the poet began his compositions in those lands and never left them. In *Somewhere Northeast* (*Algures a Nordeste*), his 1974 debut, the title of which refers to an overvaluation of space, the author is keen to guide the reader in the demanding task of locating and decoding the lyrical discourse. And when reading the poem "Northeast," it becomes clear to us that this space will be much more than a reference or a poetic topos: "Whoever picks up the compass sees / eight directions of the world, / eight methods of being. / The eighth is the northeast"[1] (Pires Cabral 2006, 12). There is instead a method of being, or "soul," as Pires Cabral explained in an interview with Carlos Vaz Marques (*Ler* October 2008): "Between Trás-os-Montes, Beira Baixa and Alentejo I find something that I can't really explain, but that sometimes I define as a soul. They have a soul"[2] (Pires Cabral 2008, 34).

The poet's lyricism thus focuses on the soul of a people, in a country's interior, evoking all its underlying material and metaphysical elements. "His world is among those hills and vineyards, those shale stones and frosts"[3] ("Ípsilon," *Público*, April 4, 2009), as Pedro Mexia illustrates in commenting on Pires Cabral's latest poetic work—*Plow* (*Arado*) (2009)—and this rural and interior world constitutes the basis of an earthy and eschatological form of poetry. Since interiority means soil, "the sea doesn't mean anything to me. Indeed, what I do care about is the soil. Maybe interiority is what I like"[4] (Pires Cabral 2008, 34–35). Pires Cabral's poetry thereby outlines its main thematic axis, like a biblical elegy, in the natural cycle formed by the element of earth, the union of life and death.

Indeed, "Terra Mater"—the first poem in *Somewhere Northeast*—already shows the Orphic intent of a poet bent on descending to the world's depths, not to resurrect Euridice but rather to marry Demeter:

I descend to the ground. I invent the resistance
and the day song.

I recognize in the cry the easy, fraudulent
emotion.
Yet I still descend to earth
I dare cry:
Terra mater, painful urge to create,
bright secret of giving birth,
oh earth, I want you to sing![5] (Pires Cabral 2006, 9)

By giving voice to the earth and putting its fertility in verse, Pires Cabral, as a starting point, appears to draw from Miguel Torga, whose art heavily influenced his poetic lyricism:

I also want to open up and sow
A grain of poetry in your womb!
Everyone is plowing,
Everyone is burying rye,
And it's time now that I plant
The seed of the verses that I grow. (Torga, "Earth," *Iberian Poems*, 1952)

And this law of telluric force in creating and destroying matter, as revealed in Torga's verses—"Everyone is burying rye / And it's time now that I plant"—is what most fascinates Pires Cabral, as shown yet again in "Terra Mater":

. . . my grandparents rest
gently wrapped in you:
some flowers are also born of them,
some green-colored act
a friendly greeting
of perfume.[6] (Pires Cabral 2006, 10)

We are born from the earth and upon the earth we die, and death is to us, in the northeast of Portugal, often presented as "the last and bravest learning,"[7] because in that land "we do not die differently—just colder. / Hellenic women pour upon us / undeceived, livid cries. / Our friends canonize us, they remember things / of camaraderie and a lot of emotion. / We are in our house, soluble and unbelieving / boycotted, in solidarity with time."[8] (Pires Cabral 2006, 14). As has been implied, the dialectic between life and death seems to repeatedly populate the mind of the poet, together with a bucolic space metaphorically rich in poetic elements, such as the river, soil, flowers, bugs, vines, and olives. Underneath this dialectic, and in his poetic compositions, there is an emphasis on temporal distance: on the one hand, life appears to be associated with an unfinished past time by the use of verbal forms in the past continuous (*pretérito imperfeito simples do indicativo*); on the other hand, death is linked to the current moment through verbs in the present simple (*presente do indicativo*). Therefore, and because the northeast is at the same time synonymous with life and death, the poetic discourse, situated between these two temporal poles, often entails melancholy and languid subject matter in relation to finite time and unrecoverable life. If

On September 26, 1973
there was still life somewhere Northeast . . .
lizards all around
staining the surface of the stones in green
raised their dizzy and mocking heads
at the flight of horseflies
in the vineyard
the fallacious labors of the harvest. . . .
Oddly enough
on September 26, 1973
there was no chemistry
life still persisted somewhere Northeast.[9] (Pires Cabral 2006, 12–13)

Therefore:

Today the walls are collapsing gradually:
close to the ground where they were born.
As if it followed
An old memento: quia es petra
et in Petram reverteris.
It's a fact: the houses are not
the same reckless vocation
of eternity
plaguing their owners.[10] (Pires Cabral 2009, 19)

Nevertheless, and due to the mutation of time, not only had the houses collapsed—and the houses are a synecdoche for the wider rural environment—

but nature itself had followed the improper passage of *chronos*; the river Douro, greatly praised by the poet in *Douro: Pizzicato and Chula* (2004), signals the changing human and material landscape of an area once primitive and free:

> The river, they said, changed.
> Something got to him.
> He emigrated from the riverbed, overflowed
> forever.
> Neither bones nor skin remain.
> . . .
> The river
> is now—limited by walls—
> a new water, stout,
> but contradicted
> and slow, something that lingers
> between vocations: of lake,
> mirror or street.
> A river hostage
> of memories from a different generation:
> when he was a rush of anger
> taken as a dagger sheath
> or a stone thrown against glass.[11] (Pires Cabral 2006, 319)

Hence, the poetic subject feels betrayed by a reality that no longer seems to belong, "as if they had been removed / the eighth compass direction, / the one that pointed to a cleaner / North." (Pires Cabral 2009, 16), and reflection, as a disintegral portion of this surrounding environment, assumes the form of a syllepsis: "Up this river / down this man." . . ."Despite traveling up this river, after all, I travel down into myself." (Pires Cabral 2006, 349–350).

On the other hand, in this reflection, memory turns out to play the decisive role of safeguarding the idea of a soil that was fertile but is now sterile; thus the evoked reality is also, and essentially, inner and interiorized, existing only inside the poet. Paraphrasing from a section about *Somewhere Northeast* in Joaquim Manuel Magalhães's essay "On the Poetry of A. M. Pires Cabral," the truth is: "Reality is not the subject of this book. It is its engine. It accompanies the slow natural rhythms, the difficulty of change, makes use of rhetorical processes accompanying this slowness (such as the relative archaism of the pronoun 'you' ['vós'] in regard to those who read), and is related to variations on popular topics"[12] (Magalhães, as cited in Pires Cabral 1998, 162–63).

And it is precisely due to this interiorization of reality that the poet claims a "conflicting mortality in existing" ["conflituosa mortalidade de existir"] (Magalhães, as cited in Pires Cabral 1998, 164), because "In the soil / nothing is lost, everything is kept." ["Na terra / nada se perde, tudo se conserva."] (Pires Cabral 2006, 9). The rhetorical question presented by the poet in an elegy for his father is quite revealing of this existential paradox:

> Or should I ask instead
> exactly how many meals your flesh gives
> to the crowd without restraint of all those worms
> to whom your death
> is a miracle of bread?[13] (Pires Cabral 2006, 15)

From this point of view, the apparent degeneration of the old and rural *transmontano* world is no more than the realization of a simple way of life, a way of getting back to one's roots, of being reborn. Indeed, in *Plow*, the poet sings again of the motherland of his birth, exalting its perpetuity in giving life and becoming the fruit of his verses. In a clear allusion to the poem "Terra Mater"—"Well, *terra mater*, forget everything / I told you in immature times. / They were all verses of poor quality"[14] (Pires Cabral 2009, 14)—the poet returns in his latest work to a homonymous poetic composition, remembering that, despite the passage of time, the engine of his poetry remains intact, an image suggested by the excessive use of adverbs:

> It is still possible to see from here,
> from this place chopped up by winds,
> *terra mater*,
> Now only a residue of commotion,
> but, golly, it still hurts,
> still thrills.
> And still calls out,
> With its remaining voice,
> an almost mute and moribund plea. (Pires Cabral 2009 14)

The soil of Trás-os-Montes remains even today a source of inspiration for the poet, and in "Terra Mater" (from *Plow*), it is considered almost sacred:

I know now, after the hollow din
after all these lost decades,
that only with silence's key can I
still open a door in your olive oil body
and penetrate you as a temple.[15] (Pires Cabral 2009, 14)

This idea of the sacredness of the soil matches the words of Gastão Cruz in "Portuguese Poetry of the Twentieth and Twenty-first Centuries." According to this essayist and poet, A. M. Pires Cabral "has remained faithful to a poetic austerity, guided by a strong sense of linguistic restraint, to some extent along the lines of poetry that seeks its paradigm in the dryness of the soil"[16] (Cruz 2008, 367). From the highlands of the northeast of Portugal, the poet Pires Cabral has carved his best verses, which reflect the poet's mood. As a farmer who returns to his working instrument, the poet confesses himself, in *Plow*, to be faint and rusty but faithful to his destination, to the natural cycle of life and death, to his craft as a poet:

But the plow perpetuates itself in me.
In fact, in times of perilous exaltation,
I like to think of these verses as
a plow that tears other lands
more volatile and less arable,
I believe I leave in them some seed.
Pure illusion.
Neither such lands allow themselves to be torn apart
so easily
nor my plow has a vocation for life.
So I return to the plow
which actually plowed.[17] (Pires Cabral 2009, 13)

The semantic game between plow and poetry is evident, as Hugo Pinto Santos notes, since "Among the Romans, the verse referred to the action of the plow. . . . Through verses we reach the earth, a witness of the plundering of time"[18] (Santos, August 5, 2009). But we mustn't think that in *Plow*, a brilliant revisiting of his first book, Pires Cabral "repeats any telluric connection extracted from Torga or Pascoaes. . . . His modernity is precisely shown when, in dialoguing with lyric tradition, he assumes a tragedy that is all the more Portuguese than universal. Poetry arises in *Plow* under the symbol of the poet, tireless worker of his verses, he who prunes, he who waters, responsible for the flourishing of the poem"[19] (Cortez 2009, 23).

In conclusion, it can be stated that the soil, and, above all, that of the arid landscapes of Trás-os-Montes, is simultaneously the point of departure and arrival of all the poetry of Pires Cabral, who, in turn, does not reduce it to a simple theme or topos. His poetry closely identifies with the soil, and the poet's work is to keep plowing his verses, engaged in dialogue with others who have plowed, digging word by word until reaching his roots. Thus, in Eduardo Lourenço's words, poetry itself "is an expression of one's roots" ["é expressão de origens"] (Lourenço 1987, 29). In this case, taking into account *Plow,* "doing it again" means "continuing with the creation, and creating means being a poet. This means that there's nothing except Poetry to shape us"[20] (Lourenço 1987, 33).

NOTES

1. In the original: "Quem pega na bússola vê / oito direcções de mundo, / oito métodos de estar. / O oitavo é o nordeste" (Pires Cabral 2006, 12).

2. "Encontro entre Trás-os-Montes, a Beira Baixa e o Alentejo qualquer coisa que não sei o que é mas que eu defino às vezes como sendo *uma alma*. Têm uma alma" (Pires Cabral 2008, 34).

3. Ibid.: "O seu mundo são aqueles outeiros e vinhas, aqueles xistos e geadas" (Mexia, "Ípsilon," *Público*, April 4, 2009).

4. "Pires Cabral's poetry outlines, as if it were a biblical elegy, in the natural cycle proposed by the earth element, the binomial life/death, his main thematic axis" (Pires Cabral 2009, pp. 34–35).

5. "Desço à terra. Invento a resistência / e o cântico diurno. / Reconheço no pregão a fácil, fraudulenta / comoção. / Desço à terra ainda assim, / arrisco o grito: // Terra mater, ânsia dolorida de criar, / radioso segredo de parir, / ó terra, eu quero-te cantar!" (Pires Cabral 2006, 9).

6. " . . . em ti repousam / docemente embalados meus avós: / deles nasce também alguma flor, / algum gesto de cor verde, /alguma saudação amigável / de perfume" (Pires Cabral 2006, 10).

7. "a última e tão brava aprendizagem," a verse from the poem "A Morte" (Death), in *Algures a Nordeste* (*Somewhere Northeast*): "Do longo desamor dos dias escorridos / a última e tão brava aprendizagem / é a morte. Nela é que repousamos / sós e desamparados como feno apodrecido, / cheirosos e jacentes" (Pires Cabral 2006, 14).

8. " . . . não morremos diferente—tão somente mais frio. / Derramam-nos em cima

helénicas mulheres / desenganados, lívidos clamores. Os amigos canonizam-nos, recordam coisas / de camaradagem e muita comoção. / Estamos em nossa casa, solúveis e descrentes, / boicotados, solidários com o tempo" (Pires Cabral 2006, 14).

9. ". . . em 26 de Setembro de 1973 / ainda havia algures vida a Nordeste . . . // lagartos aqui e além / manchando de verde o rés das pedras / erguiam a cabeça tonta e zombeteira / ao voo dos moscardos // na vinha / as falazes canseiras da vindima. . . . // "por estranho que pareça / em 26 de Setembro de 1973 / a química não passava / a vida resistia a algures a Nordeste" (Pires Cabral 2006, 12–13).

10. "Hoje as paredes vão-se aos poucos derruindo: / aproximam-se do chão que nasceram. / Como se executasse nela / Um antigo memento: quia petra es / et in petram reverteris. // Está visto: as casas não têm / a mesma estouvada vocação / de eternidade / que atormenta os seus donos" (Pires Cabral 2009, 19).

11. From the anthology *Antes que o Río Seque* (2006): "O rio, responderam, alterou-se. / Subiu-lhe qualquer coisa à cabeça. / Emigrou do leito, transbordou / para todo o sempre. // E não resta dele osso / nem pele. / . . . // O rio / é agora—sujeitado por muros—/ uma água nova, corpulenta, / mas também contrariada / e morosa, coisa que hesita / entre vocações: de lago, / espelho ou estrada. / Um rio refém / das memórias de outra geração: / quando era um ímpeto de ira / como um punhal tirado da bainha / ou pedra arremessada contra vidro" (Pires Cabral 2006, 319).

12. "A realidade não é o tema deste livro. É o seu motor. Ele acompanha a lentidão dos ritmos naturais, a dificuldade das transformações, serve-se de processos retóricos acompanhantes dessa lentidão (como o relativo arcaísmo do pronome 'vós' com que se refere a quem lê), prende-se a variações sobre temas populares" (Magalhães, as cited in Pires Cabral 1998, 162–63).

13. "Ou será que devo antes perguntar / quantas refeições ao certo a tua carne dá / para a multidão sem freio de todos esses vermes / para quem a tua morte / é um milagre de pão?" (Pires Cabral 2006, 15).

14. "Pois bem: terra mater, esquece tudo / quanto te disse em tempos imaturos. / Eram tudo versos de má qualidade" (Pires Cabral 2009, 14).

15. "Sei hoje, ao cabo da balbúrdia oca / de todas estas décadas perdidas, / que só com a chave do silêncio posso / abrir ainda uma porta no teu corpo de azeite / e penetrar em ti como num templo" (Pires Cabral 2009, 14); Gastão Cruz, "Poesia Portuguesa dos séculos XX e XXI," in *A Vida da Poesia* (Lisbon: Assírio & Alvim, 2008), 361–67.

16. "[A. M. Pires Cabral] tem-se mantido fiel a uma poética de austeridade, norteada por um forte sentido de economia de linguagem, de algum modo na linha da poesia que procura na aridez da terra o seu paradigma" (Cruz 2008, 367).

17. "Mas o arado perpetua-se em mim. / De facto, em horas de arriscada exaltação, / gosto de pensar nestes versos como sendo / um arado com que rasgo outras terras / mais

voláteis e menos aráveis, / e nelas julgo deixar alguma semente. // Pura ilusão. / Nem as tais terras se deixam rasgar / assim facilmente, / nem o meu arado tem vocação de vida. // De modo que retorno ao arado / que de facto arou" (Pires Cabral 2009, 13).

18. "Entre Romanos, verso remetia para a acção de arado, que, findo o seu curso, torna ao mesmo tempo, por uma volta, versus. Por versos se chega à terra, testemunha da razia do tempo." See Hugo Pinto Santos, "Arado," http://www.rascunho.net/critica.php?id=1505.

19. "[A. M. Pires Cabral] repete qualquer ligação telúrica extraída dum qualquer Torga, ou Pascoaes . . . é moderno na medida exacta em que, dialogando com a tradição lírica, assume toda a tragédia que é tanto mais portuguesa do que universal. A poesia surge em *Arado* sob o símbolo do poeta, trabalhador incansável dos seus versos, aquele que poda, aquele que rega, o responsável pelo medrar do poema." See António Carlos Cortez, "Parábolas, palavra, poética," *JL* (June 3–16, 2009): 22–23.

20. " . . . é continuar a criação e criar é ser poeta. O que significa finalmente não ter outro senão o que a Poesia nos modelar" (Lourenço 1987, 33).

WORKS CITED

Cortez, António Carlos. "Parábolas, palavra, poética." *JL* (June 3–16, 2009): 22–23.

Cruz, Gastão. *A Vida da Poesia*. Lisbon: Assírio & Alvim, 2008.

Lourenço, Eduardo. *Tempo e Poesia*. Lisbon: Relógio d'Água Editores, 1987.

Marques, Carlos Vaz. "Hoje não é tempo de poetas laureados." *Ler*, no. 73 (October 2008): 28–39.

Mexia, Pedro. "Nordeste, parte dois." *Público* ("Ípsilon" supplement), April 4, 2009.

Pires Cabral, A. M. *Artes Marginais*. Lisbon: Guimarães Editores, 1998.

———. *Antes que o Rio Seque*. Lisbon: Assírio & Alvim, 2006.

———. *Arado*. Lisbon: Cotovia, 2009.

Santos, Hugo Pinto. "Arado." *Rascunho*. Accessed August 5, 2009, from http://www.rascunho.net/critica.php?id=1505.

Torga, Miguel. "A terra." *Poemas Ibéricos*. Coimbra: Coimbra Editora, 1952.

DUARTE PINHEIRO is a temporary assistant professor of Portuguese language at the University of Salerno (Italy). He also lectures in language courses at the University of L'Aquila. His PhD thesis—already published and available online—drew a general perspective of the Portuguese crime novel and discussed, through a comparative approach, Ana Teresa Pereira's literary work. He has also published many articles on contemporary Portuguese literature and literary theory in magazines and newspapers. He may be reached at dpinheiro@camoes.mne.pt.

OSVALDO MANUEL SILVESTRE AND PEDRO SERRA. *Século de ouro—Antologia crítica da poesia portuguesa do século XX.*

Despite the scarce critical discourse about them, literary anthologies have played an important part in Portuguese poetry in the twentieth and beginning of the twenty-first centuries. They were a crucial tool for different members of the literary field to actively deal with the need to organize this field, and poets in particular made use of this format, among other purposes, to establish their position in it by assigning value to their peers and themselves. That was the case, for example, of poets such as Fernando Pessoa, Jorge de Sena, Eugénio de Andrade, and Herberto Helder, just to name a few of the most consecrated, in a tradition that in fact has seen an expansion at the turn of the millennium.[1]

The apparent paradox that lies in the reality of a large tradition of anthology making and little academic research about the topic owes to an assumption at different levels, in Portugal, that anthologies have in a more or less natural way reflected the best of a continuously changing or developing system.[2] However, a closer look will reveal that several anthologies have provoked—and oftentimes stemmed from—feelings such as fear or anxiety regarding history writing, authorial visibility, posterity and consecration, and of course oblivion and exclusion. As it happens, frequent position-takings that illustrate those same feelings can be found among Portuguese authors, critics, scholars, and, as we will see, even among those in political power. Published in November 2002, *Século de ouro—Antologia crítica da poesia portuguesa do século XX* is a clear case of a volume that illustrates both the interest in the anthology format and its impact in the literary field. By choosing to question the limits of literary historiography, *Século de ouro* led many authors, critics, and public officeholders to take varied stands on the anthology's methodology and selection of texts, which evidenced misconceptions and fears regarding the relation of anthologies and the literary canon.

Século de ouro was edited by Osvaldo Manuel Silvestre and Pedro Serra (professors at the universities of Coimbra and Salamanca, respectively) and sponsored by the cultural program Coimbra—Capital Nacional da Cultura 2003

(Coimbra—National Cultural Capital 2003), also called Coimbra 2003. The title of the anthology adopts an expression that started circulating among poets and critics at the end of the twentieth century in reference to the period's Portuguese poetry. The editors state in their introduction that there is a "critical consensus . . . about the golden nature of the Portuguese twentieth century" and reference personalities in the field who used the expression ("Desaprender (com) a história," 2002, 34). But if the book's title and front cover seem to state that twentieth-century Portuguese poetry indeed corresponds to a golden century, the back cover warns that this anthology presents itself as "the critical place where the consensus on the topic of the golden age of Portuguese poetry itself is questioned." The decision to simultaneously affirm this golden century and question the consensus about it marks the entire project, from conception to reception. Moreover, the questioning of this consensus is tightly connected with a theoretical stance that chooses to challenge the limits of literary historiography.

For a number of reasons, ranging from its title to its high number of collaborators to its status as a critical anthology, *Século de ouro* gathered the conditions to be perceived as a definitive assessment of twentieth-century Portuguese poetry. Nevertheless, this anthology is highly inspired by postmodern thought, and the editors resorted to radically uncommon organizational criteria in an attempt to question historiography itself and obtain an unpredictable result. The final outcome generated strong controversy, fueled by its having been partly financed by public funds. This polemic rippled across the Portuguese literary field, involving poets, the press, and academia, but it went far beyond these borders and, perhaps surprisingly, reached the Portuguese parliament.

The standing of Coimbra 2003 as the first of the National Capitals of Culture was relevant, as in the discussion of *Século de ouro*, some critics argued that the editors' lack of familiarity with the cultural program's guidelines resulted in the volume's inadequacy. To this contributed the metonymy in the designation of the cultural program. One could ask *which* Coimbra was the Capital of Culture? The city? Or the university founded in 1290? Or even a projected Coimbra? Naturally the concept of the program, even if directly referring to the city, partly encompassed all of the connotations associated with its designation. One of the relevant metonymical understandings of the title Coimbra 2003 with regard to *Século de ouro* is what Lakoff and Johnson call "the place for the institution" (38), in this case the name of the city representing the main university contained in it. The organizers of the cultural program developed in the city of Coimbra could easily legitimize the designation by associating it with the university, a national reference. On the other hand, as we will see, criticism of *Século de ouro* could just as easily question a lack of local representation, by focusing on the particular geographic space of Coimbra and pointing out the absence of a number of poets who lived in or referred to it.

Século de ouro presents itself as an unusual project, both in its scope and criteria. As the editors' introduction tells us, seventy-three critics collaborated in the anthology, and each was asked to choose three poems "of the corpus of twentieth-century Portuguese poetry" ("Desaprender (com) a história," 2002, 20). The two editors subsequently selected one of the three poems chosen by each critic, so as to include as many poets as possible. According to the editors, no poem or poet who had not been chosen was afterward included in the volume. The editors requested that the critical essays that follow each poem be written in the format of a close reading. Finally, and the most unusual characteristic of the project, the poems ultimately chosen were organized according to a computer-generated MATLAB matrix, therefore avoiding a more conventional order. The seventy-three poems were assigned a number (1 to 73, following alphabetical order); the MATLAB software produced ten matrixes with a random organization of these numbers; and finally a second random draw selected the matrix to be followed, which dictated the final organization of the volume's poems. The outcome was an anthology with seventy-three poems by forty-seven authors, in which some poets usually seen as canonical obtained few or no nominations, several less consecrated poets were included, some poets were represented by more than one poem, and—surprisingly or not, given the process—Fernando Pessoa was the central figure, with nine poems. As Vincenzo Russo remarks, referring to the fact that Pessoa's heteronym Álvaro de Campos was the most chosen "poet," "it is the poems of a naval engineer who doesn't exist (and never existed) that have the biggest representation" (Russo 2004, 85).

In this volume, it is the critics—mostly from Portugal, Brazil, and the United States—who are included in an attempt to create representativity, rather than the poems they have selected. The collaborators are mostly members of academia (some of them poets as well) and a few poets. The majority of the collaborators write their own literary criticism, both in the context of academia and in the press. Regarding the breadth of the collaborators, the claim by Osvaldo Manuel Silvestre and Pedro Serra that *Século de ouro* is up to the moment of its publication "surely the most ambitious [anthology] of the last century's Portuguese poetry ever made" ("Desaprender (com) a história," 2002, 19) seems undeniable.[3] In line with the selection of the poems by the collaborators, the editors' purpose was to broaden "the choices to a panorama representative of the several trends in the century . . . being faithful to the concentration of choices in certain authors . . . and avoiding the repetition of poems" ("Desaprender (com) a história," 2002, 20). Hence the criteria are unambiguous, and yet they problematize the notion of representativity. The expectation of obtaining as a result of this process of selection "a panorama representative of the several trends in the century" cannot be understood as an intention of controlling the process to guarantee such a result but rather as a tentative approach, made in order to widen the options resulting from chance. In that sense, the process of selection in *Século de ouro* works precisely in opposition to the concept of panorama itself, since what was required from the collaborators was not a personal selection of the group of voices that could make that same panorama but only three of their preferred poems from this period. As critic Rosa Maria Martelo points out, the process of selection made the collaborators themselves approach the volume as a labyrinth (2003, 200). Arguably, the conflict between the choice of adopting randomness as an organizational principle and the alleged expectation of obtaining a representative panorama mirrors the tension that, from the beginning, places this anthology between the two desires of presenting a golden age and questioning the consensus about this concept.

The criteria defined by Silvestre and Serra in principle shielded the anthology from the criticism of having committed active exclusions, a criticism that notwithstanding was still made, as we will see. More important, though, the criteria refused to provide what could be called a totalizing view of the Portuguese poetry of the twentieth century and attempted to undermine all those elements that traditionally, in critical anthologies, display historiographical characteristics. This is why the editors chose the format of close reading for the essays to follow each poem, intending namely to avoid notions such as that of "reflection," or why they used a random sequence in ordering the poems, intending to do away with subjectivity or, as Silvestre and Serra call them, the notions of "historical reason" or "processual History" ("Desaprender (com) a história," 2002, 28).

In these characteristics, *Século de ouro* is directly inspired by the discussion on historiographical methods developed in the essay "After Learning from History," by Hans Ulrich Gumbrecht, from his *In 1926: Living at the Edge of Time.*

Gumbrecht's starting point is the idea that until recently the belief existed that it was possible to "learn from History" by reflecting upon its teachings and that from a certain moment on—one he associates with the collapse of the Eastern Bloc—that belief ended. For Gumbrecht, history currently faces the paradox according to which "the claim that 'one can learn from history' has lost its persuasive power" but "books about the past continue to attract a growing number of readers, and . . . history . . . as a discipline remains unchallenged" (1997, 411). One should, however, note that while Gumbrecht states that we have stopped learning from history, what his analysis seems to indicate is that we have stopped believing that it is possible to learn from history. All the same, we should point out that this is a perception that seems to be learned from history itself, if we are to accept it as valid.

As a way to preserve the awareness of the degree of subjectivity underlying history writing, and at the same time to oppose a sort of self-castration in that act, Gumbrecht proposes "six rules of thumb for history writing, after learning from history" (425) that directly influence *Século de ouro*. These rules valorize randomness and chance as a method for selecting themes for study, and valorize the concept of simultaneity in the presentation of historical snapshots, by addressing periods of time such as "one year" through a fragmentary description of facts and artifacts, hypothetically as the individual experiences them firsthand.

Gumbrecht's suspicion regarding causality or sequence in the description of past events is in line with the fear or disbelief regarding narrative in historic discourse, as described by Hayden White: "The fact that narrative is the mode of discourse common to both 'historical' and 'nonhistorical' cultures and that it predominates in both mythic and fictional discourse makes it suspect as a manner of speaking about 'real' events" (1987, 57). In this distrust regarding historical narrative, Gumbrecht's proposal also reflects one of the most often-cited characteristics of postmodernity. Authors including Jean-François Lyotard, Linda Hutcheon, and Fredric Jameson coincide in describing a suspicion regarding any form of historical discourse that is seen as teleology. Lyotard states that the "grand narrative has lost its credibility, regardless of what mode of unification it uses, regardless of whether it is a speculative narrative or a narrative of emancipation" (1984, 37). Hutcheon puts the question in very similar terms in addressing history, when she talks about a "radical suspicion of the act of historiography" as a central characteristic of the postmodern (1988, 90). Jameson goes as far as to state that the cultural productions of history hardly can "result in anything but 'heaps of fragments' and in a practice of the randomly heterogeneous and fragmentary and the aleatory" (25). And precisely a thorough characterization of different fragments would be the best description of Gumbrecht's methodology in his aforementioned *In 1926*.

Still in line with this discussion, David Perkins's study dedicated to "The Postmodern Encyclopedia," from his *Is Literary History Possible?*, may help us better understand the characteristics of *Século de ouro*. Perkins addresses the format adopted by some histories of literature, in which essays on different topics are gathered without complying with a main plan concerned with lending internal coherence to the collection. The clearest virtue of this format, for Perkins, is that its fragmentary nature is transparent. Contrary to traditional histories, the encyclopedic format allows the reader, from the very beginning, not to mistake a representation of the past with the past itself, since the information is not presented in a causal or sequential manner. He argues: "Encyclopedic form does not distort the past at all, for in it the events that make up the past are not interrelated in a determined way. . . . Thus the encyclopedic can be a relatively open form of literary history" (1992, 55). Perkins notes that these volumes can bring together "biography, bibliography, intellectual history, social history, information about the reception of works, and criticism, moving from one to another with a flexibility that cannot easily be matched in narrative history. When a literary history has no plot, nothing appears as a digression" (54). According to Perkins, this sense of history is characteristic of the postmodern period, even if not altogether new (55). He finishes his study, however, with a negative judgment of this format, writing that its "audience is a limited one, composed mainly of specialists . . . and theorists of literary history. A literary history of this type is logically ancillary or supplemental" (58). For Perkins, therefore, this is not yet the method that answers the paradox described by Gumbrecht, since this history with encyclopedic characteristics presents the alleged crisis of literary historiography but does not go beyond it: "Encyclopedic form is intellectually deficient. . . . It precludes a vision of its subject. Because it aspires to reflect the past in its multiplicity and heterogeneity, it does not organize the past, and in this sense, it is not history. There is little excitement in reading it" (60).

Perkins's analysis is relevant here if we consider the historiographical aspect typical of critical anthologies, and that *Século de ouro* precisely refuses to provide a historical perspective of the literature of the period it covers and states that its own title corresponds to a "posthistorical" figure ("Desaprender (com) a história," 2002, 21). The editors tell us that this is a "posthistorical" project and that "posthistory is, in this book, a critical exercise that is suspicious of all pretensions to a pacified and happy posterity" ("Desaprender (com) a história," 2002, 65). In fact, more than doing away with history and therefore being ahistorical, *Século de ouro* places itself at the core of the postmodern suspicion regarding the possibility of writing history, and it is in that sense that it claims a posthistorical status.

Because of the fragmentary nature of anthologies, there are multiple ways of reading them. For every reader who is obstinate about following the laid-out sequence, another one can always be found who will read the anthology in a random or personal order. This is true even in the case of critical anthologies, despite their higher degree of contextualization. Such an understanding of anthologies as mainly fragmentary makes us inevitably ask what the consequence of preventing a more conventional order is. In this light we could consider *Século de ouro* under three very different, and all partial, perspectives. First, it can be seen as an improvement to the format of anthologies, as the editors in fact claim, in the sense that it perfects the random and fragmentary nature of any anthology ("Desaprender (com) a história," 2002, 31). Second, we can see its unusual organization as a redundant effort, if we are to consider that it only reinstates what any anthology *can* already be, that is, an object to be read in random order. Yet *Século de ouro*, more than affirming this possibility, adopts it as its main characteristic, forcing it to be factored in the reading, and making us think of the characteristics and limitations of the anthology format itself. Third, through adopting a more conservative view of history, we can consider *Século de ouro* as an impossible anthology, since the volume boycotts the option of reading in an arguably more transparent way (namely, the chronological), a group of poems gathered under a title that aims exactly at a historiographical concept. But, again, *Século de ouro* avoids this third view by drawing attention to the limitations of the format and history at the same time that it incorporates alternative indexes at the end of the book, such as indexes of poets, critics, titles or *incipits*, and even a chronological organization of the poems.

The editors' suggestion that these indexes be seen as "other potential random entries in the book" ("Desaprender (com) a história," 2002, 33) is logical in a project that claims to be posthistorical. The claim evidences the belief that none of these methods provides an understanding of twentieth-century poetry that is any clearer than the random one, given the editors' suspicion that narrative may attribute meaning to what may not possess it to begin with. However, the inclusion of these indexes can also be seen as a recognition that a random reading does not necessarily present more advantages than a traditional one and, ultimately, that the reader to whom a golden century was promised might be expecting to find a sense of history and organization of the past. To point this out is hardly any criticism, since the editors themselves raise the question of whether "historical legitimation, even if undeclared, can be dismissed in an anthology of poetry of an entire century" ("Desaprender (com) a história," 2002, 39). The question arises from the decision by many critics who contributed to the anthology with critical essays to not limit themselves to close reading after all, but instead to contextualize the poems both with regard to the authors' works and their periods or movements. In my view, this preference illustrates a recognition that literary value also lies in factors that may go beyond the textual constructions, although it does not exist without these. At the same time, these critics' stance undermined the option of considering the entire century as a simultaneous unit, since they preferred to highlight processes of influence between the century's different poetic trends. Ultimately, by questioning if historical legitimation can be dismissed in an anthology dedicated to a century, the editors decide, more than questioning history, to take up the very concept of posthistory that has been operative for their own work, and leave it to the readers—and time—to provide an answer.

The impact of a project that questioned both the consensus about the figures of the century as well as the possibility of writing that history to begin with was quite significant. The early elements of a polemic were already present in the first references to *Século de ouro* found in the press in November 2002, although the general reception has been frankly positive. The anthology is considered "polemical and eccentric" (Silva 2002), owing to the oddity of the criteria, and the important *Diário de notícias* dedicated a full page to the volume, under the title "Os 73 ouros do século XX" (The 73 Golds of the Twentieth Century; November 15, 2002), including a small box titled "*Intelligentsia* deixa de fora mais de 30 autores" ("Intelligentsia Leave Out More than 30 Authors"). Although the title seems to point to active exclusions, the article considers these absences the contingency of all anthologies. *Século de ouro* is therefore said to have the very same sort of fallibility of *all* anthologies, despite its radically different criteria. With the exception of José Carlos Vasconcelos (*Jornal de letras*), who writes that the anthology "doesn't give a minimally coherent panorama" of what he agrees is a golden age, most critics praised *Século de ouro* in the period immediately following its publication. Ana Marques Gastão (*Diário de notícias*) considers it "essential in any library." Sara Belo Luís (*Visão*) evaluates the anthology as a "great essayistic work about twentieth-century Portuguese poetry." In a text symptomatically titled "666"—an apocalyptic reference that plays on the anthology's page count and alludes to its intrinsic oddness—João Barrento (*Público*) states that the volume's preface displays "a solid theoretical basis, for its critical and informative clairvoyance," and António Guerreiro (*Expresso—Cartaz*) valorizes the originality of the project.

Nonetheless, between November 2002 and late January 2003 the discussion would evolve and the reception change drastically, and already in the months of February and March the anthology would be highly criticized. Ana Marques Gastão (*Diário de notícias*) reports what is by then seen as "the anthology of disagreement" ("A antologia da discórdia"; January 28, 2003). The news was no longer the volume itself but rather the polemics attributed to the noninclusion of poets associated with Coimbra, illustrated by statements provided by poets, professors, and critics. Particularly outstanding was the position by Manuel Alegre, a well-known poet from the area of Coimbra, a former opponent of the fascist dictatorship and a member of parliament who later ran to be president of the republic (in 2006 and 2010). Alegre rejects the project by stating that "Nobody can understand that in an anthology sponsored by Coimbra 2003 Afonso Duarte, [Miguel] Torga, and myself are not included. This story is all the more unfortunate since these poets, connected to Coimbra, were already censored during the dictatorship" (January 28, 2003). Helena Roseta, another member of parliament, criticizes the use of public funding to sponsor "an editorial project based on a methodology whose results are incompatible with the objectives of Coimbra 2003" ("Tiro nos Pés," January 30, 2003). Most strikingly, a month later the members of parliament of the two main—and rival—Portuguese political parties elected in the district of Coimbra presented a self-titled "Manifesto contra uma antologia poética grosseiramente discriminatória" ("Manifesto against a Grossly Discriminatory Poetic Anthology," Gabinete de Imprensa, February 25, 2009). In this manifesto the members of parliament expressed their "sincere indignation" regarding the criteria of the compilation and provided a list of poets who, in their view, were excluded or *saneados*, a Portuguese word that means "banned" and is associated with political persecution.

It is worth analyzing in more detail the three main arguments used against

Século de ouro with regard to its stance on historiographical discourse. The first one—the absence of some authors of Coimbra in an anthology sponsored by Coimbra 2003—implies a misunderstanding or a rejection of the criteria of the anthology. Manuel Alegre's position (and that of his fellow members of parliament), in particular, is paradigmatic, since the poet understands these criteria but rejects them as inadequate. According to his position, an anthology should be representative of the concept or product that sponsors it, and not of the topic chosen or the corpus addressed. The reaction lets us understand that Alegre believes he should be part of any anthology of twentieth-century Portuguese poetry, since he knows the scope of the book and considers his absence a flaw. But in defending the argument for his presence, he cites his own connection to the city of Coimbra, because he believes an anthology sponsored by Coimbra 2003 should have a representation of local authors.[4] However, by reducing the scope of the compilation from a collection of Portuguese poetry to a group of poets whom Coimbra would choose, or by stating that the anthology should at the very least include the most consecrated authors of the city, Alegre inadvertently reduces the reach of his own poetry to a local dimension, since for all purposes he emphasizes this local component as the real oversight. Ultimately, his argument expresses a deeper anxiety regarding the posterity of his work in the framework of twentieth-century Portuguese poetry. Alegre certainly believes he already belongs in what could be called the canon of poets of Coimbra, as well as the canon of twentieth-century Portuguese poetry—something that, no doubt, most critics recognize. But his dismissal of the criteria of *Século de ouro* seems to evidence a writer's common fear that exclusion from an anthology may imply exclusion from a hypothetical canon. This happens namely because, at first glance, this anthology in particular presents itself as a sort of balance book of the century and also because it originates from within the university, which along with the school, as John Guillory explains with regard to the concept of the literary canon, is the most important threshold for authorial consecration.

The controversy furthermore illustrates a confusion associated with the parliament members' status as elected figures of Coimbra. Both Manuel Alegre and the members of parliament who signed the "Manifesto" attempted to transfer to the literary field the authority conferred upon them in a political election and claim legitimacy to represent the population in aesthetic and critical judgments. The public funds used in *Século de ouro* gave the argument of legitimacy that the parliament members needed to express their opinion. Bourdieu reminds us that

"The state . . . has the power to orient intellectual production by means of subsidies, commissions, promotion, honorific posts, even decorations, all of which are for speaking or keeping silent, for compromise or abstention," and that this applies particularly to "artists and especially professors coming from the petite bourgeoisie [who] are most directly under the control of the state" (1993, 125). In this case, the public money allowed the parliament, a synecdoche for the state, to chastise the members of the literary field involved in the production of this anthology. Essentially, the political authority criticized the performance of the cultural authorities precisely when the cultural authorities destabilized consensus and questioned the limits of history writing. *Século de ouro* also offered to the most consecrated poets the unique opportunity of denouncing a proximity to power of the youngest and least consecrated, who, precisely because of their lesser degree of institutionalization, allowed for an accusation of misspending public funds. In fact, for the parliament members, the "minor poets" included in *Século de ouro* were gold of "a lesser carat."

The third argument used by critics of the anthology has to do with the rigor expected from members of academia. For these academics, the ability to define literary value, more than any power, is indeed an obligation. Some critiques of *Século de ouro* focused particularly on the argument that the anthology originated in the intellectual space of the University of Coimbra, and sometimes in violent terms stated that the readers "expected more" from those ironically called "enlightened brains" (Braga 2003), that is, the editors of the volume, now cast back to the hypothetical ivory tower of academia.

In conclusion, the editors' choice of an anthology to present their own challenge to the format of literary history and its epistemological limits is particularly relevant since anthologies, even if prolific and celebrated in Portugal, have been seen as unproblematic in their format, even when they have polarized multiple anxieties about their representations. In the literary field, the need to write the history of a given period is felt all the more intensely the closer one is to that period; therefore, raising an immediate expectation of historicism, a critical anthology was the ideal match for the editors' desire to question the limitations of historiography. The reactions to *Século de ouro* reflected an obvious fear that an anthology with apparent characteristics of a balance book of a literary century seen as one of the most valuable, if not the most valuable, of Portuguese poetry would lead to the exclusion or the absence in the memory of the literary field itself, in other words, of what is usually called under different perspectives the canon. *Século de ouro* reminds us that anthologies tend to the writing of history by organizing the past, and because readers and authors will expect, or still do expect, such to be the case, that is an expectation anthologists also deal with. In other words, contrary to what anthologists and poets sometimes want to convey, often with evident effort to hide their belief otherwise, anthologies do not merely reflect a natural selection of the best works but rather try to add to the shaping of the canon with their own perspective. *Século de ouro* destabilized the idea, relatively common in Portugal, that the literary canon represents an honor list—or pantheon—into which authors enter peacefully. The anthology that chose not to choose was the wrench needed to remind us that authors are remembered due to different processes of consecration, namely recognition at the university level, which may lead them to influence subsequent writers, and that this is something most authors know rather well.

Moreover, *Século de ouro* was the perfect emblem for the paradox, expressed by Gumbrecht, of being attracted to history while doubting the possibilities of learning from it. The anthology celebrated the conflict inherent in proposing a sample of a century beforehand considered golden, while programmatically trying to avoid a historical approach and questioning a general consensus all too easy to reproduce in print. As far as its reception is concerned, *Século de ouro* was trapped in that same conflict, as it received a high volume of criticism and demagogical positions generated by the misunderstanding or the rejection of its heterodox methodology and theoretical proposal. An assessment of its merits and flaws directly depends on whether the reader agrees that a historiographical methodology such as the one used provides a better knowledge of the past, and/or that we have stopped learning from history, to begin with. The project of *Século de ouro* should therefore be applauded not only for choosing to face the difficulty of writing the history of a literary period so close in time, but even more for trying to do so with a strong awareness of the limitations of historical discourse and a clear willingness to question it and, by doing so, contributing to a debate that is largely open.

NOTES

1. I thank Osvaldo Manuel Silvestre for agreeing, in the early stages of my research for this paper, to talk with me about *Século de ouro* and for providing me with a number of press articles that were invaluable in documenting the reception of this anthology.

2. For an accurate listing of anthologies published in Portugal in that period and a

thorough discussion on the topic, see Patricia Odber Baubeta's *The Anthology in Portugal: A New Approach to the History of Portuguese Literature in the Twentieth Century*. For an analysis on the role of anthologies in the literary field and the relation between authorship and anthology making, see Ricardo Vasconcelos's "Quem tem medo de antologias?—Antologias de poesia portuguesa e brasileira do século XX no meio literário português."

3. Also evidencing the strong attention currently paid to this format, a number of anthologies have since been published. A volume that is impressive for its dimensions, both in terms of the number of collaborators and its sheer number of pages (2,149), is *Poemas portugueses—Antologia da poesia portuguesa do séc. XIII ao séc. XXI*, eds. Jorge Reis-Sá and Rui Lage (Porto: Porto Editora, 2009). The many collaborators assisted in the production of the bio-bibliographic notes of the 267 poets included. Although the anthology covers close to eight centuries, about half of it is dedicated to the twentieth and twenty-first centuries, both reinstating the belief that this is a golden age and, of course, raising the issue of whether time will allow that belief to be kept.

4. Manuel Alegre also invokes the imaginary of regional anthologies dedicated to Coimbra, such as those edited by Afonso Lopes Vieira (*Cancioneiro de Coimbra*, Coimbra: França Amado, 1918) or Eugénio de Andrade (*Memórias de Alegria—Antologia de Verso e Prosa sobre Coimbra*, Porto: Inova, 1971).

WORKS CITED

Alegre, Manuel. Answer to the inquiry "Concorda com os critérios?" *Diário de notícias*, January 28, 2003, 45.

Barrento, João. "666." Review of *Século de ouro*. In "Mil folhas," *Público*.

Baubeta, Patricia Odber. *The Anthology in Portugal: A New Approach to the History of Portuguese Literature in the Twentieth Century*. Bern: Peter Lang, 2007.

Bourdieu, Pierre. *The Field of Cultural Production*, edited by Randal Johnson. New York: Columbia University Press, 1993.

Braga, João. "Antologia ou antrologia?" Review of *Século de ouro*. *A Capital*, March 9, 2003.

Coelho, Eduardo Prado. Answer to the inquiry "Concorda com os critérios?" *Diário de notícias*, January 28, 2003, 45.

Gabinete de Imprensa do Grupo Parlamentar do Partido Socialista. "Coimbra Capital da Cultura: Manifesto contra antologia poética grosseiramente discriminatória." February 25, 2009. http://www.ps.parlamento.pt/?menu=actualidade&id=237.

Gastão, Ana Marques. "Os 73 ouros do século XX." Review of *Século de ouro*. *Diário de notícias*, November 15, 2002, 51.

———. "A antologia da discórdia." Review of *Século de ouro*. *Diário de notícias*, January 28, 2003, 45.

Guerreiro, António. "Campo de batalha." Review of *Século de ouro*. *Expresso—cartaz*, November 23, 2002.

Guillory, John. *Cultural Capital*. Chicago: University Chicago Press, 1993.

Gumbrecht, Hans Ulrich. *In 1926: Living at the Edge of Time*. Cambridge: Harvard University Press, 1997.

Hutcheon, Linda. *The Poetics of Postmodernism*. London: Routledge, 1988.

Jameson, Fredric. *Postmodernism; or, The Cultural Logic of Late Capitalism*. Durham, NC: Duke University Press, 1991.

Lakoff, George, and Mark Johnson. *Metaphors We Live By*. Chicago: University of Chicago Press, 2003 [1980].

Luís, Sara Belo. "Antologia—O livro do desassossego." Review of *Século de ouro*. *Visão*, November 21, 2002, 198.

Lyotard, Jean-François. *The Postmodern Condition: A Report on Knowledge*. Minneapolis: University of Minnesota Press, 1984.

"Manuel Alegre fala de 'ódio' no texto de opinião sobre antologia de poesia." *Público*, March 3, 2003, 35.

"Manuel Alegre incapaz de 'comentar o ódio.'" *Diário de Coimbra*, March 3, 2003, 3.

Martelo, Rosa Maria. "No labirinto: Notas para a leitura de *Século de ouro*." *Inimigo Rumor* 14 (2003): 199–205.

Pereira, Andreia Marques. "Poesia portuguesa do século XX—a antologia . . ." *O primeiro de Janeiro*, November 20, 2002, 22.

Perkins, David. *Is Literary History Possible?* Baltimore: Johns Hopkins University Press, 1992.

Russo, Vincenzo. "L'antologia della fine: Il '*Século de Ouro*' Portoghese." Review in *SO: Rassegna Iberistica* 79 (2004): 83–86.

Silva, Patrícia Isabel. "Ensaístas reflectem sobre 'Século de ouro' da poesia portuguesa." *Diário de Coimbra*, November 16, 2002, 5.

Silvestre, Osvaldo Manuel, and Pedro Serra. "Desaprender (com) a história." Introduction to *Século de Ouro—Antologia crítica da poesia portuguesa do século XX*, edited by Osvaldo Manuel Silvestre and Pedro Serra. Lisbon: Angelus Novus, Cotovia, 2002. 15–65.

———, eds. *Século de ouro—Antologia crítica da poesia portuguesa do século XX*. Lisbon: Angelus Novus, Cotovia, 2002.

"'Tiro nos pés' de Coimbra 2003" [news article about a statement by Helena Roseta]. *Diário de notícias*, January 30, 2003, 42.

Vasconcelos, José Carlos. "Livros—Antologia crítica do século XX." Review in *SO: JL—Jornal de Letras, Artes e Ideias*, November 27, 2002, 26.

Vasconcelos, Ricardo. "Quem tem medo de antologias?—Antologias de poesia portuguesa e brasileira do século XX no meio literário português." PhD diss., University of California, Santa Barbara, 2010. ProQuest, July 9, 2012.

White, Hayden. *The Content of the Form: Narrative Discourse and Historical Representation.* Baltimore: Johns Hopkins University Press: 1987.

RICARDO VASCONCELOS is an assistant professor of Luso-Brazilian literature and culture, and Portuguese language, at the University of Wisconsin, Milwaukee. He received his doctorate from the University of California, Santa Barbara, with a dissertation entitled "Quem tem medo de antologias? Antologias de poesia portuguesa e brasileira do século XX no meio literário português." He holds an MA in modern and contemporary Portuguese literature, and a BA in Portuguese and English, from the University of Porto (Portugal). He is the author of *Campo de Relâmpagos—Leituras do Excesso na Poesia de Luís Miguel Nava* (Lisbon: Assírio e Alvim, 2009) in addition to various articles. He may be reached at ricardov@uwm.edu.

Fiction

CAROLA SAAVEDRA
Translated by Hsiao-Shih Lee

Brief Beginning of the World (Episode in Three Movements)

I.

The world had finished taking its place. All was still so new that night has not even fallen. The whole world was one burst of light. The hours passed, but the day remained the same, as if all hours were the same hour, insistently repeating, in the sky and at the edge of the sky. Until the sky began to fade, and its edge turned to the color of flames, the color of forest, the color of a dark sea, and the sky ended up resembling the color of earth. Resembling an anteater. First only at the edges, then the entire sky the color of earth, the color of an anteater. In the beginning a red anteater, a gold anteater, afterward a flash darker and darker and even darker until the sky itself was no longer an anteater, and in its place stars, which were previously the gleam of the anteater's body, and in its place the moon, which used to be the gleam in the anteater's left eye, then just the gleam of the anteater without the anteater. And the moon was not called moon, and the stars were not called stars, and night was not even called night, they were nameless things, as all things existing for the first time are.

And men stayed there, on that first night, along with the gleam of the body and the left eye of an anteater. And the men were very scared, because fear is the second sentiment that accompanies the nameless things, because the first sentiment is a kind of astonishment, which is what emerges when things emerge for the first time and are still neither good nor bad. Because in the instant in which things emerge, they haven't had time yet to be what they are, and they themselves do not even know their own nature. So the night was neither good nor bad in the first moments, and men unfolded strange smiles. But afterward, time continued to pass, and the night continued there with its eye and with its nameless starry gleam. And men began to feel apprehensive because they perceived that the night began to search for something that would sustain it. And they began to hear noises from creatures that until then did not exist. And men did not know that so many two-, four-, or many-legged creatures could exist within the night.

And men felt a fresh fear on that first night, and they spent all the hours that never ended looking at the gleam and the eye of the anteater. Until at some point the anteater fell asleep and closed its only eye. Until little by little, the anteater's gleam began to dim, and the sky shifted colors, and the anteater disappeared completely. Until it was day again, as it has always been, and men recognized that, and they recognized the sun and its gleam that was very different from the anteater. And the fear dissipated because now the things that emerged were things that had names and creatures that had names, and they could see them with their own eyes and their own astonishment.

II.

It happened very far away from there. In the beginning, there were not houses, nor huts, nor shacks, nor cabins, nor things that carried those names, and the earth was just earth and a closed forest and a river that ran through it. It was an earth run through by many rivers that went and came in the direction of the north and south, and they made the sounds that rivers are accustomed to making when there is only earth and forest and rivers. And the noise repeats and repeats for days and nights and days, until incorporated into the landscape, until becoming a noise that does not exist, until becoming a kind of silence. Because silence has always been a noise. Because silence is music that never ceases. But once in a while the silence is broken. The music. And there came steps and rhythms and days and nights that passed. Afterward, the steps and everything else went away, following their path, and all returned to the previous moment. The silence of the earth and the forest and the rivers. The music. Until one day, amid the steps and rhythms running through, someone stopped for a few moments and said, surprised—or just with some kind of delight—look, a tree, or a river or a monkey or an anteater. Someone said, look, and everyone was silent, the music was restored, and the one who spoke remained in suspense waiting for the answer, while everyone looked at the tree, or the river or the monkey. Only after a long time, perhaps days and nights and days, someone also stopped and repeated, indeed, a tree, or a river or a monkey—an echo, a second voice, or some sort of response. And that was when something took place, or finished taking place. There, everyone remained still, surprised with what they had seen, the tree, the river or monkey, as if watching for the first time, and unfolded strange smiles, because the tree or the river or the monkey has also remained still, as if they themselves have discovered something. And when night arrived, men built a cot there in order to keep looking at the tree, or the river or the monkey, and pointing and repeating, look, a tree, or a river or a monkey, turned into rhythm, into music. And the night emerged with its anteater eyes and seemed less frightening to them. For the first time, less frightening. And they slept and dreamt dreams that were strange and similar at the same time, as if they dreamt the same dream, as if they sang the same song. As if they smiled. And when day broke, someone else said, look, a tree, or a river or a monkey, and they continued in that strange surprise, as if "look" were not an imperative, but a question. And they stayed there, waiting, and repeating, and waiting. Until night fell again. And again the anteater and the eye of the anteater, and again they had strange and similar dreams. And many nights passed like this, and things began to transform, as if the body and the name of the things had become more compact, become slower and heavier. And as if the music suddenly were another, and the silence were another. And they decided then to construct a roof that would separate them from the nocturnal birds and the stars, which have also become slower and heavier and other. So the time passed, and time continued, and they discovered that the roof separated them from the night, but also from the day and the rain and the canopy of trees, and created a strange acoustic there. And they remained there, around the cot and the roof and the leaves that have scattered under the roof, always slow and heavy and always other, thinking that tomorrow, tomorrow they will leave.

III.

First, everything was born: the stars and the planets and the rivers and the sea and the monkeys and the anteaters. And things continued being born and being born and being born and populating the world, which was still very big and never ending. And for a long time things continued being born and populating and never ending, until one day, or one night or one day, the first thing ended. And with it, other things and creatures, four-legged creatures, and two-legged creatures, and even none-legged creatures, until one day, a man, a two-legged creature, unleashed a shriek, which was not the shriek of monkey or bird, it was the shriek of things ending, of a man ending, and since they did not know what was a man ending, they did not know it was a shriek, they did not have a name for the shriek that came from a two-legged creature like them, like so many others of them. A man ending. And for the first time they saw what was a man who was ending and not being born anymore nor populating the world, the world that never ended. For the first time they heard the shriek, which was a frightening and insistent shriek that insisted for a long time, a long time that never finished passing for the man that shrieked so that other men could hear, and for the shriek itself that for a long time insisted, and insisted, until becoming rhythm, becoming music. Until bit by bit it went dying down, diminishing, diminishing, until transforming into a groan, until transforming into a long and tired groan, until disappearing. And they saw for the first time the first person who stopped being a person. They saw the moment in which he stopped being a person and they did not know what name to give that body that remains and that was nothing, only a two-legged body that no longer stirred nor emitted sounds, nor groans, not even a fright, not even the inconsistency of the music. And so they made a circle around the man who stopped being a person, while outside the circle the children played with the monkeys, which also had two legs and continued existing and stirring and shrieking. And the men and children and monkeys remained there, from outside the circle, for many days and nights, to the side of the man inside the circle, for many days and nights, and the men sang and told stories, and the children played with the monkeys, and the man inside the circle did not do anything. And the time passed, and the children grew, and they also went to keep the man company, inside and outside the circle, and to sing and to tell stories. Inside the circle, where one did not get up. Outside the circle, from where one looked inside the circle with astonishment and fascination. And during this the man inside the circle, who was every time less of a person, his flesh eaten by other creatures of two and four or no legs, and his face eaten by other creatures was that of someone who could never have had a face. Until one day, someone approached and, impatient and cold and scared, threw a fistful of soil over the man's face, because the face of a man who has stopped being a person was a face in silence. The earth that separated him from the days and the nights and the days, made into a roof, house, and the circle disbanded and covered the entire man in earth so that they could finally leave. And so the circle disbanded, and they all left. Meanwhile, under the earth, in place of eyes, there were now two orbits, and in place of mouth, a cavity, and from where there would be gleam and music, now only orbits, cavities, and the creatures that were nestling in them. Until everything became one body and one creature.

CAROLA SAAVEDRA is one of the most acclaimed young authors of Brazilian contemporary literature. She has published the novels *Toda terça* (Companhia das Letras, 2007), *Flores azuis* (Companhia das Letras, 2008; which received the award of the Associação

Paulista dos Críticos de Arte for best novel of the year and was also a finalist for the prestigious São Paulo de Literatura and Jabuti awards), and *Paisagem com dromedário* (Companhia das Letras, 2010; which received the Rachel de Queiroz award for young writers and was a finalist for the São Paulo de Literatura and Jabuti awards). Her titles are currently being translated into English, French, Spanish, and German. She was included among the twenty best Brazilian young writers by *Granta*. She is a PhD candidate in comparative literature at the Universidade do Estado do Rio de Janeiro (UERJ). She may be reached at carolasaavedra@gmail.com.

MICHEL MELAMED
Translated by Micaela Kramer

regurgitophagy

REGURGITOPHAGY
Enters stage after the third signal. *OFF:*
"Good-night, the performance Regurgitophagy was made possible by a Rioarte 'art and technology' fellowship. Thanks to it, an interface named 'pau-de-arara' was developed, which captures all sonorous reactions from the audience, and transforms them into electrical discharges onto the actor's body. Please turn off your cell phones. Or turn them on. Enjoy the performance."

Before anything else, everything. Because—unlike the avid anthropophagists—we've already swallowed too many things. Which is why, if they say 'point,' I don't know if it's to the point, g point, meeting point, point of sale, of no return, of view, of honor, of duty, needle point, case in point, that guy who'd prompt actors with their lines, exclamation point, boiling point, point blank, beside the point, zero point. Which is why, if they say 'pulling,' it can be pulling it off, pulling the plug, the trigger, teeth, strings, one's leg, ahead, the old switcheroo, pulling it together, pulling a face, the rug from beneath your feet, pulling out all the stops, pulling your weight, a fast one, pulling punches, pulling rank, through, over, apart, back the curtain. This is the story of the butterfly that fell in love with a punch. The platonic love of a butterfly for a punch . . . and this eternal feeling of buying money, frying pans, digging shovels, photographing photos . . . exchanging what one already has for what one still has . . . Alreadyet. They don't make used to's like futurely

because the three stars of Orion + the seven seas are the ten commandments
and the 7 wonders of the world minus the 3 little pigs
are the 4 seasons
or the 4 knights of the apocalypse or the 4 musketeers.
because
the three stooges or the Chick Corea Trio
+ the seven Capitol Hill sins, or the 7th art of Captain Ahab's seven-day-diet, or the seven dwarves,
would add up to ten,

would score 10! 10!
but this, minus the moon or life
would add up to nine brothers for nine sisters
and wouldn't exceed the 12 tasks of Hercules or the Strange Pilgrims' Twelve Stories
minus a four of Ace minus tea for two
because the three hundred and sixty-five days of the year,
minus the Jackson Five
minus three payments with no interest
minus Shakespeare's 154 sonnets
the forty thieves, the ninth symphony and the 500 miles of Indianapolis
would lead us
—even if one has to change the order of the factors or futures—
to fight
so that every P.S. has a W.C.
and not so that every V.D. has an O.K.
but so every E.R. has an A.C.
every P.C.: I.Q.
H.B.O.: T.H.C.
L.S.D.: G.R.E.
O.B.: N.Y.
I.M.F.: G.S.U.
P.T.A.: SKI
I.O.C.: B.B.Q.
FED: BUT CUT: VICK BIC: BAM V.I.P.: S.O.S.
EVERY ZAP: ZIP
BUG: P.M.S. G.L.S.: D.M.V. U.N.: D.N.A. U.F.O.: S.O.B.
RAP: RAM IT: ALLAH B.F.G.: V.J. K.K.K.: N.B.A.
TOP: TAB CAT: FAB G.N.P.: S.A.T. ZEN: JET BIG: P.H.D. POP: N.G.O. DOG: A.T.&T.
every GOAL be STEEL
every BEEP: BOOM
very END: PEACE
so that very P.M. has a GOOD AFTERNOON
and every DISPROPORTIONABLENESS has an

ANTIESTABLISHMENTARIANISM
and every HONORIFICABILITUDINITABUS a
SUPERCALIFRAGILISTICEXPIALIDOCIOUS

You know that 'Rorschach test'? That psychiatrist's test that shows a stain, a blot on the page, and every nut immediately thinks of sex or a bat? Well, it has to do with it. Here's the deal: you get any story, love story, work story, any story you want. Then you start pushing it away, far, far away, as if it were a chain of mountains, far . . . far on the horizon. There's a distance where you put things, any thing, and it becomes real tiny, just the essential, like a shadow, an indistinct form . . . and it's either a yes or a no. Are you following? It's simple: everything, in a last analysis, is a yes or a no. It's either good or bad for you. This goes for everything. For example: think of your wife. There, did you think of her? Now throw your wife far away . . . chain of mountains far on the horizon . . . very well. Is she there? At the limit? The last shape? See that indistinct form? That teeny tiny indistinct form? Is it a yes or a no? Huh? Yes or no, man! Got it?! Think of your work . . . Now throw your work far away! Chain of mountains far on the horizon . . . very well. See that teeny tiny work? Yes or no? Yes-or-no? Think man, think! Everything in life is like that. Out of everything there can be just a no or a yes left. The world is ours! You can look. Go . . . throw the world far away and look!

267–0425, 285–1018, 556–1553, 511–3856, 259–9093, cvv, dominos pizza, debora secco, 527–3241, 286–2906, 259–0671, 274–4435, 292–4499 (77178), 558–6016, 558–7682, 259–8231, 259–5431, 287–2692, 227–1236, 294–3215 . . .

Because everything has a connection. For instance . . . bench and . . . hiccups:

bench	hiccups
park . . . no: court	fright
justice . . . no: seduce	fear
score	trembling
sex . . . no: game	movement
baseball . . . no: hunt	swing
run	ball
feet	Cinderella
shoe	

I must confess: I'm the libido incarnate. More: I only think and have sex. Since the world has a habit of work and other chores, in the absence of a woman I don't hesitate to penetrate medicine flasks, notebooks and soda cans. I've already masturbated in the computer lab, in cream cheese containers, and, with the help of a chair, I've even inserted it into the chink of the shower heater. In short, there's no live object that, seen aslant on a 'Rorschach' (that psychiatrist's test that . . .), I don't see feminine nuances. My problem began about a month ago when, after ejaculating on an electric outlet, I realized it had come to an end. There are no more virgin objects for me, and worse: having become used to this practice for some time now, I no longer feel any desire for women. I look at the house, submerged in sperm, and feel alone. From the ashtray to the toaster, from the sofa to the steak, as if crystallized, my come reflects my expressions of discontent. Yep, I guess I've reached the end. I go down the elevator and on everything I see, on streets, on cities, I see the marks of my come. There is no more sense to living. Life of come—come to nothing life.

Marry me and make me the happiest man in the world. The most handsome, the most loved, respected, taken care of . . . The one who scores the most. And the most dated man in the world, and the most married. And the most parties, travels, dinners . . . Marry me and make me the most professionally accomplished man. The most got-a-woman-pregnant man, the most father. And the most first arguments; the most new fights and same old quarrels man. Marry me and make me the most separated man in the man. The loneliest, only see-my-kid-on-weekends man. The most hit rock bottom and rebound man. The most rebuilt his life. The most met a new chick and fell in love again man . . . Marry me and make me the most "marry me and make me the happiest man in the world."

Everything in this world should be called pencil. Obviously not overnight, like with an unconstitutional amendment. But little by little, like one caresses an earlobe. And so, gradually, the pencil would take over all sentences.

—Hey man! How pencil to see you!

—How bout you? How's it pencil?

—Pen-cil! Pencil non-stop . . . Totally in pencil. And you?

—Gee, man, my mom just pencil . . .

—What a pencil . . . But hey: pencil up . . . The pencil must go on . . .

—Yeah, you're totally pencil . . . What do you say we get together for a pencil?

—It'd be Pencil!

—But it's no pencil, huh! I'm being pencil!

Imagine what a wonderful world it'd be! In the first place, it would put an end to communication problems. Secondly, it would do away with illiteracy . . . Now, of course, pencil is only an idea—and it'd cause trouble for someone actually buying or borrowing a pencil . . . But we could have a plebiscite:

—Hey man! How money to see you!

—How bout you! How's it money?

—Mon-ey! Money non-stop . . . Totally in money. And you?

—Gee, man, my mom just money.

—What a money. But hey: money up . . . The money must go on . . .

Imagine what a wonderful world it'd be! In the first place, it would put an end to communication problems. Secondly, it would do away with illiteracy . . . Now, of course, money is only an idea—and it'd cause trouble for someone actually buying or borrowing money . . . But we could have a plebiscite:

—Hey man! How dead to see you!

—How bout you! How's it dead?

—De-ad! Dying non-stop . . . Totally in dead. And you?

—Gee, man, my mom just died.

ATTENTION

Heuristics? Gestalt?

Hermeneutics?

Wordology

Have the most important facts

of your life

revealed to you

with mathematical precision,

be they:

sexual frigidity,

lowering crop yields

drinking problems

make someone long gone come back into your life . . .

READ CLOSELY

Deeply enrooted in religion, it has devoted itself to the sacred for over 100 years. Used by spiritual callings to unveil secrets pertaining to health, love, business and success. Or failure. All of this in a deadly honest game, laid bare through the crakerjackology of fortune, in a divinatory practice as old as humanity itself. Although most distinguished in this arena, it also shines in the reading of tarot cards and of seashells. All of these allied, of course, to its extraordinary powers of clairvoyance. CRACKERJACKOLOGY has a firm manner while respectfully speaking of the religion that it embraces and carries within its box as a divine obligation.

PERSONALIZED CONSULTATIONS

* CRACKERJACKOLOGY *

KEEP OUR STREETS CLEAN * DO NOT LITTER * INTERNAL DISTRIBUTION

Regurgitate: to expel, to cast out (what, in a cavity is in excess, especially in the stomach).

Phagy: to eat.

In 1922, the week of modern art took place in Brazil, a kind of armory show that changed the course of national culture. Until then, the Brazilian cultural production was almost exclusively based on the importation of European schools. Romanticism surged in Europe, Brazil reproduced the Romantic school; the Parnassian movement took place, Brazil reproduced it; and so forth. In 1928, the writer Oswald de Andrade published the Anthropophagist Manifesto: based on a scene that had actually taken place, where a colonizing bishop was eaten by Brazilian cannibal Indians, Oswald proposed that, like the Indians, Brazilians swallow the European vanguards, mixing them with our own traditions and references in order to create a genuinely Brazilian art.

And what about today? Almost eighty years after. Do we continue to 'swallow vanguards' or have we had all sorts of information—concepts, products—pushed down our throats?

(And today, do we keep on 'swallowing vanguards,' or either all kinds of information have been pushed down into our throats? Concepts? Products?)

In short, what to do with the impossibility of assimilation, the state of acceleration, the excessive information syndrome (*dataholics*), the millions of visual, auditory, daily stimulations, which increase in a rhythm diametrically opposed to reflection?

Regurgitophagy:

'throw up' the excess in order to evaluate what we actually want to swallow again.

The de-objectification of man via the critical conscience, the "programmed ignorance." I will eat when I want to what I will to.

"extra! extra! The media is over!"

for you who didn't disappear in 68 only because you weren't born yet:

pleonastic oxymorons, chaosmos, electroconvulsiontherapy . . . Pavlov would use chemical artifices to stimulate vomiting so as to produce a conditioned reflex. the human being uses, at the most, 10% of his brain, sees 1% of all light, and hears sounds up until 20,000 cycles per second . . .

. . . we are what we eat, carnivorous chewing gum . . .

. . . In Brazil, people wear ribbons named after the Bonfim Saint from Bahia, tied around their wrists. Wishes are made with each knot that ties it on, and these are believed to come true when the ribbon falls off. A "Senhor do Bonfim" ribbon has been especially designed for the Japanese market, programmed to fall off in three days: artificially aged . . .

The Lego complex: if you are a legocentric, a legoist, everything fits in . . .

. . . finally, a cure that will take scientists years to find the illness. Which is why, if I believe in the future of humanity it's because there will always be a new Beatles song. At the dawn of day, I don't take part in the end of the world, and yet, I identify with the majority of thighs, I love everything that is strange, I only believe in exceptions.

. . . in the saunas of the Young Men's *Muslim* Association, and of the Young Men's Hebrew Association, the heat of the discussions will come only and exclusively from the well functioning of the machinery. un-tested waves, I repeat, damaged waves head toward the beach. wingantennae, antennaewings. almost Roseanne and Marilyn Manson presenting the Fox news . . .

. . . I'd take this sentence to a deserted island. This, this sentence. Hasta la Buena Vista Social Club, Baby: alreadyet. The Big Apple: That Big Adam received from Big Eve . . . Be a patriot: go to Vietking kong. Look at the hands . . . up . . . YOURS . . . Truly. Manwo. Wohuman. Wommon. Humanwo. Wommyn. Island is a piece of man surrounded by tears on all sides. All men are islands. The jingle bells toll for thee. I become a transparent paintball, I am nothing, I stain all. Just say say say . . . NO.

. . . Nobody beats the fees. The opposite of Maximilian is minipenny. SOS (sell our souls). I was consumed by a feeling of general déjà vu: looking at the can of rosebudweisernegger, listening to Billie Holiday on ice or Nat King Cole Porter reading the unbearable lightness of being or not to be superman-at-workaholics in progress at the end of the second halftime is money can't buy you happiness is a warm gun:

in des-photography it's like this
first the flash, then the smile

the development before the click
you remember and therefore live
it's the little birdy that looks at you
and all the while you're saying seeeeeeeeeech
Down with!!! Down with!!! Down with!!!

In an upcoming study, to be published in a respected magazine of the scientific world, not only will the existence of the mental cavity be proven, but the alarming indications of its occurrence will be shown as well. As expected, this phenomenon, which affects peoples of different countries, has, as one of its main causes, the terrible dietary trends of these populations, who are raised, for the most part, on the consumption of canned laughter from exported American TV series, sugary soap operas, and beating around the George Borscht.

In order to prevent the extraction of the organ, under risk of irreversible consequences, such as, for instance, lame thinking, one highly recommends the continuous and correct use of the brain brush and mental floss.

Let us join efforts to make the world a place with a smile that is white . . . and black and Afro-American and Afro-Asian-American and Afro-Asian-Native American and . . . with interracial breath!

I'd like to write a book in which everyone died got fucked a book of stories where adjectives and verbs were all wonderful and cruel metaphors a book that spoke of drowsy afternoons with crinkling clouds eleven year-old boys fags women and, at last, that everyone died, got fucked that every story ended with a drop of blood streaked down his body the air groping his hands and his transfigured throat or even that it ended abruptly like an impression, a still from a movie and only the music hovering over the flicker of the blank page it's that at one point she told me of the impossibilities of her depression and of how she saw no perspective and the saturation of everything her children the bills and I said but in this world everything is possible in this world everything can exist but she said no and so I said do you think in this world nobody eats shit?! That there aren't millions of people in this world who don't eat shit?! That at this very moment there isn't a young beautiful couple in buenos aires loving each other furiously in the midst of their own excrement?!? that in Bangkok a man hasn't, with one virulent spurt, just brought a right handful of shit to his mouth?!? in the Tacoma desert a solitary Indian doesn't say a prayer and doesn't lick his very own shit?!? In paris-berlin-cairo-moscow-in-every-single-place?!? In Japan a lonely middle-aged extremely rich man big stock market investor in his high-tech apartment solemnly conveys his shit on a tray until resting it on the table romantically set to candlelight . . . that this man lives for this?!? That the stock market job is a way of keeping away suspicion so that he may invest?!? In shit?!? In desire?!? And so she asks me:

—what is the opposite of eating shit?

—sadness . . . no! frustration.

but she insists and says she wants to know in terms of taste and I make an effort to feel what the taste of shit might be like

Hel-lo? Hel-lo? Anybody on the line? Is there nobody on the line? Are we rolling? We're not rolling yet . . . But I'd like to take this opportunity to thank mom and dad, grandma and grandpa, kids—who are the future of this country—and to our youth—who are completely lost. Because it's thanks to you, thanks to you!, that I have more than 100% of the national viewing audience! Would you please give us a close-up here: can you see: the Rapist Show? 100% Now our competitors: the Murderer's Show? It's a blank. The Robber's Show? It's a blank!! The Fascist's Show? Blank!!! Blank!!! Blank!!! Only the Rapist Show has 100% of the national viewing audience!!! Thank you very much . . . May God illuminate you all . . .

But today's show is unmissable, you can't miss it . . . The tremendous Condom Camera!!! Just look at how well this episode has been worked out: we kidnapped this guy, we kept him in captivity, naked, in chains . . . He ate bread and water whenever there was any!!! Otherwise he ate only sugar . . . We tore off the nails from his feet! We put superglue in his nostrils . . . on his eyelashes . . . he was raped by five sex maniacs . . . In fact, I'd like to thank Effervescent Talents, which supplies us with its fabulous actors, and thank especially the participation of Robert DeNixon, great actor shortly to be seen in the next Hollywood movie, in a theater near you. But it's not over yet. Look at how well worked out it was! One day the guy wakes up and finds out that: the chains are unlocked and the door is open . . . He leaves, wait and see how fabulously we worked it out: taxis start passing by every five minutes . . . and no one stops!! No one stops!! But it's not over yet. . . . Stop!!! Stop!!! Stop!!! Are you sure you want to keep watching?!? Very well, the guy gets home and his building is being robbed! It's the actors of Effervescent Talents, my big thanks once again. So then there's this robber who's the most hot-tempered one . . . Robert DeNixon . . . Great character work . . . he's a talent . . . the guy didn't even notice . . . And he shoots him straightaway in the head and at his spinal cord!!! You should see the look of joy on the guy's face waking up from his coma, and finding out he had just participated in another CONDOM CAMERA!!! Hello? Hello? Is there anyone on the line? Are we rolling? Spin the VT!

[Enter Michel and Antonio Banderas's commercial onscreen]

But let's change the course of this prose a bit, let's change the subject, because the time has come for a sketch that everyone loves . . . A sketch that has already become a part of the American family's Sunday afternoons . . . HOWLS. THE FUCKED UP'S GAME!!! VIGNETTES AND HOWLS. You already know the rules: the most fucked up, the most wretched, worthless, the most miserable wins!!! Let's call last week's champion and his companion to the stage!!! You can come in . . . VIGNETTES AND HOWLS. Excellent, excellent . . . Is he prepared to win this week as well? Yes, Mr. Rapist, he's been preparing himself intensely this week. HOWLS. You mean to say that you've prepared yourself, sir? (The candidate drooling . . .) Well, I am going to tell you that our production team has been doing its homework . . . Our production team has been doing its work and is here with a fellow who the doctor accompanying believes he will win! Says that today he's the one going home with the prize!!! HOWLS. So let the challenger come in!!! VIGNETTES AND HOWLS. What's his name? The doctor who accompanies the challenger: he doesn't have a name. Whoa, man!!! Now this is getting ugly!! I'm warning you, this week our production team has given it its all . . . This one here isn't going to be easy!!! It's going to be tuff for the winner today . . . But since our time is rather short, VIGNETTES AND HOWLS, let's get going, let's begin this competition right away. VIGNETTES AND HOWLS. What does he have? Throat cancer, replies the champion's assistant. And him? He's blind, replies the doctor who accompanies the challenger. Now you! Coronary bypass surgery. You! Asthma. You? Parkinson. You? Arteriosclerosis. Come on, folks, let's get to it! Typhus! Tetanus! Tumor! Castrated! Dumb! Deaf! Leper! Aids! Alzheimer! Epilepsy! Diabetes! Tuberculosis! Excellent!!! Excellent!!! Our time is almost coming to an end . . . Aaaaahhh . . . And our candidates are extremely well prepared!!!! HOWLS. A round of applause!!! VIGNETTES AND HOWLS. Now let's go straight to the part everyone likes, from Physically Fucked let's go to Socially Fucked!!! VIGNETTES AND HOWLS. You? Terrible credit. You? Name in the IRS. You! Attempted suicide eight times: took: strychnine, ant poison, insecticide, rat poison, cyanide, arsenic . . . OK, OK! And him? Also attempted suicide eight times (with spiteful sarcasm): cut his wrists, set fire to his clothes, turned the gas on and closed the window, jumped through a closed window, threw himself in front of a moving truck, lay down on the train tracks . . . Come on, folks, I don't have all my life here . . . And the Show must go on!!!! He's a Jew! He's a Palestinian! He's black! He's a homosexual! A woman! Native American! Lives in the slums! Lives in the suburbs! Killed his wife and kids! Buried his mom and dad alive! . . . Texas Emergency Reserve! Neo-Nazi! Al-Qaeda!! CIA!! Develops biological weapons!!! Develops atomic weapons!!! Gentlemen, gentlemen! The competition is excellent, really wonderful, but unfortunately our time has run out!!! Aaaaahhhhh . . . But they'll be back next week!!! HOWLS. For the big clincher!!! HOWLS. So prepare yourselves well, because as you know, when the dispute is this tight . . . it's the details that solve it!!! HOWLS. Diarrhea!!! HOWLS. Lice!!! HOWLS. Wryneck! Ingrown nail! Warts!!! Hiccups!!!!! HOWLS. HOWLS. HOWLS. And don't forget to take care of yourselves!!! Keep yourselves alive!!! Ha ha ha!!! (Rape! Rape! Rape!) Stay tuned for the SLAUGHTER OF THE FRESHMEN!!! (Rape! Rape!) Now let's go to commercials!!! HOWLS AND VIGNETTES. COMMERCIAL BREAK.

for Luciana
at our last dinner
we sat at the table and ate in silence. The silence.
we drank wine and did not toast
there are only toasts when there are plans
that night, at that table
our last dinner was our only certainty
someone, spying at us perchance through our window
would see cutlery and cups floating over the candles
at our last dinner
we sat at the table and ate transparently
someone, spying at us perchance through our window
would see the food being digested inside us
at our last dinner
we sat at the table and ate ourselves away
someone, spying at us perchance through our window
would see us for a very short while

people are circles with two dots a line like this one like this and another like this I'd like to dissolve myself in water because more than anything more than you love of my life more than daddy mommy and god and sex and money I love the water things can happen naturally it often happens that people say hi to me and I think they're telling me I'm high! a cocacolic slip is impossible when would anyone say " . . . that soda . . . what's its name again . . . goddammit . . . that black one . . . the one that looks like pepsi . . ."? never! It'd be unforgivable you can forget the light on your father's age what was it again it's ok it's acceptable but the cocacolic slip is in extinction there are things that can't be hurt but it's not because of that that I haven't yet written the most beautiful thing I've ever written till today (the end of ideologies is a fallacy on the contrary today we live its zenith in my case for instance I have to fight to be a michelist melamedian and not a pre-michelist post-melamedian) it's never happened that someone's asked me "movie?" and I've understood "groovy!"

It's official, I died. I'm only here to clarify that there is no life after death. We die and that's it. Everything's over. In the exact second that we die, we lose consciousness and . . . Therefore there is no soul, no reincarnation, no hell and no heaven. The obvious question, you may point out, is: how is it possible, if there is nothing after death, that, having died, I be here, seeking to confirm inexistence? It's quite simple: I'm writing this text before I die. It's a mixture of insight and prediction. The rest is left to chance and I'm betting all my cards. After all, there being nothing after death, there is nothing to describe. Only this confirmation and I am certain that, wherever I may be, I'll continue to endorse it. I'd like to take this opportunity to give thanks for having lived. XOXOs to the whole world, and I wish luck and courage to you all. See you later, folks, that is, never again!

peeling onions
I thought of you
and cried

It's official, I died. I'm only here to clarify that there is life after death. We die and that's when it all starts. Everything begins. In the exact second we die, we gain consciousness and . . . Therefore there is a soul, there is reincarnation, hell and heaven. The obvious question, you may point out, is: what is there after life? It's difficult to explain. Because I'm writing this text before I die. It's a mixture of insight and prediction. The rest is left to chance and I'm betting all my cards. After all, there being life after death, I'll do my best to manifest myself and tell you every little detail. In the meantime, only this confirmation and I am certain that, wherever I may be, I'll continue to endorse it. I'd like to take this opportunity to give thanks for having lived. XOXOs to the whole world, and I wish luck and courage to you all. See you later, that is, fancy seeing you here!

INVERSION OF THE AXIS (audience scene)

I need a volunteer, a candidate.

You no . . .

You?

No . . .

You!

Come here, man! Don't be shy!

Co-ome! Co-ome!

There you go! What's your name? Speak up, man! Are you a fag?! What's your name?!

So if you're not a fag, you must have a girlfriend . . . a wife . . .

When you're home with your wife, in private, do you like to suck farts?

Do you suck farts, man?!

You're a fag . . .

Fa-ag!! Fa-ag!!

So do the following: sing and shake your ass. Sing and shake your ass, man! Sing-and-shake-your-ass! Sing-and-shake-your-ass!

You don't know how to sing shaking your ass?! So . . .

Imitate an agouti!! Imitate an agouti, man!! I-mi-ta-te an agou-ti! I-mi-ta-te an agou-ti!!

(. . .)

SHOWS THE ELECTRICAL SHOCKS TO THE AUDIENCE

To be a Piscean, a Jew, a poet and a Carioca (someone from Rio) and to have an account at Citibank is—besides the flea behind the ear—to live the eternal and generalized déjà vu.

There are no novelties in the world. It's easy to hear a story and to begin to think of it as yours. More: to hear about a place, like for instance, Brookwood, and yeah, sure, great, Brookwood, fantastic, know it really well, etc. How's Billy?

A while ago I went to a street carnival. While noticing, from in between the tits of the masses, a lit window on the last floor of a neighboring building, this buffoon here was suddenly assailed with a pungent nostalgia. I even saw the old man at that window—myself—from the altitude of my eighty something years remembering me here, in the recess of youth, in between kisses and sips, in this same street where I see myself there, reminiscing of me over here being watched from over there.

And then I was certain of the futile life. And I quaffed a half can of beer in one gulp. And I burnt my parched lips with mint tea. And I chanted a samba. And I yawned with tremulous hands. And I kissed the girl. And my old lady placed a hand on my shoulder. And I grew melancholic about the future. And I smiled remembering the past.

You who are a Taurus, Catholic, dentist, from Texas—with an account at Chase; or a Libra, Muslim, publicist from South Carolina—Britney Spears Bank; or even a Leo, atheist, actor, from L.A.—Bank of Boston, you should know, it's very strange to be a Piscean, Jew, poet, Carioca—with an account at Citibank. To have the feeling that everything you've just said has been said before. Thought of. Forgotten.

* AQUI FALTA UM TXT PARA LER: "DEUS"? ELIANA? MARIÁ CARDOSO?

REBECCA?

Because everything is a metaphor for life. Take, for instance . . . the sea. The sea is a metaphor for life. One day the tide is low, others high . . . There are days when you read the morning paper and the current of events pulls you under. And there are times when life is just plain surf . . . Because everything is a metaphor for life . . . For instance . . . a butcher's shop! Everything is there, exposed . . . But each thing has its price and you have to make your choices. So then you can ask for the butcher's advice or be a self-made . . . And so reap what you sowed: a tenderloin phase, an entire year when everything seems to be baloney, a job where you're just hitting the daily meat grind . . . a time when you just want to get to the meat of things. Because everything is a metaphor for life . . .

EVERY THING IS A METAPHOR.
BUT ONLY GOD IS HYPERTEXT.
Be there a marginal, be there a hero
when the swept winds of the curves
hit your loose screws
—with no pony tail, chignon, or pig tails:
underneath the curls of your loose screws like a sail:
be there a marginal, be there a hero
—to fly screws:

kite in a cage and loose screw.
Substitute the quickly as pieces as possible substitute.
Change everything: Brands new!
The machinery urinating pubic hairs and blisters . . .
Axle, crank, cylinder?
Kite in a cage and loose screw.
Condo, viaduct, slum:
Loose screw.
Prison, asylum, condom:
Loose screw.
Handcuffs, belly, trouser fly:
Loose screw:
Beer, weed, money, stitch . . . :
Loose screw:
The gear has begun to itch
There, where the axle bites its tail
Gel on the kite's tail
Kite in a cage and loose screw.
[now, all the words you can think of]
what's the meaning of life—of machines?
Where do they come from, where do they go?
How do you explain their existence?
Glass shards on their tails!
There, where the axle bites their tails.
Kite in a cage and loose screw . . . to fly sails:
Be there a marginal, be there a hero

The tin-man sinks his paw on the accelerator of his automobile of meat and bones. He pushes forward into the nervous center of the unsouled city so as to cast his heart like a grenade. the mission accomplished tosses him into routine. tin-man wraps up the direction of his home in a flight propelled by cuffs on his nape, thumps on his skull—running on lethargy—as if hoisted by his pubic hairs of steel wool by tweezers. he parks in the garage of the building of meat and bones. inserts his key of meat in the lock of bone. sits on the sofa of liver and opening a dirt cheap can of blood, encrusts himself onto his cartilage television set. Sleep tin-man, sleep. push your way into this optical-fiber forest under this sky of electric fuses. Look how beautiful the sea of gasoline is, breaking upon the bytes of the beach. dream tin-man, dream. What doesn't make you stronger will kill you. There must be a place where life is only steel, wood, iron, plastic. The world also belongs to those who only dream they can conquer it. tin-man awakens with a start. where can there be stone in this world, he wonders, I'm tired of semi-machines. he sits at his desk of fat and, recalling tomorrow, writes in his laptop of striated tissue.

rio de Janeiro
minus 20 degrees.
the ice-skaters gallop side-by-side on the iced mirror of the lake
the statue of the Christ,
almost unrecognizable,
with the snow covering
the back of its hands feet arms shoulders head . . .
were it not for its correct localization and size
one might suspect it was somebody else in its place:
a king-kong petrified on the mount's peak
a sphinx, standing on its feet, proposing the pantomime of its enigma
the statue of liberty—renouncing its torch,
its arms half-raised like wings, free;
perhaps the Eiffel Tower, obese,
or even a pathetic gigantic scarecrow chasing away the sun . . .
the snow falls upon the city.
tumbling slowly braced by the absolute silence,
This silence that has hibernated for over five hundred years,
lapidating the flake's helices
for the white epiphany.
couples on skis descend the sugar loaf.
on the guanabara bay a father pulls his son on a sleigh.
penguins applaud the boreal dawn on Ipanema beach
and brazil wood may well insist on fading in poland
and a bird to gargle in russia
uzbekistan and its palm trees from the rainforest . . .
siberia 40° Celsius . . .
here,

today,
it's the snows of march that end the summer.
and no more promises.
ever again.

MICHEL MELAMED is an award-winning Brazilian artist. He is considered one of the most outstanding talents of his generation. Indeed, besides excelling in his performances as an actor, Melamed is an acknowledged playwright as well as a noted screenwriter. His innovative work is interdisciplinary in scope, featuring a mixture of artistic languages (e.g., theater, literature, TV, music, technology), and it has been shown in some of the most important cultural capitals, including New York, Paris, and Berlin. In 2013, Melamed is releasing the television series SEEWATCHLOOK for the Brazilian cable channel Canal Brasil. He may be reached at melamedmichel@gmail.com.

SELECTED RECENT WORKS

Television

Capitu—Rede Globo—2008
[Lead role]
http://www.youtube.com/watch?v=XoZjXHDBatw&feature=related

Theater

Adeus à Carne or Go to Brazil—RIO—2012
[Creator, actor, and director]
http://vimeo.com/40138393
password: 2012gotobrazil2013
SEEWATCHLOOK—High Line—NYC—2011
[Creator, actor, and director]
http://www.nytimes.com/2011/10/29/theater/seewatchlook-street-scenes-at-the-high-line.html
REGURGITOPHAGY—Public Theater—NYC—2008
[Author, actor, and director]
http://www.youtube.com/watch?v=IMZCJC9kAx4